CRITICAL INSIGHTS

Ray Bradbury

Ray Bradbury

CRITICAL

INSIGHTS

Ray Bradbury

Editor
Rafeeq O. McGiveron

Lansing Community College

SALEM PRESS
A Division of EBSCO Information Services, Inc.
Ipswich, Massachusetts

GREY HOUSE PUBLISHING

Publisher's Cataloging-In-Publication Data
(Prepared by The Donohue Group, Inc.)

Names: McGiveron, Rafeeq O., editor.
Title: Ray Bradbury / editor, Rafeeq O. McGiveron.
Other Titles: Critical insights.
Description: [First edition]. | Ipswich, Massachusetts : Salem Press, a division of EBSCO Information Services, Inc. ; Amenia, NY : Grey House Publishing, [2017] | Includes bibliographical references and index.
Identifiers: ISBN 978-1-68217-571-2 (hardcover)
Subjects: LCSH: Bradbury, Ray, 1920-2012--Criticism and interpretation. | Speculative fiction, American--20th century--History and criticism. | Science fiction, American--20th century--History and criticism.
Classification: LCC PS3503.R167 Z739 2017 | DDC 813/.54--dc23

Contents

Resources

About This Volume

Rafeeq O. McGiveron

Critical Insights: Ray Bradbury explores the work of perhaps the most immediately recognizable, and also influential, name in speculative fiction, a wide field that includes not only science fiction and even fantasy but also horror, the "weird tale," and works of that ilk. Ray Bradbury (1920-2012) was a perennially imaginative soul, one who both drank in the world of sensation and excitement and wonder, and then helped transform that world with his own relentless artistic creativity. What literate person, after all, has not at least heard the premise of "A Sound of Thunder" (1952), in which a time traveler stepping on a butterfly in the dinosaur era reshapes the reality of the future? And who does not know, courtesy of the slim yet monumental *Fahrenheit 451* (1953) with its book-burning "firemen," the temperature at which book paper supposedly ignites?

Even from his earliest years, the shy, myopic Bradbury reveled in the mysterious, the supernatural, the fantastic—films like *Frankenstein* and *Metropolis*, radio shows such as *Chandu the Magician*, Edgar Rice Burroughs's novels of John Carter transported by astral projection to a canal-girded Mars, and comic strips about Buck Rogers and Flash Gordon. With a dial-a-letter toy typewriter the young author-to-be laboriously yet lovingly created his own retellings of such works—what we now would call *fan fiction*—and he also came to write and draw his own completely original creations as well. At age nineteen he wrote and published his own fanzine, and at twenty-one he sold his first paid story. As Bradbury learned his trade in short stories in the early 1940s, he also was befriended by big-name science fiction writers like Leigh Brackett, C. L. Moore and Henry Kuttner, and Robert A. Heinlein. In the postwar years, though, Bradbury broke out of the less lucrative and less prestigious genre markets, gaining wider readership, receiving national prizes for two short stories in *Mademoiselle* and *Charm*, and also receiving from influential literary critic Christopher Isherwood a glowing review of *The Martian Chronicles* (1950). Further books such as *Fahrenheit 451*, *Dandelion Wine* (1957), and *Something Wicked*

This Way Comes (1962) solidified Bradbury's growing popularity, as did his numerous short stories; he worked in film and television as well, extolled the quest of the Space Age, and, rightly or wrongly, for a good fifty years became the public face for science fiction and for space travel.

With this text, then, we examine the writings of Ray Bradbury and their growing legacy. This volume is divided into four main sections. In the introductory section, I discuss Bradbury's career and certain themes of his writings in fairly broad terms, while Karen S. Garvin gives a biography of the man behind the literature. The book's concluding section contains helpful resources such as a brief chronology of Bradbury's life for quick reference, a list of his major works, a bibliography of critical essays and books for further study, and an index of key terms used within this text. Bracketed between the opening and closing apparatus is the meat of this project: a four-chapter section of critical contexts to help inform and set up readers' understanding of Bradbury and his art, and a nine-chapter section of critical readings exploring many and varied facets of the stories, novels, television adaptations, and occasional piece of nonfiction.

Karen S. Garvin begins our critical context by discussing the cultural and historical milieu of Bradbury's early career, including the postwar era's McCarthyite climate of fear, and the threat of nuclear war, both of which helped shape classic works such as *The Martian Chronicles* and *Fahrenheit 451*. Garvin shows Bradbury's art stemming in part from his childhood interests in the Gothic and in fantasy, and yet even more importantly, she turns the lens around to examine Bradbury's influence on the culture at large, especially in the area of censorship, free speech, and political correctness.

W. C. Bamberger helps us understand the various ways critics throughout the decades have treated the writings of Bradbury. Using three early major books as representatives—the fix-up episodic novel *The Martian Chronicles*, the story collection *The Illustrated Man* (1951), and *Fahrenheit 451*—Bamberger surveys Bradbury criticism from the first contemporary reviews through the judgments of the present day. Evaluators include not only book reviewers and professional academics but also fellow writers and even one president of the United States. Bamberger finds that although some early reviewers tried to elevate Bradbury from genre writing and into mainstream literature, the label of genre writer never quite goes away—which, indeed, may be a good thing.

Andrea Krafft then explores Ray Bradbury's fiction through an intriguing and provocative feminist lens. Although critics and ordinary readers alike occasionally have criticized Bradbury's female characters as being flat and stereotypical, Krafft finds that "if we dig deeper into how Bradbury depicts women, we can locate cracks in their veneer of homebound bliss" and thus discern "significant moments of resistance to cultural expectations for feminine behavior." Bringing in the work of prominent feminist critics such as Simone de Beauvoir, Betty Friedan, and Hélène Cixous, Krafft explores not only the obvious *Fahrenheit 451* but *Something Wicked This Way Comes* and a wide range of short stories to reveal in Bradbury's trapped housewives and rebellious witches an underlying critique of the social and economic strictures too often preventing women's attainment of personhood.

I conclude our context section by examining early Bradbury stories about censorship and book burning—"The Exiles" (1949) and "Usher II" (1950)—in relation to the now-classic portrayal in *Fahrenheit 451*. Although the novel was published only a few years after the short stories, its treatment of the topic is far subtler, depicting censorship not almost as parental spoilsportism, as the stories tend to, but as something for which we also can blame ourselves. The more mature *Fahrenheit 451* thus serves as a much more realistic and useful warning.

Starting our section of critical readings is perhaps the last essay of the late William F. Touponce, an interesting discussion of Ray Bradbury's literary libraries. In his own life, of course, Bradbury was nourished artistically and intellectually by libraries; it began in childhood, and yet the hunger for reading grew even more important, with public libraries being the self-taught youth's main source of enlightenment. Touponce examines not only such obvious choices as *Fahrenheit 451*, *Something Wicked This Way Comes*, and "Usher II," (1950), but also less familiar novels such as *Death Is a Lonely*

Business (1985) and "Somewhere a Band Is Playing" (2007), and even "There Will Come Soft Rains" (1950) and "The Million-Year Picnic" (1946) with its burning of the remaining articles, papers, and records of a world that has committed nuclear suicide.

Timothy E. Kelley then analyzes faith and religion in the major novels of *Fahrenheit 451, Dandelion Wine,* and *Something Wicked This Way Comes.* Although Bradbury throughout his career of course uses many Christian motifs, Kelley notes that the author actually "works out a pantheistic philosophy more easily explained in Nietzschean than religious terms..." Even as Bradbury's works highlight the uncertainties of the mortal world, they eschew the bleakness of much existential writing, and instead show "a faith in the beauty, the mystery, and the value of life."

Next, Guido Laino examines the role of robots and artificial intelligence in such stories as "I Sing the Body Electric" (1969), "The Veldt" (1951), and others. Though occasionally portrayed as antitechnology, Bradbury in fact was leery less of machines in general than of the misuse of machines. To situate Bradbury's work in its philosophical and artistic contexts, Laino discusses the Hebraic concept of the golem as a servant—yet a potentially dangerous one—created from clay, nods to earlier literature like E.T.A. Hoffmann's *Der Sandmann* (1816) and Mary Shelley's *Frankenstein* (1818), and ties in with our modern fears about artificial intelligence that might outstrip humanity. Bradbury's treatment of the issues, Laino argues, is "far more ambiguous" than even the author perhaps intended.

Just as the threat of nuclear annihilation hung over postwar America, so, too, did the issue color Bradbury's writings of the late 1940s and 1950s. Focusing on "Embroidery" (1951) and "The Million-Year Picnic," stories which prominently, and terrifyingly, feature the devastation of the Bomb, Anna McHugh details the way Bradbury portrays the phenomenal new power not just as the product of modern science and technology, but, very interestingly, also in terms of the literary and rhetorical trappings of myth.

Bradbury of course was a wildly prolific short story writer, yet also a relentless reimaginer of his own earlier works, including for reuse in other media such as radio, film, and television. In discussing

The Ray Bradbury Theater series that ran on cable television from 1985 to 1992—every script of which was written by Bradbury himself—Phil Nichols examines three representative episodes in relation to their original printed source stories: "The Murderer" (1953), "The Lake" (1944), and "The Crowd" (1943). Nichols shows that whether dealing with science fiction, fantasy, or horror, the entertaining Bradbury remains "a writer who is not afraid of modifying his stories as he adapts them, and one who is strongly aware of how to match story to medium."

Next, Robin Anne Reid gives us a nuanced stylistic investigation of three of Bradbury's so-called autobiographical novels: *Dandelion Wine, Death Is a Lonely Business*, and *Green Shadows, White Whale* (1992). Using data analyzed by computer software, Reid examines representative samples in terms of key words and clauses. She finds that although these novels involving writers incorporate the different genre elements of fantasy, detective fiction, and memoir, they all share some great similarities of stylistic construction—elements that Reid also puts into perspective with comparison to pieces of classic literature from *The Sun Also Rises* and the US Constitution to *A Tale of Two Cities* and *The Call of the Wild*. Rather than stop there, though, Reid also has recommendations for stylistic research into Bradbury's canon.

Ádám T. Bogár follows this by examining the role of books in *Fahrenheit 451* and *The Martian Chronicles*. It is a commonplace, of course, to note that books occupy a central place in Bradbury's famous novel of book burning, or even in his breakthrough book whose tales of Mars include, say, the Poe-based revenge-upon-the-small-minded of "Usher II." Bogár, however, looks at books not only as metaphors but also as something that creates a sense of comfortable domesticity and as something that, with the opening or closing of a Bible, for example, can punctuate a literary scene. In addition, the chapter also explores the physicality of Bradbury's books, draws connections between some of Bradbury's lyrical fancies, like the metal Martian book that sings when its raised lettering is stroked, and the postbook technology of our own world.

Imola Bülgözdi discusses Bradbury's depiction of Mars—both in stories collected in *The Martian Chronicles*, and in others as well—in relation to the notion of translocality, the concept of being situated in different places and times. As social scientists have theorized, the individual's sense of self is tied in part to a sense of place, both physical and cultural. Critics and ordinary readers alike across the decades have noted the echoes of the Cold War in Bradbury's Martian stories, along with the parallels between the colonization of the planet and the westward movement of settlers in the nineteenth-century United States. Bülgözdi, however, also looks at the complexities and contradictions of identity and being as individuals and populations uproot, shift, and attempt to reestablish themselves—movements that she reminds us are emblematic of the post-Second World War era of *The Martian Chronicles*.

In our final chapter, Andrea Krafft provides a refreshing discussion of Bradbury's mundane heroes. While the focus of much early pulp science fiction naturally was upon brilliant inventors and brave explorers, Bradbury looks far more at the ordinary, even marginalized, people who would be caught up in a future of rocket travel and the colonizing of other worlds. Examining classic stories such as "The Gift" (1956), "The Rocket Man" (1951), "The Rocket" (1950), and others, Krafft notes that despite the irresistible allure of space exploration, Bradbury shows the alienation that occurs both to the seemingly glamorous rocket men isolated by their exalted positions and also to those ordinary people left behind. Yet, as Krafft concludes, Bradbury nevertheless remained characteristically optimistic, his spacefaring futures portrayed "as an opportunity whose benefits will outweigh the costs."

On Ray Bradbury and His Works

Rafeeq O. McGiveron

Even if Ray Bradbury (1920-2012) had never published anything but *Fahrenheit 451* (1953), that now-classic novel of a book-burning near-future America, which remains perennially popular and also is assigned reading in countless high school and college English classes over half a century later, likely would have guaranteed his lasting fame. After all, Harper Lee, author of *To Kill a Mockingbird* (1960), until the very last year of her life was known and revered for a single classic of similar ubiquity. Yet the relentlessly imaginative and evocatively poetic Ray Bradbury of course was no one-hit wonder. Indeed, the creative output of this prolific and popular writer spans a full seventy years, and includes not only prose fiction— short stories and occasionally novels—but also poetry, drama, radio plays, screenplays, and teleplays, along with occasional reportage infused with his characteristic artistry, and opinion pieces ranging from subtle to downright exhortations; in speeches and interviews he was never particularly shy either. Bradbury's writing style—the length and meter of his sentences, the crispness of his word choices, the familiarity and yet also newness of his imagery—can be, as critics and general readers alike have observed, a delight to read, and yet just as uplifting and satisfying are the sense of wonder and the humane sensibilities that underlie his many, many tales.

The Birth of the Author, the Birth of His Craft

Ray Douglas Bradbury was born on 22 August 22 1920 in the then-small town of Waukegan, Illinois. The second surviving child of Leonard Spaulding Bradbury and Esther Mogen Bradbury, Ray was four years younger than his brother Leonard Jr., known as Skip. Whereas Skip, like the boys' father, was strong and athletic, young Ray grew up smaller, frailer, and myopic. Jonathan R. Eller notes that while "[i]t took years for father and brother to come to terms with the dreamy and bookish 'Shorty,'" the family nevertheless was "close and loving"—and Esther was particularly indulgent toward her coddled little darling (Becoming 10).

A dweller in imagination from childhood on, young Bradbury devoured the fantastic arts, whether films like *The Phantom of the Opera* and *Metropolis*, the Barsoom novels of Edgar Rice Burroughs, the pulp fiction of *Argosy Weekly*, or Buck Rogers and Flash Gordon comic strips. Even as a child, though, Ray clearly had a spark of the creative himself. He wrote stories by hand on rolls of butcher paper, then shifted to working with a primitive toy typewriter that selected one letter at a time via a circular dial, a device with which at age 12 he created a sequel to one of Burroughs's John Carter of Mars novels (Eller, "Miracle" 14). In junior high, Ray had the lead in a school play, and he actually broke into professional radio in a small way by performing sound effects and, eventually, voice roles for shows broadcast from the CBS station in Tucson, Arizona, where the elder Leo's job as telephone lineman had taken the family (Eller, "Miracle" 13, 15-16).

Ray broadened his horizons still further in the sprawling, multiethnic Los Angeles in which the family finally settled in 1934. Although in high school the teased boy was shy and introverted, he nevertheless hunted autographs from big name stars in Hollywood with irrepressible aplomb. Just short of age 16, the aspiring author had a poem published in his hometown Waukegan newspaper, and in January 1938 Forrest Ackerman's fanzine *Imagination!* gave Bradbury his first short story publication, unpaid though it was. Bradbury wrote and published his own fanzine of science fiction and fantasy, *Future Fantasia*, in 1939 and 1940, while August 1941 saw publication of his first paid story, coauthored with Henry Hasse, in *Super Science Stories*.

In these early years, Bradbury sold newspapers to pay for his pulp magazine reading habit, and he schooled himself, as he had for years, with relentless prowlings through libraries—indeed, the library is a location of wonder and excitement that appears again and again throughout his career.[1] He also counted as mentors such prominent SF authors as Jack Williamson, Henry Kuttner, Edmund Hamilton, Leigh Brackett, and Robert A. Heinlein (Eller, Becoming 64-69). By the end of 1942 Bradbury had become a full-time writer. Although he certainly was not wealthy—in fact, he did not move out of his parents' house, where he slept on a foldout bed in the living room with his brother, until he married at age 27 (Weller 148)—Bradbury was honing his craft in tale after tale. After the Second World War he, like Heinlein, broke out of the ghetto of pulp science fiction and into more respected mainstream magazines, and Bradbury even won prestigious literary prizes in 1947 and 1948. In 1950, Doubleday published *The Martian Chronicles*, a lyrical, bittersweet saga of the conquest and colonization of an already inhabited Mars, and then the ultimate destruction of Earth in nuclear holocaust, a book that influential critic Christopher Isherwood reviewed glowingly—and thus began Bradbury's rise to wider fame.

Bradbury's Place in Science Fiction
No one can argue Bradbury's craft, his popularity with readers over the decades, or his influence on science fiction, fantasy, and popular culture in general. His exact place in science fiction, though...well, that definitely bears some discussion.

On the one hand, Ray Bradbury's name cannot help but remain popularly synonymous with the genre of science fiction—stories about the future, space travel, aliens, robots, and whatnot, to put it broadly. Certainly the editors at Bantam found SF a handy marketing label, splashing "'THE WORLD'S GREATEST LIVING SCIENCE-FICTION WRITER'" prominently upon the covers of several 1970s editions. Even they seemed a bit ambivalent about the term, however. The quotation marks, after all, suggested that someone's judgment was being quoted, though that someone was never identified; by the 1980s they simply had removed the peculiar punctuation. Yet still, despite their full-capital science-fictional assertions, Bantam often backpedaled amusingly, with the same cover also referring to the given work as "A MASTERWORK OF FANTASY"...a phrase placed higher than the "world's greatest," yet in type of softer color and slightly smaller font. The average reader could be forgiven for some confusion about cubbyholing.

Bradbury of course has written works that are clearly science fiction: *Fahrenheit 451* (1953), for example, that "most skilfully [sic] drawn" (Amis 109) dystopic future of consumerist conformity and book burning, or "A Sound of Thunder" (1952) with its time machine crackling noisily with energy, or "The Veldt" (1951), which features, among other futuristic gizmos, what we now would call immersive virtual reality. Yet he has also written a great deal of outright fantasy: *Something Wicked This Way Comes* (1962), for example, whose eerie traveling carnival contains, along with other creepy supernatural oddities, a carousel that can force hapless riders to grow one year older or younger per revolution, to death or to helpless infancy, depending on which direction its sinister owner sends it. Occasionally Bradbury's work focuses on the completely nonfantastic, such as in *Dandelion Wine* (1957), that nostalgic opus to the rosy Midwestern childhood of summer 1928. But sometimes— and here is where labels get the most problematic—the artist blurs the lines and mixes elements in supposed SF, completely without any stodgy concerns about genre.

The Martian Chronicles (1950), the book that first brought Bradbury to wider recognition beyond readers of the pulp SF and fantasy magazines, is a particularly interesting one to examine in this respect. On the one hand, futuristic science-fictional elements abound: gleaming rockets carrying first crewcut explorers and then settlers to Mars, mysterious Martians of ancient wisdom and otherworldly telepathy, references to the globe-spanning canals that astronomer Percival Lowell around the turn of the century imagined he saw, and a cataclysmic nuclear war. Yet, really, such then-current SF tropes are used without almost any reference to the science, or even nods to scientific plausibility, at all.

Modern readers should not fault Bradbury for giving Mars a breathable atmosphere, as this was a commonplace in 1940s and 1950s science fiction, before it was understood that the planet's main gas was carbon dioxide rather than oxygen; even Robert A. Heinlein, the dean of "hard" SF, did a similar thing in *Red Planet* (1949) just the year before.[2] But what about all those classic science-fictional rocket ships appearing throughout Bradbury's book? Are they chemically powered, like the sleek but deadly V-2s the Germans so few years before the time of writing had rained upon London? Are they driven by water or other fluids pumped through a nuclear reactor to spray, superheated and rapidly expanding, from the tail? Or are they moved by some even grander super-science?[3] In Heinlein's *Space Cadet* (1948) a character who cannot tell the difference between chemical and nuclear rockets receives some mild derision (35), but in *The Martian Chronicles* the issue is immaterial. The Martian "canals" are treated even more superficially. Percival Lowell asserted out that what was being seen was "not the canal proper, but the vegetation along its banks" (*Mars* 165), and later, after various trigonometric experiments, he suggested that the canals nevertheless were 15 or 20 miles wide (*Mars and Its Canals* 182). Whereas Heinlein, whose early editions of *Red Planet* incorporated a Lowellian map of Mars on its endpapers, alludes to the miles-wide nature of these supposed artifacts (25), in *The Martian Chronicles* a canal, with its "rim" over which a man can dangle his feet in the water (58), appears little different from those of, say, Venice.

Christopher Isherwood, who shrugged tolerantly at Bradbury's "characteristically casual implausibility" (57) even as he helped bring the author to a wider mainstream readership, noted at the very beginning that "[i]t may even be argued that *The Martian Chronicles* are not, strictly speaking, science fiction at all" (56). Bradbury himself, almost half a century later, seemed to chuckle at those "furious that [he] get[s] away with murder" by "us[ing] a scientific idea as a platform to leap into the air and never come back" (52). Such poetic rather than "scientific" uses of the trappings of SF can be seen throughout Bradbury's work, of course, enough that the term *speculative fiction*, which encompasses not only science fiction but also fantasy, horror, "weird fiction," and the like, seems a significantly better fit for most of his tales.

Still, critics and fans have gnawed the "Is Bradbury really a science fiction writer or not?" bone across the decades, always finding one more little strip of meat or drop of marrow. The issue has become so well known in popular culture that even the animated television show *The Simpsons* has addressed it: Middle school brainiac Martin Prince, running for class president, vows a library featuring the ABCs of science fiction—Asimov, Bester, and Clarke— and when a student asks, "Well, what about Ray Bradbury?" the SF snob simply replies with a dismissive wave of the hand, "I'm aware of his work" ("Lisa's Substitute").

The wry scene is amusing, and yet it also should remind us of the fruitlessness of trying to determine how many science fiction authors—and which ones—can dance on the head of a pin. Such quibbling over genre, after all, ignores perhaps the true draw of art: the delight of the interplay of idea, story, and language. Archaeologist Jeff Spender of *The Martian Chronicles* asserts that although a killjoy scientist examining a painting "can prove that color is only the way the cells are placed in a certain material to reflect light," it would be far better simply to judge the work as coming "from the hand and the mind of a man inspired," an artist who produced a "thing [that] is good" (67). This latter, really, is the way to approach Bradbury, who created works with "idea[s] and...color[s] [that] are drawn from life" but who at the same time "never let science crush the ae[s]thetic and the beautiful" (*Martian Chronicles* 67). If, as Jonathan R. Eller and William F. Touponce put it, "...Bradbury is primarily a fantasist, a mythmaker, a writer of moral fables" (2), it is his relentlessly genre-crossing approach that allows him the widest scope possible, in both idea and execution.

The Delight of Bradbury

As so many millions can attest, the art of Ray Bradbury—his print, naturally, but also his work in other media—is a delight. To comment that the central characteristic of Bradbury's artistry is its wild and vivid imagination is a truism...and yet of course a truism is true, and this one must be repeated now as well.[4] Who, after all, could envisage a story about a woman giving birth to a small blue pyramid with tentacles? Only Bradbury, in "Tomorrow's Child" (1948). Who could imagine a space captain's rocket chasing an elusive Jesus from planet to planet across the galaxy? Bradbury, in "The Man" (1948). A tattoo that can coalesce to depict the entirety of a person's life, including future death? *"The Illustrated Man"* (1951). A lighthouse calling up a lonely sea creature that has slumbered in the depths since the dinosaur age? "The Fog Horn" (1951). An advertisement in the back pages of *Popular Mechanics* as the Trojan horse for an extraterrestrial invasion? "'Boys! Raise Giant Mushrooms in *Your* Cellar!'" (1962). All of these ideas, and a dozen dozen more, are unmistakable Bradbury.

Yet regardless of whether he is writing about the science fictional, the utterly fantastic, or even simply the sunlit green lawns of an idealized Midwest, Bradbury has always been a very fine stylist and an engaging storyteller—a "master," Sarah-Warner J. Pell terms it, of "able craftsmanship, of beauty and poetry of style" (188). And of course that style, as Robert Reilly observes, "is like a great organ—it has many registers through which he ranges, counterpointing dark against light, simple against complex, beautiful against grotesque" (73). Such rich description and unexpected juxtapositions can be seen, for example, in "A Sound of Thunder," in which hunters from the year 2055 travel back in time on a safari for the biggest and most dangerous game animal of all, a Tyrannosaurus rex.

"'Jesus God,' whisper[s] Eckels," the jittery man whose stumbling, muddy bootprints soon will stomp and rend the fabric of history itself, and then Bradbury gives us our first look at the beast, a look that starts on the outside, then penetrates like an x-ray of the sickly entranced watcher's imagination:

> It came on great oiled, resilient, striding legs. It towered thirty feet above half of the trees, a great evil god, folding its delicate watchmaker's claws close to its oily reptilian chest. Each lower leg was a piston, a thousand pounds of white bone, sunk in thick ropes of muscle, sheathed over in a gleam of pebbled skin like the mail of a terrible warrior. Each thigh was a ton of meat, ivory, and steel mesh. (94)

When the viewpoint surfaces again for an external, almost cinematic view, Bradbury mixes imagery of frightfulness, size, and power with imagery of ironic delicacy:

> And from the great breathing cage of the upper body those two delicate arms dangled out front, arms with hands which might pick up and examine men like toys, while the snake neck coiled. And the head itself, a ton of sculpted stone, lifted easy upon the sky. Its mouth

gaped, exposing a fence of teeth like daggers. Its eyes rolled, ostrich eggs, empty of all expression save hunger. It closed its mouth in a death grin. It ran, its pelvic bones crushing aside trees and bushes, its taloned feet clawing damp earth, leaving prints six inches deep wherever it settled its weight. It ran with a gliding ballet step, far too poised and balanced for its ten tons. It moved into a sunlit arena warily, its beautifully made reptile hands feeling the air. (94)

And when the tyrannosaur finally spots its potential "toys," Bradbury juxtaposes "glitter[ing]" beauty with literally disgusting repellence: "Its armored flesh glittered like a thousand green coins. The coins, crusted with slime, steamed. In the slime, tiny insects wriggled, so that the entire body seemed to twitch and undulate, even while the monster itself did not move. It exhaled. The stink of raw flesh blew down the wilderness" (94). All of it is classic Bradbury style from one of his most classic stories.

Yet Bradbury is equally at home, and just as moving, when looking "only" at the beautiful and wondrous. In "The Rocket Man" (1951), for example, a high schooler stands in awe of his father's seemingly romantic profession as spaceship pilot, which takes him all over the solar system. Yet whereas other boys' spacemen fathers bring home as mementos the exotic rocks and sands of other worlds, the narrator's father does not, and just as he "never comment[s]" on his son's collection of "Martian rocks and Mercurian sands"— received in trade from friends—"fill[ing] his room," neither does he ever wear his uniform going to or from the rocket port, because he does not want to appear "vain about being a Rocket Man" (68). One night when the man comes home after a long stint in space, however, the youngster sneaks his father's suitcase:

And from the opened case spilled his black uniform, like a black nebula, stars glittering here or there, distantly, in the material. I kneaded the dark stuff in my warm hands; I smelled the planet Mars, an iron smell, and the planet Venus, a green ivy smell, and the planet Mercury, a scent of sulfur and fire; and I could smell the milky moon and the hardness of stars. I pushed the uniform into a centrifuge machine I'd built in my ninth-grade shop that year, set it whirling. Soon a fine powder precipitated in my retort. This I slid under a microscope. And while my parents slept unaware, and while our house was asleep…I stared down upon brilliant motes of meteor dust, comet tail, and loam from far Jupiter glistening like worlds themselves which drew me down the tube a billion miles into space, at terrific acceleration. (66)

The description is gorgeous and longing, and when at last the boy sleeps again, it is "with the little vial of magical dust in [his] pajama pocket, over [his] beating heart" (67).

For Bradbury, though, even rainwater collected in an old wooden barrel is a thing of evocative beauty. In *Dandelion Wine* (1957) a boy's grandfather makes the titular concoction; the mere words are "summer on the tongue," while the drink itself is "summer caught and stoppered" (9). Yet the base material is magic, too, both a reflection and a product of a grand, swirling, interconnected Nature:

> Nothing else in the world would do but the pure water which had been summoned from the lakes far away and the sweet fields of grassy dew on early morning, lifted to the open sky, carried in laundered clusters, nine hundred miles brushed with wind, electrified with high voltage, and condensed upon cool air. The water, falling, raining, gathered yet more of the heavens in its crystals. Taking something of the east wind and the west wind and the north wind and the south, the water made rain and the rain, within this hour of ritual, would be well on its way to wine. (10)

For the summer of 1928, long before vast weather fronts could be tracked by satellites in space or the knowledge, images, and sounds accumulated through the entirety of history could be called up in cities and towns around the globe with effortless speed, such a view is a beautifully poetic and stirring description that calls the imagination across spaces that the novel's characters otherwise could not experience.

While Bradbury's art ranges wide in time and space, in genre, and even in chosen medium, this quest of the imagination to draw together understanding or sympathies is common in his work. Willis E. McNelly has noted Bradbury's "nostalgia for either the past or future" (20). We can see this perhaps most prominently in *The Martian Chronicles* when the rocket from the Third Expedition lands, with the beautifully incongruous wish fulfillment of a dream, upon a sunlit lawn among the Victorian houses of a small town familiar to the main character "[b]orn in 1920 in Illinois" (35). Bradbury of course was born in this same year, in this same state, and yet just as he harks back to the cozily secure and simple times of his own small-town childhood, when the song "Beautiful Dreamer" drifted in the air (35) and Maxfield Parrish paintings hung in countless middle class parlors (37), he also harks forward, like many of his original readers, who may have hoped that "through the grace of God" and "science that…knows how to make *some* old men young again" (35; italics Bradbury's), they, too, might visit other planets in the year 2000. The huge medical advances may be a bit hokey, but the hokum can be difficult to resist.

Whereas the backward-looking gaze ends up being a trap laid for the Third Expedition by telepathic Martians, when the next Terran mission arrives, the nostalgia for the past—though ultimately bringing results little less deadly—at least is morally and intellectually more questing, and at least attempts to hark toward an enlightened future. In longing for a world without materialism and greed and the destruction of the beautiful, archaeologist Jeff Spender looks into an anchoring Martian past whose philosophy "knew how to live with nature" and "didn't try too hard to be all men and no animal" (66). It "sounds ideal" (66), his captain admits, but when Spender's path to paradise includes killing off his crewmembers one by one, and those of any succeeding expeditions as well, this imagined future proves as mirage-like as the earlier crew's departed relatives miraculously restored to life. Captain Wilder, conflicted but duty-bound, then closes off that path with a clichéd single "clean" shot to the chest, in the almost bloodless style of the old cowboy movies.

And that cinematic visual aesthetic is another classic piece of Bradbury's style, one that occurs again and again across his career. As Bradbury himself has observed, the love affair with film begun in his early childhood helped shape "the direction [his] writing has taken over the years, the type of writing [he] ha[s] done, and the way [he] ha[s] expressed [him]self" (qtd. in Weller 28). Certainly he ended up doing quite a lot of writing for visual media: "I Sing the Body Electric!" (1962) for *The Twilight Zone* television series, and films like *It Came from Outer Space* (1953) and *Moby Dick* (1956), for example, along with many other projects both successful and abortive.[5] Even throughout his print works, however, Bradbury often punctuates scenes with exquisite little set pieces of visual beauty and dramatic power. Such a technique is all the more effective for being something of a counterpoint to the way he often delves into characters' inner worlds with interior monologue or with third-person authorial observation.

Captain Wilder of *The Martian Chronicles*, for example, has agonized over the need to kill Spender, first with a huge half-page interior rant about the self-righteousness and blindness of the "rotten majority" (69), and then with silent urging to his quarry: "Go on, now, man, before it's too late" (70). Soon, though, once the echoes of the captain's rifle shot die away, Bradbury gives a tableau straight out of any of countless old black-and-white Western movies:

> They gathered around the body and someone said, "In the chest?"
> The captain looked down. "In the chest," he said. He saw how the rocks had changed color under Spender. (71)

Such juxtapositions of interior uncertainty and exterior movielike closure can be seen throughout Bradbury's breakthrough work. In *The Martian Chronicles* it occurs, to name just a few, in the inexplicable and ironic small-town funeral the still-disguised Martians stage for the members of the Third Expedition killed in their sleep (47-48), in the poignant image of the robot family staring up at the dead and "green[ly] burning" postnuclear Earth after the passing of their lonely old maker (166), and in the reflection of the last humans, now considered Martians themselves, staring back from the waters of a canal (181). Bradbury's entire canon, of course, is infused with this characteristic and striking cinematic aesthetic. Open nearly any tale, and we can find such lovely, affecting jewels of verbal and visual brilliance.

None of these elements of writerly craft gleams for the sake of mere prettiness, however. Beautiful this author's writing may be, but underlying it all—his fiercely fertile imagination, his versatile verbal style, his visual aesthetic and plotting—are a sense of wonder even in the seeming ordinary and a hopefulness in the face of threats large or subtle that are characteristically Bradburian. Bradbury can write movingly enough of, say, the nostalgic joys of rosily imagined small town life, and yet even when depicting greed or racism or the threat of nuclear annihilation, he does not lose sight of the enduring humaneness to which we should aspire.

Conclusion

Near the end of *Fahrenheit 451*, Granger, the leader of the dissident book memorizers, tells us that "[e]veryone must leave something behind when he dies..." (182):

> "A child or a book or a painting or a house or a wall built or a pair of shoes made. Or a garden planted. Something your hand touched in some way so your soul has somewhere to go when you die, and when people look at that tree or that flower you planted, you're there. It doesn't matter what you do..., so long as you changed something from the way it was before you touched it into something that's like you after you take your hands away." (182)

Ray Bradbury, whose first experimentation in art began in early childhood, and whose publications ranged from the 1930s all the way to the 2000s, certainly has left behind "something"—and what he has changed are generations of the recipients of his talent. This wildly imaginative and stylistically pleasing writer helped bring fantasy and science fiction to a broader audience, becoming not only perhaps the most recognized name in speculative fiction but also an enthusiastic voice for the Space Age. Bradbury's exuberance ranged widely, from the short stories that began his career, across hugely successful and instantly recognizable novels such as *The Martian Chronicles*, *Fahrenheit 451*, and *Dandelion Wine*, through radio, television, and film, to plays, poetry, and nonfiction. From the dinosaur-haunted jungles of prehistory to futures of robots and rocket ships, from the lightless bottom of the sea to the farthest stars, from the depths of the human psyche to humanity's most fundamental goodness, Ray Bradbury's unique genius ensures that his work will continue to be relished for many more decades to come.

Notes

1. In the foreword for the printing on the fortieth anniversary of *Fahrenheit 451*, Bradbury claims "probably [to] have written more poems, essays, stories, plays, and novels about libraries, librarians, and authors than any other writer today" ("Burning Bright" 17). William F. Touponce discusses some of these in the current volume.

2. Heinlein, however, gave very conscious attention in the plot to the underlying scientific principles, not to mention the careful calculations he had made beforehand (*Grumbles* 50).

3. The chapter of the Second Expedition, after all, contains a single, never-repeated reference to "gravitizers" (29).

4. We may quibble about an overexuberant metaphor here and there, but to sniff that "[h]is imagination is mediocre," as Damon Knight has (109), seems mistaken indeed.

5. See, for example, Eller's *Ray Bradbury Unbound*. See also Phil Nichols's discussion of *The Ray Bradbury Theater* in this volume.

Works Cited

Amis, Kingsley. *New Maps of Hell: A Survey of Science Fiction*. 1960. Arno, 1975.

Bradbury, Ray. "'Boys! Raise Giant Mushrooms in Your Cellar!'" 1962. *The Machineries of Joy*. 1964. Bantam, 1983, pp. 57-69.

———. "Burning Bright: A Foreword by Ray Bradbury." 1993. *Fahrenheit 451*, pp. 11-21.

———. *Dandelion Wine*. 1957. Bantam, 1964.

———. *Fahrenheit 451*. 1953. Ballantine, 2001.

———. "The Fog Horn." *The Golden Apples of the Sun*. 1951. Bantam, 1970, pp. 1-8.

———. "The Illustrated Man." *The Illustrated Man*. 1951. Bantam, 1969, pp. 1-5.

———. "I Sing the Body Electric!" Writ. Ray Bradbury. Dir. James Sheldon and William Claxton. *The Twilight Zone* season 3, episode 35. 18 May 1962.

———. *It Came from Outer Space*. Writ. Ray Bradbury and Harry Essex. Dir. Jack Arnold. Universal, 1953.

———. "The Man." 1948. *The Illustrated Man*. 1951. Bantam, 1969, pp. 42-53.

———. *The Martian Chronicles*. 1950. Bantam, 1975.

———. *Moby Dick*. Writ. Ray Bradbury and John Huston. Dir. John Huston. Warner Brothers, 1956.

———. "Playboy Interview: Ray Bradbury." *Playboy* May 1996, pp. 47+.

———. "The Rocket Man." 1951, *The Illustrated Man*. 1951. Bantam, 1969, pp. 65-74.

———. *Something Wicked This Way Comes*. 1962. Bantam, 1972.

———. "A Sound of Thunder." *The Golden Apples of the Sun*. 1952. Bantam, 1970, pp. 88-99.

———. "Tomorrow's Child." 1947. *I Sing the Body Electric*. 1969. Knopf, 1978, pp. 32-49.

———. "The Veldt." *The Illustrated Man*. 1951. Bantam, 1969, pp. 7-19.

Eller, Jonathan R. *Becoming Ray Bradbury*. U of Illinois P, 2011.

——— "Miracles of Rare Device: Bradbury and the American Southwest." Gloria McMillan, ed. *Orbiting Ray Bradbury's Mars: Biographical, Anthropological, Literary, Scientific and Other Perspectives*. Critical Explorations in Science Fiction and Fantasy Series 41. McFarland, 2013, pp. 11-23.

———. *Ray Bradbury Unbound*. U of Illinois P, 2014.

———, and William F. Touponce. *Ray Bradbury: The Life of Fiction*. Kent State UP, 2004.

Heinlein, Robert A. *Grumbles from the Grave*. Edited by Virginia Heinlein. 1989. Del Rey, 1990.

———. *Red Planet*. 1949. Del Rey, 1978.

———. *Space Cadet*. 1948. Del Rey, 1978.

Isherwood, Christopher. Rev. of *The Martian Chronicles*, by Ray Bradbury. *Tomorrow* Oct. 1950, pp. 56-58.

"Lisa's Substitute." Written by Jon Vitti, directed by Rich Moore. *The Simpsons* season 2, episode 19. Apr. 25, 1991.

Lowell, Percival. *Mars*. Houghton, 1894.

———. *Mars and Its Canals*. Macmillan, 1906.

McNelly, Willis E. "Ray Bradbury—Past, Present, and Future." *Ray Bradbury*. Ed. Martin Harry Greenberg and Joseph D. Olander. Writers of the 21st Century Series. Taplinger, 1980, pp. 17-24.

Knight, Damon. *In Search of Wonder* 2nd ed. Chicago: Advent, 1967.

Pell, Sarah-Warner J. "Style is the Man: Imagery in Bradbury's Fiction." *Ray Bradbury*. Edited by Martin Harry Greenberg and Joseph D. Olander. Writers of the 21st Century Series. Taplinger, 1980, pp. 186-94.

Reilly, Robert. "The Artistry of Ray Bradbury." *Extrapolation* 13 (1971), pp. 64-74.

Weller, Sam. *The Bradbury Chronicles: The Life of Ray Bradbury*. Harper, 2005.

Ray Douglas Bradbury_____

Karen Garvin

Ray Douglas Bradbury (1920-2012) was one of the most well-known and respected science fiction authors of the twentieth and early twenty-first centuries. During a career that spanned seven decades, Bradbury authored nearly sixty books and wrote numerous radio scripts and screenplays for both movies and television (Jonas, par. 6). His lyrical writing style and romantic optimism appealed to readers of all ages, and he was instrumental in bringing science fiction to a mainstream audience (Jonas, par. 3).

Bradbury was born on 22 August 1920 to Leonard Spaulding Bradbury (1890-1957) and Esther Marie Moberg (1888-1966). After losing an elder child to Spanish influenza, Bradbury's mother doted on him, and Bradbury grew into an emotionally sensitive child who latched onto his mother's fears and developed a strong interest in the macabre (Weller, *Chronicles* 31).

Bradbury grew up in Waukegan, Illinois, a small town on the outskirts of Chicago that would become the model for Green Town, a fictional setting that Bradbury used in several of his works. As a child, Bradbury was surrounded by artistic influences. His mother took him to movies on a regular basis, while his aunt, Nevada "Neva" Marion, inspired him by her art and read stories to him. Bradbury learned to read at age five and became an avid reader (Weller, *Chronicles* 30).

Like many American families, the Bradburys were hit hard by the Depression. Bradbury entered first grade in 1926, but in November his unemployed father packed up the family and headed West. They settled in Roswell, New Mexico, for a couple of weeks before continuing on to Tucson, Arizona. They lived close to the University of Arizona, where Bradbury spent afternoons sneaking into the campus halls and falling in love with the dinosaur fossils and other exhibits (Weller, *Chronicles* 35-37).

On 27 March 1927, Bradbury's mother gave birth to Elizabeth Jane (1927-1928). Bradbury's father, still unable to find work, reluctantly moved the family back to Waukegan. Bradbury was jealous of the attention that his baby sister received, and when she died from influenza in February 1928 he felt responsible. Guilt-stricken, he turned to movies, magic, and books for solace (Weller, *Chronicles* 40-41).

The family returned to Tucson in 1932. Bradbury, now in seventh grade, auditioned for a school play and nurtured dreams of becoming a writer. He began hanging out at KGAR, the local radio station, and was offered a stint at reading comic strips aloud on air. He received "pay" in the form of movie tickets. Bradbury loved the job, but once again, his father could not find work, and the family returned to Illinois (Weller, *Chronicles* 65-66).

In the spring of 1934, the Bradburys moved to Los Angeles, California. This time, Bradbury's father managed to find employment as a lineman just as they were about to run out of money (Weller, *Chronicles*, 71). Bradbury hung out in front of local film studios with his autograph book on the chance that he would meet a movie star. On one occasion he met George Burns and told him that he had written speculative scripts for the Burns and Allen radio show. Burns was polite and used one of Bradbury's pieces for his show (Weller, *Chronicles*, 76-77). Encouraged by this moderate success, Bradbury began submitting stories to the slick New York magazines, but his unpolished work was rejected (Weller, *Chronicles* 82).

While attending Los Angeles High School, Bradbury wrote and produced a play for the school's annual talent show as well as writing movie reviews for the school newspaper (Weller, *Chronicles* 83). He graduated in June 1938 and in August began selling afternoon newspapers on a local street corner. He spent the rest of his day writing and watching movies. Bradbury applied to and was accepted at Los Angeles City College, but he decided that college was not for him (Weller, *Chronicles* 91). Instead, he became an autodidact, spending time at the local libraries where he devoured books on a variety of subjects (Bradbury, *Hot Topic* par. 2).

In 1939, Bradbury was contributing to a local science fiction group's fanzine when he decided to start his own publication, which he named *Futuria Fantasia* (Weller, *Chronicles* 93-105). That summer, he attended the First World Science Fiction Convention and the New York World's Fair, both of which would leave lasting impressions on him (Weller, *Chronicles* 93-97).

In the fall of 1940, Bradbury published a story in *Script*, a Hollywood literary magazine (Weller, *Chronicles* 102). The next year he collaborated with Henry Hasse (1913-1977) to coauthor "Pendulum," which sold in July 1941 to *Super Science Stories* magazine (Weller, *Chronicles* 104). It was Bradbury's first professional sale, quickly followed by the horror story "The Candle," in *Weird Tales* in 1942 and "Promotion to Satellite" in *Thrilling Wonder Stories* in 1943 (Weller, *Chronicles* 109, 115).

In 1944, Bradbury sold twenty-two stories, including "The Lake," which was published in the May 1944 issue of *Weird Tales* (Weller, *Chronicles* 119). It was the first story that he had written that was nonderivative and entirely his own (Weller, *Chronicles* 112). His gift was the ability to create a viable first draft in a few hours, but ever the perfectionist, he would revise the work many times (Weller, "Art"). Bradbury worried that he was not producing enough quality work at this early stage of his career, and even sought counseling to help allay his fear of failure (Weller, *Chronicles* 120).

Bradbury scorned the distinction between serious and mainstream literature and felt that his work was taken less seriously because he had contributed to so many pulp magazines (Weller, *Chronicles* 160). He rejected the idea that science fiction was less worthy than other forms of literature and allowed a friend to persuade him to submit stories to mainstream magazines, including *Mademoiselle* and *Collier's* (Weller, *Chronicles* 124).

A road trip to Mexico with a friend in 1945 introduced Ray to a new world, new foods, and new celebrations. He attended a Día de los Muertos festival and visited the mummies of Guanajuato, which provided fresh inspiration for his work (Weller, *Chronicles* 125-30).

In 1947 Bradbury's first story collection was published. *Dark Carnival* contained science fiction and fantasy stories based on a traveling carnival theme, including "The Homecoming," "The Night," "The Man Upstairs," "Jack-in-the-Box," and the terrifying story "The Small Assassin" (Jonas; Weller, *Chronicles* 141-44).

That spring, he met Marguerite Susan McClure (1922-2003) in a bookstore (Weller, *Chronicles* 137-38). They were married on September 27 and rented an apartment close to Venice Beach, where Bradbury wrote during the day while Marguerite worked as a secretary (Weller, *Chronicles* 147-49). After the birth of their first child, Susan Marguerite, on 5 November 1949, Bradbury began working out of his parents' garage, where he pumped out one story a week.

The Martian Chronicles was Bradbury's first novel, comprised of earlier short stories with a Mars theme that had been pulled together into a single book. Published in May 1950, it became one of his best-known works (Weller, *Chronicles* 162).

In February 1951 Bradbury published another collection, *The Illustrated Man*, which contained eighteen short stories, including "The Veldt," "The Long Rain," and "The Rocket Man." On May 17, his second daughter, Ramona Anne, was born. Bradbury maintained his writing pace and released another story collection, *The Golden Apples of the Sun*, in 1953 (Weller, *Chronicles* 166-67, 179, 197).

The McCarthyite political climate of 1950s America inspired one of Bradbury's most famous works: *Fahrenheit 451*, a novel set in the dystopian future where books are outlawed (Weller, "Bradbury's 180" par. 2). Published in October 1953, the novel was comprised of earlier short stories, including "Long after Midnight," which was later renamed "The Fireman" and published in the January 1951 edition of *Galaxy* magazine. *Fahrenheit 451* also was serialized in three parts in *Playboy* magazine, the first installment appearing in the March 1954 issue (Bradbury, *Hot Topic* par. 12-14).

Bradbury wrote the first draft in nine days, cloistering himself in the basement of the UCLA library, where he fed money into a coin-operated typewriter (Weller, *Chronicles* 201). Ballantine Books later expressed interest in the work, but requested that Bradbury extend the manuscript by another 25,000 words (Bradbury, *Hot Topic* par. 5). The book won the 1954 American Academy of Arts and Letters Award in Literature and the Commonwealth Club of California Gold Medal.

In September 1953, Bradbury and his family went to Ireland, where he worked on the screenplay for John Houston's film *Moby Dick* (Bradbury, "Speech"). Bradbury had a difficult time with Houston, and when he returned to the United States and received other offers to write screenplays, he turned them down (Weller, *Chronicles* 224-31). However, Bradbury continued to write for radio and television, producing scripts for shows that included NBC's *X Minus One*, the *ABC Radio Workshop*, CBS's *Suspense*, *Alfred Hitchcock Presents*, and Rod Serling's *Twilight Zone* (Weller, *Chronicles* 237).

In 1955 Bradbury's third daughter, Bettina Francion (1955-), was born on July 22. That year, Bradbury's first children's book, *Switch on the Night*, was published by Pantheon Books (Weller, *Chronicles* 235-36). On 13 August 1958, Bradbury's fourth daughter, Alexandra Allison (1958-), was born, and shortly after her birth the family moved into a larger house (Weller, *Chronicles* 249). Bradbury wrote three more books during the 1950s: *The October Country* (1955), *Dandelion Wine* (1957), and *A Medicine for Melancholy* (1959).

The 1960s were another busy decade for Bradbury, who published eight books, including *Something Wicked This Way Comes* (1962), *R Is for Rocket* (1962), *The Vintage Bradbury* (1965), *S Is for Space* (1966), and *I Sing the Body Electric!* (1969). In 1962 he was offered work as a consultant on the United States government exhibit for the 1964 New York World's Fair, and François Truffaut purchased the film rights to *Fahrenheit 451* (Weller, Chronicles 262-64, 273). The film premiered in New York on 2 November 1966, but received poor reviews. *The Illustrated Man* and *The Picasso Summer* were also made into films, but failed to capture the essence of Bradbury's writing (Weller, *Chronicles* 275, 279).

Bradbury showed no signs of slowing down; eight more books followed in the 1970s, fifteen during the 1980s, and between 1990 and 2007 he produced another nineteen books. His first collection of poetry, *When Elephants Last in the Dooryard Bloomed*, was published on October 1973, and contained fifty-one poems.

In 1976, Disney hired Bradbury as a consultant to write the script for their Florida-based EPCOT Center's "Spaceship Earth" ride. Situated inside a geodesic dome that would become a focal point for the Florida theme park, the ride carried visitors on a journey through time from Earth's prehistoric age to the Space Age (Weller, *Chronicles* 296-98).

Bradbury, who felt at home in front of an audience as much as he did behind the keys of his typewriter, hosted ABC's 1979 commemorative program, *Infinite Horizons: Space Beyond Apollo*. In 1985 he began hosting *The Ray Bradbury Theater*, which debuted on HBO and later moved to the USA Network. The sixty-five episode show ran for seven years and won a dozen Cable Ace Awards (Weller, *Chronicles* 299-300, 310-15).

Several of Bradbury's works were made into movies and television shows, including *The Martian Chronicles*, which aired as a three-part miniseries in 1980. Bradbury was not involved in writing the script and thought the show was boring, but one tale he longed to see made into a film was *Something Wicked This Way Comes*. Bradbury had written a screenplay for it in 1955 but failed to get financial support; several other attempts had been made to produce the film, but it was not until 1982 that Disney purchased the film rights. Despite production headaches, the movie premiered in April 1983 to mixed reviews (Weller, *Chronicles* 300-302, 304-10).

During his lifetime Bradbury wrote nearly sixty books. His later work included *The Halloween Tree* (1972), *The Mummies of Guanajuato* (1978), *The Ghosts of Forever* (1981), *The Toynbee Convector* (1988), the nonfiction book *Zen in the Art of Writing* (1989), *From the Dust Returned* (2001), *Farewell Summer* (2006), and *Now and Forever* (2007).

Bradbury received commendations for his work, including the 1984 Prometheus Hall of Fame Award from the Libertarian Futurist Society for *Fahrenheit 451*, the 2000 National Book Foundation's Medal for Distinguished Contribution to American Letters, the 2004 National Medal of Arts, and in 2007, a Pulitzer Prize Special Citation (Libertarian Futurist Society; Bradbury, "Speech"; Weller, *Chronicles* 331-32).

Bradbury, who denied being an optimist, never allowed himself to be defeated (Weller, "Art"). After a stroke in November 1999 that left him hospitalized for a month, he dictated *Let's All Kill Constance* (2002) to his daughter Alexandra (Weller, Art; *Chronicles* 322). After his wife died on 24 November 2003, Bradbury continued to write, and produced another five books before his death on 5 June 2012, at the age of ninety-one.

Works Cited

Bradbury, Ray. "First Spark: Ray Bradbury Turns 90, the Universe and UCLA Celebrate." *Hot Topic*, 2011. http://www.spotlight.ucla.edu/ray-bradbury/hot-topic/. Accessed on 15 Aug. 2017.

———. "National Book Award Acceptance Speech," 15 November 2000. http://www.nationalbook.org/nbaacceptspeech_rbradbury.html#.WL7no3-CQTo. Accessed on 15 Aug. 2017.

Jonas, Gerald. "Ray Bradbury, Who Brought Mars to Earth With a Lyrical Mastery, Dies at 91." *New York Times* 6 June 2012. http://www.nytimes.com/2012/06/07/books/ray-bradbury-popularizer-of-science-fiction-dies-at-91.html. Accessed on 15 Aug. 2017.

Libertarian Futurist Society. http://lfs.org/awards.shtml. Accessed on 15 Aug. 2017.

Weller, Sam. *The Bradbury Chronicles: The Life of Ray Bradbury*. Harper, 2005.

———. "Ray Bradbury, The Art of Fiction No. 203." *Paris Review* 192, Spring 2010. https://www.theparisreview.org/interviews/6012/ray-bradbury-the-art-of-fiction-no-203-ray-bradbury. Accessed on 15 Aug. 2017.

———. "Ray Bradbury's 180 on *Fahrenheit 451*." *Dallas News* 12 April 2013. http://www.dallasnews.com/opinion/commentary/2013/04/12/sam-weller-ray-bradburys-180-on-fahrenheit-451. Accessed on 15 Aug. 2017.

CRITICAL
CONTEXTS

Big Brother, Little Sister: Ray Bradbury, Social Pressure, and the Challenges to Free Speech_____

Karen Garvin

Ray Douglas Bradbury (1920-2012) is remembered as one of the most influential science fiction writers of the twentieth and early twenty-first centuries. During a professional writing career that spanned almost seventy years, Bradbury produced more than fifty books, which included eleven novels. He wrote more than 600 short stories, many of which were gathered into multiple anthologies, and his opus included plays, radio scripts, television scripts, and screenplays.

Although he is most commonly thought of as a science fiction writer, Bradbury's genre-spanning work never fit neatly into any one literary category. He wrote not only science fiction but also fantasy, horror, mystery, nonfiction, poetry, and even a children's book. In fact, most of his stories actually are not science fiction, but are instead fantasy and horror, such as his 1962 novel *Something Wicked This Way Comes*, a coming-of-age story set in mythical Green Town, Illinois, a stand-in for Bradbury's hometown of Waukegan, Illinois, which he uses as a setting in several other works, including the 1957 novel *Dandelion Wine* and the 2006 novel *Farewell Summer*.

Bradbury read widely, even from a young age. He learned to read at age five by studying the comic strips and fell in love with L. Frank Baum's *The Wizard of Oz* series, captivated by the colorful illustrations as much as by the incredible stories the books contained. Bradbury devoured books about dinosaurs and magic, and became hooked on Edgar Rice Burroughs's Tarzan novels and Mars novels. It was Burroughs's romantic image of the planet Mars that would bury itself into Bradbury's subconscious, resurfacing when he wrote his own Mars stories that would later be compiled into the 1950 novel *The Martian Chronicles* (Weller, *Bradbury Chronicles* 30, 48).

Bradbury began writing during his childhood by penning traditional horror stories and imitating those writers whose work he fell in love with, which included Edgar Allan Poe's *Tales of Mystery and Imagination* (Weller, *Bradbury Chronicles* 42). Themes of the Gothic run heavily throughout Bradbury's works, even in his science fiction. But perhaps that is inescapable, because as Patrick Brantlinger notes, both science fiction and the Gothic have shared literary conventions: They both explore the limits of reason, and in a sense, they both are antithetical to reason (30, 38). But where the romantic Gothic tales turn to ghosts and the supernatural in order to arouse feelings of terror in readers, science fiction stories turn to alien encounters and advanced technology—perhaps so advanced that it is indistinguishable from magic—in order to arouse feelings of wonder in readers (Brantlinger 38).

Gothic literature was a reaction against Enlightenment values, which placed an emphasis on rational thought, as well as against the growing industrialization of the late eighteenth century (Brantlinger 31). Bradbury's own values fit neatly into the Gothic landscape, as he was not particularly interested in the technology that made his rockets work, nor with computers or chemistry. Bradbury was a celebrated technophobe, although that is perhaps too strong a word. Bradbury did not hate technology—he simply believed that it was a tool, and like most tools, it could be misused (Weller, *Bradbury Chronicles* 168, 180). He never used a computer, even though he bought one; instead he relied on his trusty IBM Selectric typewriter (Weller, "Art of Fiction"). He never learned to drive, and only took his first airplane flight in 1982, at the age of 62. Bradbury scorned electronic books, saying that they were not real books, that real books had to be something that you could hold in your hands and experience (Weller, "Art of Fiction").

Bradbury's influence on American popular culture and American writers, screenwriters, and filmmakers was tremendous, and his work continues to inspire today's readers and audiences. The celebrated horror writer Stephen King cited Bradbury as the "nurturing influence" on his own work (qtd. in Weller, *Bradbury Chronicles* 153), and director Steven Spielberg said that Bradbury's most important contribution to American culture was his ability to show readers that there were no boundaries (qtd. in Weller, *Bradbury Chronicles* 11).

Many science fiction writers, including Ursula K. Le Guin, Kim Stanley Robinson, Elizabeth Bear, Daniel H. Wilson, and Neil Gaiman, said that Bradbury was responsible for fueling their love of science fiction and of reading in general. Robinson called Bradbury an ambassador for science fiction, and credited his "open and welcoming style" for helping to introduce science fiction to mainstream American audiences, many of whom had never read science fiction before (Adams par. 34). Indeed, for many readers, Bradbury's appeal was his ability to relegate the technology and hard science to the background and to focus on the people in the story.

Bradbury was one of the four major science fiction authors of the mid twentieth century whose influence on the reading public elevated science fiction from the fringes of literature, the pulp magazines, and put it in front of mainstream audiences. The four authors, whom astronomer and writer David Brin referred to as "the BACH quartet," consisted of the hard science fiction writers Isaac Asimov, Arthur C. Clarke, and Robert A. Heinlein, and Bradbury. But while the other three writers focused on more traditional space adventure stories and dazzled their readers with advanced technology and scientific facts, for Bradbury the science was tangential and served merely as the backdrop (Derleth 191; Adams par. 13). For instance, the rockets in *The Martian Chronicles* are barely described; their purpose is to get the Earth people to Mars, and the technology is more or less taken for granted. Bradbury does not want to focus on how the rockets work, because his story is about the people, not the technology.

Bradbury and the triumvirate of Asimov, Clarke, and Heinlein were jointly responsible for pulling science fiction out of its "pulp-magazine ghetto" and establishing it as a legitimate form of literature, but it was Bradbury who elevated science fiction into an art form (Brin 471). Called the "poet of the pulps," Bradbury has a writing style that has been described as lyrical, and his romantic optimism appealed to readers of all ages, garnering him an international audience as well (Weller, "Art of Fiction"). Nevertheless, Bradbury denied on more than one occasion that he was a science fiction writer.

As a burgeoning author, Bradbury built his early career with sales of short stories in the science fiction pulp magazines that included *Weird Tales*, *Thrilling Wonder Stories*, and *Astounding Science-Fiction*. In 1941, he sold his first short story, "Pendulum," coauthored with Henry Hasse, to *Super Science Stories*. From that point forward, Bradbury's sales in the pulps began growing with regularity.

In the 1940s, however, there was still a stigma associated with science fiction that deemed it less worthy than other forms of literature. Bradbury hated the distinction (Weller, *Bradbury Chronicles* 160), but the only way he could change readers' minds was to break out of the pulps. After his friend Grant Beach persuaded him to submit work to mainstream publications, Bradbury decided to use the pseudonym William Elliott to avoid prejudicing editors against his work. He sold three stories, one each to *Collier's*, *Mademoiselle*, and *Charm* (Weller, *Bradbury Chronicles* 124) and established himself as not just a science fiction writer, but a *writer*.

Bradbury was influenced from a young age by newspaper comic strips, especially *Buck Rogers in the 25th Century*, which he cut out and saved from the pages of the newspaper. When his passion for Buck Rogers was ridiculed by his third-grade classmates as "childish," Bradbury threw his collection away, but it was not long before he regretted the decision. The incident became a turning point for Bradbury, who recognized that the romance and imagination inherent in the comic strips was something worth cherishing (Weller, Bradbury, *Chronicles* 45-47).

He was swept up by magic, too. Bradbury was enamored by Blackstone the Magician, whom he had first seen perform in 1928 (Weller, *Bradbury Chronicles* 41). After his parents bought him a simple magic trick, Bradbury began practicing tricks and putting on magic shows for his family (Weller, *Bradbury Chronicles* 49). At another time, he attended a carnival where he watched Mr. Electrico pour thousands of volts of electricity through his body (Weller, *Bradbury Chronicles* 56). The magician from the radio show *Chandu the Magician* was another of Bradbury's early influences, and the young Bradbury would rewrite Chandu's scripts from memory and imagine himself battling the villains of the world (Weller, "Art of Fiction"). Bradbury later would use the setting of the autumn carnival and the persona of Electrico as inspiration for *Something Wicked This Way Comes*, a novel in which he pursues the themes of good and evil, youth and maturity, using as his story's vehicle a carousel that could be run forward or backward in time to change the age of the rider (Weller, *Bradbury Chronicles* 56, 258; Weiner 83).

Bradbury had only a high school education, but he furthered himself by reading widely at the local library. His love affair with libraries dated from his childhood in Waukegan and would continue during his high school days. "I discovered me in the library," Bradbury said in a 2010 interview for *Paris Review* (Weller, "Art of Fiction"). After graduating from high school in 1938, Bradbury went to the library three nights a week, drawing inspiration from literary sources as well as popular novels. His favorite literary authors included George Bernard Shaw, John Steinbeck, and Thomas Wolfe, and the poets Shakespeare and Robert Frost (Weller, "Art of Fiction"). Bradbury also acknowledged reading Heinlein and Clarke, but he credited the works of nineteenth-century authors H. G. Wells and Jules Verne as being the major influences on his science fiction writing. Bradbury compared himself to Verne, calling himself a "writer of moral fables, an instructor in the humanities." For Bradbury, as for Verne, humans could hope to overcome the difficult situations they found themselves in through moral behavior (Weller, "Art of Fiction").

Bradbury's stories are clearly products of the age in which he worked, the midcentury American culture where the men went out to work in unfulfilling jobs while their wives stayed home, tending to the equally unfulfilling chores (Weiner 85-86). Although Bradbury uses this story device in both of his most influential novels, *The Martian Chronicles* and *Fahrenheit 451*, his stock characters manage to tell the story without exposing readers to deeper, personal motives of the characters. This approach makes Bradbury's work suitable for a wide age range of readers and is important because at the time many science fiction fans were juvenile readers (Weiner 87).

But in his creation of rather shallow characters, Bradbury was not alone. Indeed, many of the early twentieth-century science fiction writers were swept up by the science, and their characters lacked depth. This was a problem with science fiction that was recognized early on by avid readers of the genre and only gradually came to be recognized by science fiction writers and editors. Science fiction, with its already hard-to-define boundaries, needed to appeal to readers because the story was good and the characters were worthy of consideration, not because the story was filled with facts and predictions (Derleth 189-90).

In 1952, science fiction writer August Derleth wrote that "Unquestionably in top place among contemporary American writers of science-fiction is Ray Bradbury, whose two collections, *The Martian Chronicles* and *The Illustrated Man*, stand head and shoulders above all other science-fiction in our time." Bradbury accomplished this by writing about humans, not gadgets. After going on to describe Bradbury as "the most literate and original of writers in the [science fiction] genre," Derleth explained that part of Bradbury's appeal was his willingness to embrace ideological themes in his stories, including racial prejudice (Derleth 191).

The best science fiction is, after all, about people, not technology. The aim of good science fiction is to explore ethical questions, and that means being willing to examine the failings of our societies and having the courage to work toward making difficult changes in order to avoid future disasters. Bradbury, despite his somewhat formulaic characters, managed to imbue them with a sense of purpose, hopes, fears, and dreams (Harlow 311).

Mars, the Red Planet, Bringer of War
Mars features prominently in Bradbury's imagination, and it had done so since his childhood when he first read Burroughs's Mars novels. During the early 1940s, Bradbury began writing a series of short stories set on Mars. He sold the first one, "The Million-Year Picnic," to *Planet Stories* in 1946, and within three years had

enough stories to warrant publishing an anthology of science fiction shorts. When an editor at Doubleday suggested that Bradbury pull the separate stories into one novel, he began organizing them into what biographer Sam Weller called "a narrative mosaic that would literally change the field of science fiction" (Weller, *Bradbury Chronicles* 155).

The resulting novel, *The Martian Chronicles*, reads like a chronological history of the Red Planet, from the arrival of Earth men to the extinction of the Martians, and finally, to the Earth men becoming the new Martians. Bradbury's stories, now chapters, dealt with a variety of political and social issues, including censorship, a topic of growing importance for Bradbury, who had become increasingly disillusioned with politics when the House Un-American Activities Committee began scouring Hollywood during the late 1940s for Communist sympathizers (Weller, *Bradbury Chronicles* 193-94). Bradbury also compared his image of the invasion of Mars to the taming of the American West (Weller, *Bradbury Chronicles* 155-56):

> Mars was a distant shore, and the men spread upon it in waves. Each wave different, and each wave stronger. The first wave carried with it men accustomed to spaces and coldness and being alone, the coyote and cattlemen, with no fat on them, with faces the years had worn the flesh off, with eyes like nailheads, and hands like the material of old gloves, ready to touch anything. Mars could do nothing to them, for they were bred to plains and prairies as open as the Martian fields. They came and made things a little less empty, so that others would find courage to follow. They put panes in hollow windows and lights behind the panes. (*Martian Chronicles* 114-15)

Given the ideological subject matter of the novel, in which the various human colonists import the worst of humanity's behaviors to Mars when they arrive, *The Martian Chronicles* could read as one long lecture, but there is enough distance, figuratively and literally, from Mars, that it allows Bradbury to write about compelling real-world topics including racism, environmental disaster, disease, extinction, and censorship, without making his readers go on the defensive. Instead, Bradbury's skill as a storyteller shines through, allowing readers to get caught up in a romantic vision of Mars in which Earthlings reinvent themselves on a new world (Harlow 311-12), even as the arrival of humans on the Red Planet inadvertently brings about the Martian genocide. In the chapter "—And the Moon Be Still as Bright," Earth men from the fourth expedition to Mars discover that all of the Martians are dead, killed from chicken pox, which "burnt them black and dried them out to brittle flakes" (*Martian Chronicles* 66).

The description of the dead Martians, whose bodies Bradbury describes as piles of autumn leaves, is surreal, and serves to distance readers from the rotting of dead bodies while managing to instill a sense of horror (*Martian Chronicles* 65). While the space explorers lament the passing of the Martian race, later characters treat their bodies as debris. Young boys, hiking through the Martian countryside and investigating the ancient, empty Martian cities, imagine they are running through autumn leaves. But these are not leaves—they are the blackened flakes of dead Martians. As the boys run from house to house they find Martian bodies and kick the debris, where the first to arrive gets to be the Musician and play the "white xylophone bones beneath the outer covering of black flakes" (*Martian Chronicles* 117).

The image of autumn leaves weaves itself into several of Bradbury's works, including *The Martian Chronicles* and *Something Wicked This Way Comes*. But another image crops up in *The Martian Chronicles* that would resurface in Bradbury's later work, too: the Firemen. The Firemen—with a capital F—whom Bradbury describes as "antiseptic warriors," burn clean all traces of Martian bodies from the cities, "separating the terrible from the normal," and cleaning the planet so the Earth people would not have to see what a terrible thing they had done to the Martians, even if had been done unintentionally (*Martian Chronicles* 118).

The lessons inherent in *The Martian Chronicles* about humanity's impact on the environment tell a serious tale that continues to resonate with modern readers. Bradbury's masterpiece has been described as a pivotal work, with a profound influence not only on literature but on the thought processes of scientists and citizens (Harlow 314). His mundane humans on Mars are regular people who find themselves swept into novel situations and locations but nevertheless find ways to adjust to their new home while retaining the attributes that make them human—for better or worse (Derleth 191).

One of those people is businessman Sam Parkhill, who in the chapter "The Off Season" has just opened the first hot dog stand on Mars, an aluminum building that he erected from the surplus metal of a crashed rocket. Bursting with pride, Sam tells his wife Elma that "Sam's Hot Dogs" is going to rake in a fortune because Sam has wisely chosen a spot near the intersection of two main roads to locate his restaurant. It will be only a month before the next rockets arrive from Earth, carrying hungry customers, and Sam is anxious for their business.

His wife is less sure of their success, and after a Martian visits them and Sam overreacts and kills the Martian, the couple are faced by more Martians. Sam is fearful of revenge, but the Martians are there to bring bad tidings. Sam and Elma look up at the sky in time to see Earth engulfed in flame. Unfortunately for the would-be entrepreneur, his customer base is now extinct. Elma, who never seemed enthusiastic about the hot dog stand, remarks to her husband, "This looks like it's going to be an off season" (*Martian Chronicles* 191).

The Martian Chronicles is a compilation of short stories Bradbury pulled together into a single book at the behest of an editor from Doubleday. Several of the stories were published separately, including the chapter "There Will Come Soft Rains." In this story, the protagonist is an automated house that is going about performing its daily chores despite its human occupants being gone. Bradbury's brooding, Gothic atmosphere is evident in the description of what has happened to the Featherstone family, the former occupants of the house:

The entire west face of the house was black, save for five places. Here the silhouette in paint of a man mowing a lawn. Here, as in a photograph, a woman bent to pick flowers. Still farther over, their images burned on wood in one titanic instant, a small boy, hands flung into the air; higher up, the image of a thrown ball, and opposite him a girl, hands raised to catch a ball which never came down. (*Martian Chronicles* 222)

Bradbury makes no direct reference to an atomic bomb, yet his description is chilling. Here an ideal American suburban family is at ease in their yard, oblivious to danger even as they are vaporized by the blast from an atomic bomb. Bradbury had seen a photograph of a house in Hiroshima that had "nuclear shadows" of people burned into its sides and was so moved by the image that he was inspired to write the story (Weller, "Art of Fiction").

While *The Martian Chronicles* remains in print and continues to entertain readers, it is another of Bradbury's novels that takes center stage: his runaway bestseller, *Fahrenheit 451*.

The Pleasures of Fire
In the mid-1940s, Bradbury read Arthur Koestler's novel *Darkness at Noon*. Set in 1930s Russia during the Stalin show trials, the story is about Nicholas Rubashov, a former Soviet revolutionary who is arrested and tried for treason under Stalin's rule. Rubashov, betrayed by the very political party that he helped install into power, is put into prison, where he endures psychological torture and confesses to crimes that he has not committed. Koestler's dystopian novel was inspired by his own experience as a political prisoner in Spain during the Spanish Civil War, and served as inspiration for George Orwell and Aldous Huxley. Bradbury would draw inspiration from Koestler's work, too.

By early 1946, Bradbury had an idea for a story in which firemen burned books rather than putting out fires. He put his notes for the story aside, but the seed of an idea had been planted; it only needed time to germinate. Meanwhile, Bradbury drafted "Where Ignorant Armies Clash by Night," a short story about book burning in a post-apocalyptic world, and set to work on another story, "Long After Midnight," which would be renamed "The Fireman." Bradbury typed the draft for the story during the summer of 1950 in the basement of the UCLA library, using a rental typewriter, and his agent, Don Congdon, sold the 25,000-word novella to *Galaxy Science Fiction* magazine.

"The Fireman" was published in February 1951, and for a time, that was the end of it. But this was during the early 1950s, when the American political climate was rife with censorship and virulent anti-Communist sentiments, such as those promulgated by Senator Joseph McCarthy, whose demagogic efforts to stem the "Red Scare" became known as McCarthyism. Bradbury spoke out publicly on the topic of free speech and even ran a full-page newspaper ad in which he denounced censorship. His experiences during this tumultuous era helped form the core of what would become one of his most famous works: *Fahrenheit 451*, a novel set in the dystopian future where books are outlawed.

During a trip to New York City in 1951, Bradbury saw Sidney Kingsley's play based on Koestler's *Darkness at Noon*. Bradbury became interested in revising and expanding "The Fireman" (Eller 175-76). In early 1953, Bradbury signed a contract with Ballantine Books to write a collection that would include "The Fireman," but the editors wanted him to expand the story by another 25,000 words. Bradbury was determined to flesh out the story into a full-length novel, which had a variety of working titles, including "Fahrenheit 270" and *Fahrenheit 204*, before Bradbury called the fire department and asked them at what temperature paper burns (Eller 176).

Fahrenheit 451 is set in the not-too-distant future, with fireman Guy Montag as the protagonist. It is Montag's duty—and pleasure—to burn books for a living. Books are dangerous because they contain ideas, and for the inhabitants of Montag's world, the twin goals of happiness and harmony must not be disturbed by unwelcome thoughts that might lead to antagonism (Patai 43). The citizens are lulled into complacency by inane television shows and constantly bombarded by advertising, retreating into a kind of childlike stupor where they consume whatever is on the television while avoiding anything that would require them to think or analyze.

Montag starts out as a complacent member of society, but after meeting a new neighbor, Clarisse McClellan, who asks him whether he is happy, Montag begins to do some soul searching. Eventually he begins to question his job and wonders what is in the books that make them so dangerous. Montag smuggles a book home, thinking that no one has noticed, but his boss, Fire Chief Captain Beatty, knows that something is up. As Montag becomes ever more rebellious, even daring to read a book aloud to a group of his wife's friends, Bradbury stages a scene in which Beatty has a showdown with Montag. Here Beatty is a stand-in for society, a sort of Grand Inquisitor whose role it is to bring Montag back into the fold (Patai 43).

When Montag calls in sick to work one day, Beatty, who suspects Montag has squirreled away some books, visits him at home and warns him about the dangers they pose. Authors were "full of evil thoughts" (*Fahrenheit 451* 55) that threatened the happiness of society because those thoughts might inadvertently make someone, somewhere, feel bad. Beatty explains:

> "Now let's take up the minorities in our civilization, shall we? Bigger the population, the more minorities. Don't step on the toes of the dog-lovers, the cat-lovers, doctors, lawyers, merchants, chiefs, Mormons, Baptists, Unitarians, second-generation Chinese, Swedes, Italians, Germans, Texans, Brooklynites, Irishmen, people from Oregon or Mexico. The people in this book, this play, this TV serial are not meant to represent any actual painters, cartographers, mechanics anywhere. The bigger your market, Montag, the less you handle controversy, remember that! ... It [censorship] didn't come from the Government down. There was no dictum, no declaration, no censorship, to start with, no! Technology, mass exploitation, and minority pressure carried the trick, thank God. Today, thanks to them, you can stay happy all the time, you are allowed to read comics, the good old confessions, or trade journals." (*Fahrenheit 451* 54-55)

When asked what influence Orwell and Huxley had on his thought processes as he wrote *Fahrenheit 451*, Bradbury commented that it was Arthur Koestler who was his main inspiration. "Koestler got the full range of desecration, execution and forgetfulness on a mass and nameless graveyard scale ... [He was] true father, mother, and lunatic brother to my F. 451" (qtd. in Eller 167).

Although the message of *Fahrenheit 451* is widely cited as an argument against censorship, for many years Bradbury maintained that the book was really about the distractions of technology and the increasingly short attention span of the population, who have been lulled into complacency through the voyeuristic television shows they watch (Patai 42). "*Fahrenheit 451* is less about Big Brother and more about Little Sister," Bradbury told Sam Weller, his official biographer. But Weller disagreed with Bradbury's protestations, citing a 1953 letter he wrote for *The Nation* about censorship, as well as a 1966 introduction that Bradbury wrote for a later edition of *Fahrenheit 451* (Weller "Ray Bradbury's 180"). Bradbury, however, correctly recognized that the suppression of independent thought could come from social pressure as well as from the government, and indeed, the core premise of *Fahrenheit 451* is that it is not government censorship that initiates the book burning in Montag's world, but rather a gradual erosion of free speech as the citizens, anxious to avoid any kind of disagreements or discomfort, go to great lengths to eradicate any kind of speech that might be considered hurtful or inflammatory (Patai 43).

In *Fahrenheit 451*, Bradbury introduces several technologies, including the wall-sized television screens and the tiny earbud radios, which he calls Seashells, that would become technologically realized in our time. But the devices are always less important to Bradbury's work than the plot or characters, and his focus is on how people would react to their tools and surroundings and how the technological progress would impact human relationships (Weiner 85).

Fahrenheit 451 is a dystopian novel, and near the end the city that Montag has lived in, the city in which his wife Mildred is still living, is atom-bombed. The war is over in an instant, the nameless city dead and its inhabitants dust. While in the hands of other science fiction writers it would have remained a dark story, in Bradbury's capable hands the book ends with a ray of hope. Montag, who has escaped into the wilderness, is now living with a group of people who are determined to rebuild civilization, even though it may take many years. In a 2010 interview with Sam Weller for *Paris Review*,

Bradbury said that he did not believe in optimism, but rather in optimal behavior. Bradbury detested cynicism, which he believed was akin to treason against the human race (Brin 471).

Fahrenheit 451, which Ursula K. Le Guin called a "Myth for Our Time" (Adams par. 4), was not an immediate success. Released in October 1953, the book received favorable reviews and enjoyed a steady stream of sales, firmly establishing a place for itself on the literary shelves and eventually becoming Bradbury's bestselling book (Weller, *Bradbury Chronicles* 209). Oddly enough, the novel itself was subjected to censorship during the 1960s when editors cleaned up the text for classroom use, exorcising swear words and references to nudity and other adult themes (Smolla 900-901), but when Bradbury found out about the changes, he ordered the original text restored (Eller 185).

The impact that *Fahrenheit 451* has had on discussions of censorship and free speech cannot be underestimated. Around the time that Bradbury wrote his novel, two major Supreme Court cases, *Chaplinsky v. New Hampshire* (1942) and *Beauharnais v. Illinois* (1952), upheld censorship based on the premise that it was useful if it could prevent the kind of hate speech that led to the Holocaust (Smolla 903). Bradbury, however, essentially argues against the high court's decision, intuitively understanding that allowing free speech, even the occasional ugly idea, is the best way to prevent such behaviors and social decline (Smolla 904).

Bradbury understood, too, that social pressure could restrict independent thought. It did not require a totalitarian regime to restrict free speech when the population was filled with special interest groups that could do the job just as well. The phrase "political correctness" did not exist in Bradbury's time, but he understood that the public's desire to quell hate speech to prevent some people from becoming upset was merely a step on the path to full censorship (Smolla 902). And books, filled with the thoughts of individuals, represent real danger to Montag and Beatty's happy society, so much so that the Firemen are compelled to burn books to keep the masses safe.

Despite Bradbury's earlier protestations that *Fahrenheit 451* is about the misuse of technology, censorship is clearly the central theme of the novel, although he also touches on themes of humanity, such as the ability to cultivate inner peace (Smolla 911). Today, when we are surrounded by the very technology that Bradbury could only dream of in the 1950s, the ability to turn off the electronic gizmos and sit back with a book is a rare luxury. But thanks in part to Bradbury's courage to defy censorship, *Fahrenheit 451*— restored to its uncensored version—continues to entertain, inspire, and teach another generation the valuable lessons of free speech and independent thought.

Works Cited

Adams, John Joseph. "Sci-Fi Scribes on Ray Bradbury: 'Storyteller, Showman and Alchemist.'" *Wired* 6 June 2012. https://www.wired.com/2012/06/ray-bradbury-writer-memories. Accessed on 16 Aug. 2017.

Bradbury, Ray. *Fahrenheit 451*. 1953. 60th Anniversary Edition. Simon, 2013.

Brantlinger, Patrick. "The Gothic Origins of Science Fiction." *NOVEL: A Forum on Fiction* 14.1, 1980, pp. 30-43.

Brin, David. "Ray Bradbury, an Appreciation." *Nature* 486, 28 June 2012, pp. 471.

Derleth, August. "Contemporary Science Fiction." *College English* 13.4, January 1952, pp. 187-94.

Eller, Jonathan R. "The Story of *Fahrenheit 451*." *Fahrenheit 451*. By Ray Bradbury. 1953. Simon, 2013, pp. 167-87.

Harlow, Morgan. "Martian Legacy: Ray Bradbury's *The Martian Chronicles*." *War, Literature & the Arts: An International Journal of the Humanities* 17.1-2, 2005, pp. 311-14.

Patai, Daphne. "Ray Bradbury and the Assault on Free Thought." *Society* 50.1, February 2013, pp. 41-47.

Smolla, Rodney A. "The Life of the Mind and a Life of Meaning: Reflections on *Fahrenheit 451*." *Michigan Law Review* 107.6, April 2009, pp. 895-912.

Weiner, Lauren. "The Dark and Starry Eyes of Ray Bradbury." *The New Atlantis: A Journal of Technology & Science Summer* 2012: 79-91.

Weller, Sam. *The Bradbury Chronicles: The Life of Ray Bradbury*. Harper, 2005.

————. "Ray Bradbury, The Art of Fiction No. 203." *Paris Review* 52, no. 192, Spring 2010, pp. 181-210. https://www.theparisreview.org/interviews/6012/ray-bradbury-the-art-of-fiction-no-203-ray-bradbury. Accessed on 16 Aug. 2017.

————. "Ray Bradbury's 180 on *Fahrenheit 451*." *Dallas News* 12 April 2013. http://www.dallasnews.com/opinion/commentary/2013/04/12/sam-weller-ray-bradburys-180-on-fahrenheit-451. Accessed on 16 Aug. 2017.

From *Dark Carnival* to "Carnivalization": The Critical Reception of Ray Bradbury's Works_____

W. C. Bamberger

Ray Bradbury was one of the most well-known, most celebrated and honored, and most widely published writers of the twentieth century. Critical reception of an author's work is usually taken to mean reviews of the work as it appears, and, additionally, as a career gains momentum, essays; if the author is considered to have made a serious contribution, then books, perhaps journals or fanzines, and even conferences might be devoted to the author and his or her works. All of this has come to pass for Ray Bradbury.

Upon Bradbury's death in 2012, President Barack Obama issued a statement that also was a critical judgment of his work:

> His gift for storytelling reshaped our culture and expanded our world. But Ray also understood that our imaginations could be used as a tool for better understanding, a vehicle for change, and an expression of our most cherished values. There is no doubt that Ray will continue to inspire many more generations with his writing... (Obama)

Yet Bradbury received his share of bad reviews as well, and had pages of dismissive critical comment written about his work. Some of the most critical judgments came from other science fiction writers, including some who were his friends. This essay will attempt to show some of the forces—both literary and otherwise—that have influenced critical comment on Bradbury's writings over the years. As prolific as Bradbury always was, both serious and even conversational criticism of his writing has tended to concern itself with a few very popular works, primarily *The Martian Chronicles* (1950), *The Illustrated Man* (1951), and *Fahrenheit 451* (1953), along with a small handful of his short stories. Because of this, the sheer mass of critical material that has accrued around these three early books these will be employed to illustrate how critical opinion about them has largely remained consistent, even as the discipline of science fiction criticism has changed around them.

Bradbury began publishing stories—in a number of genres—in pulp magazines in the late 1930s, and in October of 1947 August Derleth's Arkham House published his first collection, *Dark Carnival*. A perceived contrast between the qualities of genre writing and more mainstream and literary fiction would figure in criticism of Bradbury's work, though not his alone, from the first reviews. Author and editor Anthony Boucher, who had been reading Bradbury's magazine appearances for years, reviewed *Dark Carnival* for the *San Francisco Chronicle* and put the perceived differences between the two at the center of his assessment. He made it clear that he viewed Bradbury as "not only a fantasy writer; he is also a writer, period..." (qtd. in Eller 146). This kind of assertion, which conveys both enthusiasm for Bradbury's work and a defensive tone for the genre itself, would be characteristic of Bradbury criticism for years to come.

This conflict again can be seen playing a part Arthur Hillman's 350-word review of *Dark Carnival* in the British journal *Fantasy Review*. Hillman wrote that Bradbury had joined the ranks of writers who were successfully writing an updated macabre, a group that included Robert Bloch and Henry Kuttner. Hillman's review shows he had an eye for the way science fiction writers then were striving to move towards a modern style and a literary seriousness, and makes clear his opinion that Bradbury was more successful than most. In several of the other writers working in this modern macabre style Hillman sees "an air of self-consciousness" that suggests their modernity is a bit of a pose: "[They] seem to be striving for effect, to assert even aggressively that the weird tale can be modern." Bradbury's tales, in contrast, "are not simply patterned in a modern mold: their very foundations are laid in the minute now passing... The connoisseur finds here, not only a new writer, but new writing, and in the narrow field of the weird such an event is a phenomenon and a vital step forward" (13).

The Martian Chronicles, Bradbury's first "novel"—which, as reviewers and readers alike could see, was actually a strung-together set of related short stories—was published in 1950. Jonathan R. Eller notes that by February 1951, when the collection *The*

Illustrated Man was published, *The Martian Chronicles* had already "garnered a short legacy of reviews" (221). Most of these appeared in the pages of the magazines such as *Amazing Stories, Astounding Science Fiction,* and *The Magazine of Fantasy and Science Fiction,* publications that specialized in works of fantasy and science fiction. The reviews were written by "insiders" who already were enthusiasts of the two genres. These included authors Sam Merwin, L. Sprague De Camp, and Frederik Pohl, among others. There also were positive, but briefer, reviews in more mainstream publications, such as the *New York Times, San Francisco Chronicle,* and *Saturday Review of Literature.* Two longer positive, if still genre-centered, reviews were published in Chicago, one in the *Chicago Tribune,* written by August Derleth, and the other in the *Sun* by Anthony Boucher (Eller 222).

Arguably the most important review, written by novelist Christopher Isherwood, also appeared in a small science fiction magazine, *Tomorrow,* in October of 1950. Bradbury had encountered Isherwood in a bookstore, and had given him a copy of *The Martian Chronicles.* As Bradbury later told the story,

> …Christopher Isherwood called me and said, "Do you know what you've done?" I said, "No, what have I done?" He said, "You've written a remarkable book and I'm going to be the book editor and writer for *Tomorrow* magazine next October and this will be my first review." So he did a three-page review of *The Martian Chronicles* which introduced me to the intellectual world and saved my soul. (Acceptance Speech)

Others, pointing out the obscurity of the magazine, have felt Bradbury was being far too generous.

Isherwood finished writing the review on 25 July 1950 (*Lost Years* 247). Significantly, he chose to review it not within the confines of genre writing but as part of the larger continuum of literature, reaching back to its very beginnings. He asserts that the novel displays "the profound psychological realism of a good fairy story," and that Bradbury had achieved a mastery of the effective presentation of fantasy equal to that of Poe, without imitating him.

For Isherwood, *The Martian Chronicles* offers an alternative to the "imaginative bankruptcy" that he felt shapes the realistic story, even as Bradbury avoids the conventions of the more pedestrian science fiction works of the time: "This brilliant, shameless fantasy makes, and needs, no excuse for its wild jumps from the possible to the impossible" (qtd. in Eller 222). Isherwood concludes his review with a ringing endorsement, advising prospective readers that in the experience of reading *The Martian Chronicles*, "the sheer lift and power of a truly original imagination exhilarates you... His is a very great and unusual talent" (qtd. in Eller 222).

Isherwood would remain a lifelong fan of Bradbury's work. When *The Martian Chronicles* and *The Illustrated Man* were published in England, Isherwood wrote another review for the *London Observer*, in which he declared Bradbury a philosopher-poet. In his diary for June of 1960 he wrote of recommending Bradbury and Leslie Fiedler to Aldous Huxley's wife, Laura Huxley, as speakers for a symposium: "She was very contemptuous because she hadn't heard of them. The ass" (*Diaries* 868).

Another English novelist-critic who took early note of Bradbury was Kingsley Amis. In *New Maps of Hell: A Survey of Science Fiction* (1960), in a chapter he titled "Utopias 1," Amis considers *Fahrenheit 451* along with "Usher II" (1950), a story related to the novel in that it also is about the forbidding and destruction of literature—in this case the fantasy genre in particular. The chapter, Amis writes, is meant to "examine the role of [science fiction] as an instrument of social diagnosis and warning" (87). Amis, like Isherwood, considers Bradbury from the view of one who takes literature seriously. But unlike Isherwood, Amis—a longtime reader of science fiction and later editor of a science fiction anthology—looks down on Bradbury's work in general with a mixture of dismissal and backhanded compliments. He describes Bradbury as the

> Louis Armstrong of science fiction, not in the sense of age or self-repetition but in that he is the one practitioner well known by name to those who know nothing whatever about his field. How this has happened I am not quite sure; perhaps it was the early pat on the head

he got from Christopher Isherwood; perhaps it is his tendency to fall into that particular kind of sub-whimsical, would-be poetical badness that goes straight to the corny old heart of the Sunday reviewer... Another and much more unlikely reason for Bradbury's fame is that, despite his regrettable tendency to dime-a-dozen sensitivity, he is a good writer, wider in range than any of his colleagues, capable of seeing life on another planet as something extraordinary instead of just challenging or horrific, ready to combine this with strongly held convictions. (105-106)

And this last even after he suggests that Bradbury is too heavy-handed and pedantic in delivering his social messages. He also thinks that Bradbury exhibits a "certain triumphant lugubriousness...a relish" in his descriptions of the actions and speech of the evil characters (109). Another coupling of backhanded compliment and dismissal is used by Amis to place *Fahrenheit 451* under the chapter's "Utopias 1" heading: "Bradbury's is the most skillfully drawn of all science fiction's conformist hells. One invariable feature of them is that however activist they may be, however convinced that the individual can, and will, assert himself, their programme is always to resist or undo harmful change, not to promote useful change" (109-10).

In Bradbury's earliest serious notices, appearing as they did in the first years in which a serious criticism of the genre was only just beginning to find itself, we thus can see the contrasts and divisions that would define both the reactions to his work and the language of the criticism that itself shaped the comments.

In his meticulously researched study of Bradbury's early life and career, *Becoming Ray Bradbury*, Jonathan R. Eller details an exchange between Bradbury and Anthony Boucher, who had given *The Golden Apples of the Sun* (1953) a less than enthusiastic review in the New York *Herald Tribune*. In the exchange Boucher not only did not soften his criticism, but also warned Bradbury not to take the positive reviews published by the more literary critics too seriously as a sign of the book's success as writing: "To them there's a sort of discovery-surprise: My-isn't-this-good-for-a-pulp-writer! ...I can't look on *Golden Apples* as a 'find' in itself, but only in relation to the whole Bradbury corpus...on which light it seems something of a disappointment" (qtd. in Eller 256). This was a further indication of a career-long constant in Bradbury's reception. Almost no one, neither advocate nor dismissive critic, and whether they made it explicit or not, could ever completely set aside the knowledge that Bradbury had begun as—and for many always would be—a genre writer. Boucher, in attempting to surmount this, was harder on the work than most.

But Bradbury maintained a healthy attitude toward criticism of his work, accepting and rejecting praise on his own terms, in accordance with his personal views. Decades later, in an interview for *Paris Review* begun in 1978 but not finished and published until 2010, the question of other writers' opinions of his work is addressed directly, and his lifelong pride in being a sunny California writer figures in his answer:

INTERVIEWER
There was a time, though, wasn't there, when you wanted recognition across the board from critics and intellectuals?

BRADBURY
Of course. But not anymore. If I'd found out that Norman Mailer liked me, I'd have killed myself. I think he was too hung up. I'm glad Kurt Vonnegut didn't like me either. He had problems, terrible problems. He couldn't see the world the way I see it. I suppose I'm too much Pollyanna, he was too much Cassandra…

INTERVIEWER
Vonnegut was written off as a science-fiction writer for a long time. Then it was decided that he wasn't ever a science-fiction writer in the first place, and he was redeemed for the mainstream. So Vonnegut became "literature," and you're still on the verge. Do you think Vonnegut made it because he was a Cassandra?

BRADBURY
Yes, that's part of it. It's the terrible creative negativism, admired by New York critics, that caused his celebrity. New Yorkers love to dupe themselves, as well as doom themselves. I haven't had to live like that. I'm a California boy… (Weller).

This Pollyanna streak in Bradbury manifests itself on the page, in part, as a kind of positive view of human dignity and spirituality. Steven Dimeo in his 1972 essay "Man and Apollo: Religion in Bradbury's Science Fantasies," tracks some of the history of critics writing about Bradbury's religious bent. He quotes Sam Moskowitz's 1967 *Seekers of Tomorrow*, where Moskowitz writes that with the publication of his stories "The Man" (1949) and "The Fire Balloons" (1951) Bradbury "provided the bridge between C. S. Lewis and the main body of science fiction in the magazines" (Dimeo 970).

Earlier critics Dimeo points to are Henry Kuttner and Chad Oliver, both of whom published critical essays on Bradbury in 1952. Comparing Bradbury to James Branch Cabell, a fantasist now almost completely forgotten but whose works were popular in the first half of the twentieth century, Kuttner considers Bradbury "the converse" of Cabell, "deal[ing] realistically with a romantic theme: the value of faith" (qtd. in Dimeo 971). Oliver, writing of the tone of *The Martian Chronicles*, which had been published just two years earlier, feels that "Bradbury's faith in the essential dignity of the common man prevented him from falling into the hopelessness of T. S. Eliot..." (qtd. in Dimeo 971).

For his part, Dimeo sees Bradbury as pantheistic rather than conventionally Christian, and finds his religious metaphors often too heavy-handed:

> Only when Bradbury puts aside his penchant for homily to focus on the teleology and hierology implicit in this mortal effort to wade through darkness does he transcend a superficial didacticism. His literary interest in religion is thus at its best not a concern for morality but rather for mortality and immortality. Upon understanding Bradbury's opinion of the interrelationship between science and religion and man and god in the age of space, the Christian, divine, and transcendental allusions in his stories can be seen to underline the symbolic implications of his fictional pilgrimages into space itself (971).

Dimeo goes so far as to say that Bradbury belabors morality to death.

In 1976 Kent Forrester published "The Dangers of Being Earnest: Ray Bradbury and *The Martian Chronicles.*" Forrester writes as one who had been a fan when young, and now is returning to Bradbury's work after being away for a decade and a half. On his return he finds "disquieting elements that [he] hadn't noticed when [he] was younger. There was, for instance, a shrill devotion to the ideas at the expense of his narratives" (50). He remembers that in *The Martian Chronicles* Bradbury forces his characters "onto soap boxes... Bradbury lacks either the inclination or the skill to weave these sentiments into his plot" (51). Forrester goes on to quote Damon Knight's evaluation that Bradbury has a "mediocre" imagination, and ends his essay with a rhetorical flourish, asking himself whether he believes Bradbury's strengths outweigh his weaknesses. He concludes that because of Bradbury's ability to engage the reader, to successfully and consistently draw us into the fantastic worlds he creates, they indeed do. Clearly, what changed between Forrester's earlier and later readings of the novel was not the writing, but the reader. As Forrester, so science fiction and fantasy criticism itself.

Samuel R. Delany has written about the emergence of serious criticism of what he terms "the paraliterary genres" in his essay "Politics of Paraliterary Criticism":

> While the academics who had come to popular culture in the thirties were comparatively radical, the academics who first came to the paraliterary genres, specifically science fiction, in the late 1950s... were, paradoxically, comparatively conservative... [They] felt that their major task was to legitimate [science fiction] in the face of a larger academic situation that still dismissed most working-class art... (257).

Matthew Cheney, in his introduction to a collection of studies of science fiction by Delany, identifies J. O. Bailey's *Pilgrims Through Space and Time* (1947) as the first full-length academic study of the genre. In the years that followed, Cheney points out, interest in the genre grew in academic circles even as "criticism by fans and writers became more prevalent, with much of the best evaluative, historical and bibliographical work being done outside the academy..." (xvi).

It is interesting to note that 1947 also was the year of the publication of Bradbury's first short story collection, *Dark Carnival*. Thus, Bradbury's fantasy and science fiction work began emerging from the world of small genre magazines at the same historical moment that criticism of the genre's modern authors began as a serious discipline.

Some of the negative evaluations of parts of Bradbury's writing were prompted by science fiction criticism's defensive, at times flinty, tone as it struggled to emerge as a serious discipline. In his *Ray Bradbury* (1986) David Mogen describes what prompted this and how it proceeded. In Mogen's view, some critics in the 1950s were made suspicious of Bradbury's writing because of his growing fame outside the circle of science fiction readers:

> The case against Ray Bradbury was not made fully articulate, perhaps, until two fellow science-fiction writers turned critics, Damon Knight and James Blish, began their ironic evaluation of Bradbury's reputation and talents. Between them, they defined a paradigmatic yet literate standard of discourse for a field that lacked one. They sought to establish consistent critical principles... Blish felt that, as a "scientific blindworm," Bradbury was "in certain respects...bad for the field" (19).

Knight, for his part, felt that Bradbury's lyricism was escapist and childish, that his attitude toward science was a childish fear of machines, and that his style was too syrupy for mature tastes, among other objections (Mogen 19).

Negative judgments of Bradbury's work by other science fiction writers would continue for decades, some of them quite dismissive, even sarcastic. In 1980, for example, the year he published *The Brave Little Toaster*, Thomas M. Disch reviewed *The Stories of Ray Bradbury* for the *New York Times Books Review*. Mocking Bradbury's "reputation" as pure media puffery, Disch portrays Bradbury as "America's Official Science Fiction Writer, the one most likely to be trotted out on State occasions" (qtd. in Mogen 19). Disch goes on to compare Bradbury to Rod McKuen and Norman Rockwell as exemplars of kitsch.

George Edgar Slusser's chapbook-length study, *The Bradbury Chronicles* (1977), surveys some of the difficulties that had confronted critics intending to write more serious studies of Bradbury's works. Among these difficulties, Slusser identifies the fact that Bradbury's treatment of science is "too perfunctory" for the fiction to qualify as serious science fiction; however, it was no more correct to call him a fantasy writer, "for rarely in his stories does the machinery of fantasy exist for its own sake" (4, 5). Slusser also rejects the ideas that Bradbury is a futurist—as his works are really about the present, whatever their supposed time frame—and that he is an "abstract humanist." For Slusser, Bradbury is a "portraitist—the chronicler of lives in isolation" (5). Slusser's characterizations are meant to demonstrate that the question of genre is irrelevant, a stance that in the 1980s and beyond would, at long last, come more and more to predominate in criticism of Bradbury's work.

The 1980s saw more pedantically psychological and sociological criticism of Bradbury's science fiction, again with a concentration on *The Martian Chronicles* and *Fahrenheit 451*. Published in the journal *Social Education* in 1983, H. L. Prosser's "Teaching Sociology with *The Martian Chronicles*," for example, instructs secondary school teachers how they might use the story "Ylla" in discussions of race and ethnic relations. In "Expedition to the Planet of Paranoia" (1981), Robert Plank traces the braiding of plot elements with the crew's growing doubts, illustrating how they simultaneously come to doubt not just the reality of the transplanted small country town on Mars but the reality of everything that has happened in their lives. Plank interprets the open-ended last lines of the story—"Captain John Black broke and ran across the room. He screamed. He screamed twice. He never reached the door."—in the most obvious way, that the Martians rose up and killed him because he suddenly understood they were lulling the crew into a false sense of security until they could exterminate them. This being Plank's conclusion, it is difficult to understand the use of the word "paranoia" in his essay's title, but his highlighting of the pervasive element of epistemological doubt is compelling nonetheless.

Plank here also continues the tradition of the more literary critics' suggestions that Bradbury received more credit and praise than perhaps he deserved. In discussing some of the subtler questions that form an undercurrent in the story, Plank praises Bradbury and then immediately undercuts his own words: "It is the measure of Bradbury's skill that all these motifs are muted, unobtrusive. If the reader notices them at all, he does so subliminally. It also raises a question as to whether the author's skill may have operated more unconsciously than consciously" (54). Yet in the next sentence he cannot help again referring to Bradbury's "consummate skill."

In the twenty-first century the legitimacy of science fiction as literature is no longer in doubt, and while the traditional approaches to criticism of Bradbury's works of course go on, more rarefied approaches have also been brought to bear. The opening pages of Jonathan R. Eller and William F. Touponce's theoretically dense *Ray Bradbury: The Life of Fiction* (2004) illustrate the meeting of old-style Bradbury enthusiasm and a newer, more intellectual tone, of reader enthusiast and academic critical enthusiast, in a very stark way. Eller and Touponce consider Bradbury's work using the tools of newer, more theoretical literary criticism influenced by Continental philosophy. Their "Collateral Readings" list in the study's bibliography, for example, includes works by such giants of this approach as Roland Barthes, Jacques Derrida, and Julia Kristeva. But the book begins with an Introduction by William F. Nolan. At one point Nolan—a science fiction, fantasy, crime, and horror writer, thus another "genre" writer, who had been friends with Bradbury since the 1950s—wryly points a skeptical finger at one of the basic premises of the very study he is introducing:

> These pages provide detailed textual and thematic analysis for all of Ray's major fictional works. If—in this writer's opinion—the criticism is tipped too heavily in favor of a Nietzschean interpretation (Bradbury claims never to have read Nietzsche), Eller and Toupence have every right to interpret Bradbury's work as they see it. (xiii)

In the authors' introduction, Eller and Touponce cite Bradbury quoting Nietzsche. They qualify the statement, however, by writing that Bradbury "claimed never to have read Nietzsche directly," that is, to have become acquainted with the philosopher through secondary sources instead. So while they indeed point to Nietzsche as a major influence, readers are given no clear idea of how much Nietzsche Bradbury really might have known.

Eller and Touponce begin their study proper with a clear declaration of independence from received critical notions about their subject. They immediately clear the field of two of the usual standard bearers for the idea of Bradbury as a genre writer, even as they acknowledge that Bradbury himself identified them as inspirations: "Bradbury is not of the house of Poe on his fantasy side, nor is he of Jules Verne on his science fiction side, since in reality these (self-chosen) precursors, he inevitably transforms their writings into masks of himself anyway" (36).

The phrasing of this last point is shaped by one of the main frames Eller and Touponce employ here to shape their criticism. This is "carnivalization," the idea that Bradbury's work takes as one of its most basic story-generating devices the bringing forth of the carnival-like aspects of life as people experience it, of life proceeding by way of "masks, myths and metaphors" (xiv). In their introduction, the authors combine this idea with that of intertextuality—how Bradbury incorporates elements from many disparate sources in his work:

> Bradbury's intertextuality is rich and manifold, drawing on and transforming texts from both [popular and literary] cultures... We believe we have found a textual and cultural process— "carnivalization"—to be at the heart of Bradbury's authorship. This examination invokes current cultural interpretations of genre (Mikhail Bakhtin) and of authorship and influence (Freudian-based critiques) to explore Bradbury's involved use of genre writing... We argue that Bradbury has "carnivalized" genres in ways that are uniquely personal to him. (xvi)

This approach, therefore, is synthetic—bringing together the genre and the mainstream, and the most rarefied of literary and psychological approaches, along with the personal rather than separating and opposing such approaches. That is, whereas in earlier years much of the critical attention given Bradbury had been based on the widespread concern with the gulfs between genres and between high and low literatures, Eller and Touponce illustrate how critical thought more recently has shifted to looking at how these elements can be combined rather than how they might be different. Bradbury's work, with its clear intellectual and philosophical underpinnings and its swiftly moving surfaces, are very well suited to this newer approach. As the authors put it, again borrowing from Mikhail Bakhtin's concept of carnivalization, "For us, Bradbury's authorship involves far more than entertainment. His fiction is really a borderline phenomenon like carnival, operating between the serious and nonserious in culture and often disrupting that very opposition" (412).

Conclusion

As genres have cross-pollinated, conjoined and blurred, as the traditional high-culture wall between science fiction and fantasy on the one side and mainstream and serious literature on the other has been at least partially breached, Bradbury has been identified less frequently as a genre writer. In his introduction to the 2010 eleven-hundred-plus page Knopf Everyman's Library edition of *The Stories of Ray Bradbury*, Christopher Buckley calls Bradbury "the ultimate Writer's Writer," and suggests that "It is hard to think of a writer who has done more with the short story form than Ray Bradbury" (vii).

Yet even some critics who would praise Bradbury continue to see him as a genre writer. Curiously, as "pop culture" studies have become part of critical discourse, this at times is seen as a positive trait. The amazon.com listing for the *The Stories of Ray Bradbury*, for example, includes a quote from an enthusiastic review by Christopher Borrelli in the *Chicago Tribune*:

The truth is, reading the vast new Everyman's Library edition of *The Stories of Ray Bradbury*,...stopping to wonder why it has taken 30 years for this classic collection to join the hardcover literary canon, a thought slips in repeatedly: Stephen King was thinking way too small. ["Without Ray Bradbury, there would be no Stephen King." —Stephen King]. Without Ray Bradbury, there wouldn't be American pop culture.

He is the Shakespeare of American geek culture, which, in effect, is American pop culture. The Waukegan-born writer is a popularizer of ideas so frequently plundered, subjects so unusual yet routinely picked at, reading *The Stories of Ray Bradbury* becomes a crash course in not just genre but what its modern voice sounds like.

It seems clear that even among his most enthusiastic champions, the qualifying code word genres is destined to linger on.

Works Cited

Amis, Kingsley. *New Maps of Hell: A Survey of Science Fiction*. Harcourt, 1960.

Bradbury, Ray. Acceptance Speech for the National Book Awards Ceremony. 15 Nov. 2000. http://www.nationalbook.org/nbaacceptspeech_rbradbury.html#.WQe_uvnDGM8. Accessed on 19 Aug. 2017.

Buckley, Christopher. "Introduction." *The Stories of Ray Bradbury*. Knopf/Everyman, 2010, pp. vii-xv.

Cheney, Matthew. "Ethical Aesthetics: An Introduction." *The Jewel-Hinged Jaw*. Revised edition by Samuel R. Delany. Wesleyan UP, 2009, pp. xv-xxx.

Delany, Samuel R. "Politics of Paraliterary Criticism." *Shorter Views: Queer Thoughts & The Politics of the Paraliterary*. Wesleyan UP, 1999, pp. 218-70.

Dimeo, Steven. "Man and Apollo: Religion in Bradbury's Science Fantasies." *Journal of Popular Culture* 4, 1972, pp. 970-78. Accessed: http://onlinelibrary.wiley.com.

Eller, Jonathan R. *Becoming Ray Bradbury*. U of Illinois P, 2011.

———, and William F. Touponce. *Ray Bradbury: The Life of Fiction*. Kent State UP, 2004.

Forrester, Kent. "The Dangers of Being Earnest: Ray Bradbury and *The Martian Chronicles*." *The Journal of General Education* 28, 1976, pp. 50-54.

Hillman, Arthur. "Phenomenal Bradbury." *Fantasy Review* 1.4, Aug.-Sep. 1947, p. 13. http://efanzines.com/FR/fr04.htm. Accessed on 19 Aug. 2017.

Isherwood, Christopher. *Diaries, Volume One: 1939-1960*. Edited by Katherine Bucknell. Harper, 1997.

———. *Lost Years: A Memoir, 1945-1951*. Harper, 2000.

Mogen, David. *Ray Bradbury.* Twayne's United States Authors Series 504. Twayne, 1986.

Obama, Barack. "President Obama on Ray Bradbury." 6 June 2012. https://obamawhitehouse.archives.gov/blog/2012/06/06/president-obama-raybradbury. Accessed on 19 Aug. 2017.

Plank, Robert. "Expedition to the Planet of Paranoia." *Extrapolation* 22, Summer 1981, pp. 171-85. *Ray Bradbury.* Ed. Harold Bloom. Bloom's Modern Critical Views Series. New York: Chelsea, 2001. 51-66.

Prosser, H. L. "Teaching Sociology with *The Martian Chronicles.*" *Social Education* 47,1983, pp. 212-15.

Slusser, George Edgar. *The Bradbury Chronicles.* Mitford Series, Popular Writers of Today 4. Borgo, 1977.

Weller, Sam. "Ray Bradbury, The Art of Fiction No. 203." *The Paris Review* Spring 2010. https://www.theparisreview.org/interviews/6012/ray-bradbury-the-art-of-fiction-no-203-ray-bradbury. Accessed on 19 Aug. 2017.

Housewives and Witches: Finding Feminism in Ray Bradbury's Fiction_____

Andrea Krafft

Ray Bradbury might seem like an unusual subject for feminist analysis, given that so much of his fiction focuses on the interplanetary travels of heroic male protagonists and the childhood fantasies of inquisitive boys. Mark Jancovich critiques the author for problems of gender stratification, claiming that "his portrayals of women fall into fairly predictable categories such as the understanding, self-sacrificing wife and/or mother and the cold, selfish threat to masculinity" (107). But if we dig deeper into how Bradbury depicts women, we can locate cracks in their veneer of homebound bliss and identify significant moments of resistance to cultural expectations for feminine behavior. His suffering housewives and dark, unruly witches remind us that, in the years following World War II, the radical changes to the family and the rapidly lowering "age for marriage and motherhood" created a depersonalizing impact for women whose desires were at odds with the emergent cult of domesticity (Coontz 25). In this respect, Bradbury has much in common with the concerns of his second-wave feminist contemporary, Betty Friedan, who underscores the widespread psychological problems affecting postwar American women in her bestseller, *The Feminine Mystique* (1963).

"Something is Very Wrong": Isolation, Depression, and Gothic Entrapment

Building on Simone de Beauvoir's pioneering work in *The Second Sex* (1949), Friedan studies the discrepancy between the peppy media representation of happy homemakers, which she terms *The Feminine Mystique*, and the everyday experiences of ordinary women. After conducting multiple interviews, she argues that "something is very wrong with the way American women are trying to live their lives today" (9). Specifically, attempting to contort themselves to meet the unrealistic shape of the mystique leads to "a strange stirring, a sense of dissatisfaction," and "a yearning" that she terms the "problem that has no name" because women feel that they are alone with their discontentment (10, 20). Ylla K, the depressed alien housewife who appears at the beginning of *The Martian Chronicles* (1950), clearly experiences the patterns of behavior identified by Friedan, as she suffers in an unhappy marriage that fails to fulfill her romantic expectations. Just like the many doctors who trivialize women's psychological issues as "boredom" (Friedan 31), Ylla's husband, Yll, belittles her "emotional wailing" and suggests that she would feel better if she "worked harder" (Bradbury, "Ylla" 6, 5). By viewing the irresolvable emptiness of the homemaker through her own alien eyes, Bradbury reveals the innate abnormality of a system that leaves women asking "the silent question—'is this all?'" (Friedan 15).

Even though Ylla lives in a fantastical home whose "golden fruits" and "crystal walls" recall the glittering promises of advertisements and women's magazines, she feels incomplete, trapped in the same routine that her predecessors experienced "for ten centuries" (Bradbury, "Ylla" 2). The excitement that she feels in response to her clairvoyant dreams about the strange astronaut, Nathaniel York, underscores how she yearns for an escape from the repetitive nature of her domestic life. The possibility of going "into his ship" and "into the sky" (Bradbury, "Ylla" 11) would provide her with not just a fairytale vision of romantic partnership but, more importantly, the mobility that she currently lacks. Until this point, Ylla has been isolated, just as Friedan observes that "many women no longer left their home, except to shop, chauffeur their children, or attend a social engagement with their husbands" (17). Bradbury presents this problem in gendered terms, as Ylla's husband, by contrast, travels "twice a week to Xi City" and determines when they will go into town "to see an entertainment" (Bradbury, "Ylla" 8, 7). Furthermore, Yll jealously and violently insists that his wife will remain homebound, as he murders York and the other members of the first expedition in order to preserve the status quo of his marriage and Martian life as a whole. York's death is less tragic than Ylla's continued misery, as she "wanted to break and run" but remains "trapped" within a marriage that requires her obedience and silence (Bradbury, "Ylla" 13).

Mildred Montag in *Fahrenheit 451* (1953) likewise illustrates the potentially devastating ramifications of a culture in which women are supposed to live without complaint and have "no thought for the unfeminine problems of the world outside the home" (Friedan 18). Countless analyses of the novel disparage Mildred for indulging in "just about every form of self-narcotization available," reading her as "empty, suicidal" and "cruel," particularly because she offers no comfort to her husband (Eller and Touponce 188). However, Mildred's behavior stems from the larger problems of a patriarchal marketplace that is "served by keeping American women housewives," manipulating them into purchasing goods that always fail to resolve "their lack of identity" and "lack of purpose" (Friedan 208). The only socially acceptable choice for "Mrs. Middle Majority" is that she will absorb the "highly appealing 'personalities' for products" in lieu of developing any kind of independence (Packard 115, 46). This is precisely what Mildred does, as she emptily participates in television shows that act in the guise of a "family," leaving her to parrot the lines of "the homemaker" back to them in premade scripts (Bradbury, *Fahrenheit* 17). As William F. Touponce has noted, Mildred is "a true victim of consumer culture" (94), which demands that she should "laugh and be happy, now" and "stop crying" (Bradbury, *Fahrenheit* 97).

The escapist possibilities of consumption fail to resolve the issues that cause Mildred's suicidal depression, ironically locking her even further into domestic passivity that slowly eats away at her very personhood. As a nightmarish twin of Sleeping Beauty, she appears to be frozen in time and space, "uncovered and cold, like a body displayed on the lid of a tomb" while her "little Seashells" keep her in a comatose state (Bradbury, *Fahrenheit* 10). Just as Ylla feels unable to leave her disappointing marriage, Mildred burrows into a lifestyle that normalizes loneliness. She receives regular visits from "handymen" whose "special machines" bring her back from the brink of death, removing the sleeping pills from her stomach as one might dig "a trench in one's yard" (Bradbury, *Fahrenheit*

13, 12). The medications that fuel Mildred's self-destruction were, of course, invented during the 1950s "in response to a need that physicians explicitly saw as female" (Coontz 36). Her madness is not an isolated case but instead reflects the widespread danger of the dehumanizing domesticity that Friedan notoriously terms "the comfortable concentration camp" (282).

By placing his housewives into psychologically devastating traps, Bradbury depicts the limiting effects of postwar women's roles in Gothic terms. As Kate Ferguson Ellis argues, writers adopt this branch of the fantastic and its tropes of enclosure and haunting in order to interrogate "an ideology that imprisons them even as it posits a sphere of safety for them" (x). This genre has been linked to feminist anxieties about disempowerment and bodily control ever since Mary Wollstonecraft Shelley, whom Bradbury credits as his literary "mother," penned *Frankenstein* ("Introduction" 1). First published in *Dark Carnival*, "Jack-in-the-Box" (1947) emulates its predecessor's interests in questions of autonomy, focusing our attention on the frenetic environment of containment that prevents women from having "image[s] of our own future" (Friedan 69). In this story, the woman who is identified only as "Mother" has so internalized concerns about her own security and that of her son, Edwin, that she refuses to leave the house, turning it into "her tower, silent and white, high and alone and quiet" (Bradbury, "Jack" 193). While Edwin eventually breaks free and believes, naïvely, that he has died, his mother remains locked inside as a glamorous corpse wearing a "shiny green-gold party dress" (Bradbury, "Jack" 209), unable to leave behind the obsessive desire for perfection that led to the erasure of her life beyond the walls of the home.

"The Small Assassin" (1946) highlights how the widespread belief "that parenthood" is "the route to happiness" similarly freezes some women into untenable psychological positions whose seriousness is ignored at their peril (May 132). Bradbury here represents childbirth as a horrifying event for Alice Leiber, who feels that she is "being murdered" by an unknown assailant, who is not revealed to be a baby until three pages later ("Assassin" 154). From its very conception to its emergence into the world, the child, later named Lucifer, calls to mind "Dracula as fetus draining its mother's vital fluids" (Kahane 345), as Alice constantly worries that her life is at risk. She receives no real assistance in her struggle but is instead labeled as "hysterical" and unnatural for not jumping eagerly into the tasks of motherhood and expressing "some interest in her own child" (Bradbury, "Assassin" 156, 158). While Alice's husband and doctor ignore her concerns, the narrative restores our sympathies for her by confirming the dangerous monstrosity of the infant. As the story concludes with the mysterious death of both parents, Bradbury presents us with the dangerous costs of a culture that celebrates childhood while erasing postpartum depression and other issues affecting mothers in the real world.

"The Screaming Woman" (1951) further emphasizes the dark underbelly of marriage and suburbia, in this case highlighting the life-threatening consequences of domestic violence for its victims. The ten-year-old Margaret Leary narrates her discovery of a terrifying voice, as she hears the screams of a woman who is "buried under the rocks and dirt and glass" in a nearby empty lot (Bradbury, "Screaming" 157). Given her status as both a child and a future participant in a system that condemns women to silence, no one believes Margaret, despite her repeated insistence that the buried victim will "choke up and die" (Bradbury, "Screaming" 158). However, she refuses to be voiceless and her loud interjections to the adults around her, particularly her father, lead to the resolution of the mystery and the creation of a "fantasy of competence" for the young detective (Mussell 61). Likewise, the screams of the woman, Helen Nesbitt, disrupt the smiling tranquility of the neighborhood, and she reveals her identity by performing "sort of a sad song" (Bradbury, "Screaming" 170). Through their shared reclamation of the powers of speech and creative expression, Margaret and Helen signal how women might break out of the structures that made Ylla, Mildred Montag, and so many others into virtual automata.

Escaping "The Chains That Bind": Unruly and Disobedient Women

While Bradbury mourns those women who remain tied up in "chains made up of mistaken ideas and misinterpreted facts" (Friedan 31), he presents us with alternatives to Gothic entrapment by portraying unruly figures who frustrate the behavioral and bodily expectations of men. For example, Nettie Smith in "Marionettes, Inc." (1949) initially appears to be a sweet and compliant wife whose husband considers her to be "a little simpleminded" because of her incessant demands for his attention (213). Believing that he can dupe her into loving a robotic copy and thus enjoy more time by himself, Smith attempts to "just slip eight thousand" dollars out of their joint bank account (Bradbury, "Marionettes" 217). However, Nettie emerges as the economic and domestic victor as she beats her husband to the punch, having replaced herself with a duplicate for an unknown period of time. Nettie "unequivocally say[s] 'no' to the housewife image" (Friedan 342) by taking advantage of the very technology that so many scholars interpret as dehumanizing. Mrs. Braling speaks to a more ominous reversal of marital power in this story, as her husband suspects that she has conspired to murder him with his marionette, known as Braling Two. While we "never know" whether Mrs. Braling is complicit in this action (Bradbury, "Marionettes" 220), the narrative transforms both of the misogynistic husbands into victims of feminized vengeance, revealing how structures such as the mystique can backfire on their creators.

As perhaps the most overtly sexist of Bradbury's male characters, Walter Gripp similarly faces an ironic reversal of his expectations regarding female passivity and beauty in "The Silent Towns" (1950). Believing himself to be the only person left on Mars, when the phone rings, he assumes that it must be a woman because "only a woman would call and call," but "a man's independent" (Bradbury, "Towns" 224). He fantasizes that the caller is impossibly attractive with "lips like red peppermints" and "cheeks like fresh-cut wet roses" and that she will love him unconditionally (Bradbury, "Towns" 227). However, Genevieve Selsor disrupts his narrative of feminine delicacy as she storms into the story with an "ungainly shuffle" and looks at him with eyes "like two immense eggs stuck into a white mess of bread dough" (Bradbury, "Towns" 229). Though we could read the story as a mockery of the ungainly female form, Walter's shattered fantasy is the true butt of the joke in this case. Genevieve glories in the "specifically feminine danger" of "making a spectacle out of herself" (Russo 53) as she openly defies restrictions on excess and chooses to stay on Mars so she can "throw perfume on myself all day and drink ten thousand malts" (Bradbury, "Towns" 231). Her grotesquerie frustrates the romantic formula that Walter hopes to achieve and opens up new comic possibilities for Bradbury's female characters.

Marianne in "The Great Fire" (1953) continues this explosion of paternalistic control as she humorously undercuts her uncle's desire that she will marry quickly and thus leave his house. She acts as a kind of fantastical invader, spending night after night with her suitor as her uncle complains from a distance that she is stealing "my porch" and "my swing" (Bradbury, "Fire" 145). Though her uncle hopes that her romantic nesting in his house signals an oncoming engagement, Marianne does not limit herself to one relationship but, in fact, has a different boyfriend for every day of the week. She not only rebels against the containment that marriage would bring but also is supported in this action by her grandmother, who hides Marianne's promiscuity so that she can frustrate her son's anticipation of matrimony. As she chuckles "from her corner easy chair" (Bradbury, "Fire" 146), the grandmother calls to mind the celebration of women's open laughter that is central to the work of French feminist Hélène Cixous. As Cixous states in "The Laugh of the Medusa" (1976), women can regain narrative control through formidable and shameless creativity as "that which is ours breaks loose from us without our fearing any debilitation" and "laughs exude from our mouths" (878). This laughter is, like the gaze of the Gorgon, "petrifying" to those who fear the release of chaotic and powerful female expression (Cixous and Clément 32).

"They Need to Be Afraid of Us": Monstrous Female Empowerment
Bradbury's most powerful female characters are those who travel and speak with impunity, often with monstrous results, anticipating Cixous's warning that "they need to be afraid of us" (885). Given the frequent symbolic associations of such women with "the earthly, material, and the archaic grotesque" (Russo 1), Bradbury imbues

these figures with supernatural abilities, striking back against a culture that treats men as "the Absolute" and women as "the Other" (Beauvoir xvi). In "The April Witch" (1952), Bradbury celebrates Cecy Elliott's glorious strangeness as she magically transfers her consciousness into "every living thing" that crosses her path (10). The range of Cecy's experience is far vaster than that of any of his other characters, and the narrative places her abilities at odds with heteronormative romance, for marriage will result in the loss of her "ability to 'travel' by magic" (Bradbury, "April" 10). Yet she sacrifices neither her power nor her desire for romance, as she possesses the nineteen-year-old Ann Leary in order to "be in love through someone else" (Bradbury, "April" 11). When Cecy releases her hold on Ann and both women return to their respective homes, the story reminds us that freedom and mobility are far more crucial than "accepting a total dependence" (Beauvoir 654).

The ominously feminine sea creature in "The Women" (1948) further underscores how a monomaniacal obsession with romance leads to stagnation, flipping the Gothic script so that the man, rather than the ingenue, becomes the sacrificial victim. Loosely constructed from "brainlike trees of frosted coral, eyelike pips of yellow kelp," and "hairlike fluids of weeds," this siren frustrates binary understandings of gender and bodily normality, but has "a woman's ways" (Bradbury, "Women" 39). Like all abject beings, she "does not respect borders, positions," or "rules" (Kristeva 4) but seeks to blur the line between herself and others, threatening to absorb them. She achieves this by fetishizing the body of the "sun-darkened man" (Bradbury, "Women" 40), hypnotically beckoning him into the water and killing him in the process. Like Cixous and Clément's depiction of the sorceress, this underwater creature possesses all the grotesque power of nature, rendering everyone else helpless in her wake (38). She frustrates scripts of masculinist dominance, observing that men are "like dolls" in their fragility and their inactivity, as her prize "just lie[s] there" (Bradbury, "Women" 46).

Like the siren, the witches in "The Exiles" (1950) and *Something Wicked This Way Comes* (1962) surpass physical boundaries and masterfully control the bodies of others, refusing to be passive as they transform domestic tools into the stuff of magic. They most frequently opt for needles as their weapons of choice, shoving these symbols of women's work into the hearts of wax dolls and embroidering on men's flesh. For the exiled Martian witches, these formerly insignificant slivers of metal become the deciding factor in their battle with the "expensive, talented...obedient and quick" invaders who threaten to disrupt their control of the planet (Bradbury, "Exiles" 121). Similarly, the Dust Witch calls on the power of the "darning-needle dragonfly" to sew up the eyes, ears, and mouths of her victims, transforming them into senseless "statues" (Bradbury, *Wicked* 165, 166). Although the witches' victories are short-lived, they inscribe themselves on the bodies of their victims and the memories of Bradbury's readers, embodying a kind of "marked writing...that can serve as a springboard for subversive thought" regarding the relations of gendered power (Cixous 879; italics Cixous's). Hélène Cixous refers to this kind of writing as *écriture feminine*, a process through which authors "write about women and bring women to writing, from which they have been driven away" (875). Bradbury's witches "seize" his narratives, inventing new kinds of creative texts that "shatter the framework of institution" (Cixous 887, 888). The most notable example of this kind of powerful female authorship is the unseen witch who is the topic of discussion in the prologue to *The Illustrated Man* (1951). *The Illustrated Man* recalls how, after breaking his leg, he had to seek new means of carnival employment and stumbled upon an innocuous-looking "old woman in a little house in the middle of Wisconsin" (Bradbury, "Prologue" 4). This woman tattoos him, but her artwork defies the limitations of ink and flesh as the images that she inscribes predict the future. This witch seems to be unstuck in time, appearing "a thousand years old one moment and twenty years old the next" (Bradbury, "Prologue" 4), carrying within her the dark secrets of history and dooming her freakish canvas to a life as a pariah. Everything that occurs in *The Illustrated Man* is ultimately authored by the tattooing witch, who merges the needle, the pen, and nature to produce a powerfully imaginative text that questions the marginalization of both women and the symbolic Other.

"They Can Create the Universe": Women's Transformative Knowledge

For Bradbury, women are essential bearers of artistic evolution, as "they can create the universe" and "are the future" ("Playboy" 151). Oddly enough, he declared these sentiments in a 1996 interview with *Playboy*, highlighting his commitment to reversing the systemic devaluation of female voices by speaking back to arguably the most masculinist and potentially sexist audience. He credits much of his growth as a writer to "all the women in my life [who] have been librarians, writers, teachers, or booksellers" (Bradbury, "Interview" 119), particularly his wife, who "typed the manuscript for *The Martian Chronicles*," and Leigh Brackett, who mentored him at the start of his career (Bradbury, "Ray Guns" 7; Eller 65). Clarisse McClellan of *Fahrenheit 451* embodies the writerly energies of all these women, saving Guy Montag by introducing him to the transformative power of literacy. Bradbury speaks about Clarisse not as his creation but as an indispensable coauthor who "helped me to write the book" ("Temperature" 44).

Labeled as insane and destroyed by the violence of the dystopian world that she inhabits, Clarisse reminds us of the need to bring women's voices back from the margins, particularly when they have so much to teach us. Bradbury's intuitive and often magical women additionally draw our sympathies towards the freaks who populate many of his stories. For example, Aimee in "The Dwarf" (1954) purchases a funhouse mirror for the unfortunately named Mr. Big and admires the murder mysteries that he writes. Such alliances between women and other outsiders represent the ultimate goal of intersectional feminism to dismantle the systems of domination that determine normative language and identity. Of course, Bradbury is not alone in this project, but is only one participant in the proud tradition of feminist speculative fiction that we also can trace in the work of James Tiptree Jr., Ursula K. Le Guin, Octavia Butler, Margaret Atwood, and many others. Given the increasing cultural backlash against "nasty women" and their allies, such writers remain crucial voices who shout a resounding "Yes!" to Betty Friedan's question, "can women be people?" (50).

Works Cited

Aggelis, Stephen L., Editor. *Conversations With Ray Bradbury*. UP of Mississippi, 2004.

Beauvoir, Simone de. *The Second Sex*. 1949. Translated and edited by H. M. Parshley. Knopf, 1964.

Bradbury, Ray. "The April Witch." 1952. Bradbury, *Golden*, pp. 10-20.

———. "The Dwarf." 1954. Bradbury, *October*, pp. 3-18.

———. "The Exiles." 1949. Bradbury, *Illustrated*, pp. 118-35.

———. *Fahrenheit 451*. 1953. Simon, 2013.

———. *The Golden Apples of the Sun and Other Stories*. 1953. Avon, 1990.

———. "The Great Fire." 1953. Bradbury, *Golden*, pp. 141-47.

———. *The Illustrated Man*. 1951. HarperCollins, 2011.

———. Introduction. Bradbury, *Space*, pp. 1-2.

———. "Jack-in-the-Box." 1947. Bradbury, *October*, pp. 192-213.

———. "Marionettes, Inc." 1949. Bradbury, *Illustrated*, pp. 211-21.

———. *The Martian Chronicles*. 1950. HarperCollins, 2011.

———. *The October Country*. 1955. Del Rey, 1996.

———. "*Playboy* Interview: Ray Bradbury." 1996. Aggelis, pp. 150-69.

———. "Prologue: *The Illustrated Man*." Bradbury, *Illustrated*, pp. 1-6.

———. "Ray Bradbury: An Interview." 1982. Aggelis, pp. 112-21.

———. "Ray Guns, Robots, and Rockets: The Influence of Ray Bradbury on the Future." Weller, pp. 1-22.

———. "The Screaming Woman." 1951. Bradbury, *Space*, pp. 157-71.

———. "The Silent Towns." Bradbury, *Martian*, pp. 219-33.

———. *S is for Space*. Bantam, 1966.

———. "The Small Assassin." 1946. Bradbury, *October*, pp. 154-78.

———. *Something Wicked This Way Comes*. 1962. Bantam, 1979.

———. "The Temperature at Which Books Burn." Weller, pp. 39-56.

———. "The Women." 1948. *I Sing the Body Electric, and Other Stories*. Harper, 1998, pp. 39-47.

———. "Ylla." Bradbury, *Martian*, pp. 2-18.

Cixous, Hélène. "The Laugh of the Medusa." Translated by Keith Cohen and Paula Cohen. *Signs* 1.4, 1976, pp. 875-93.

———, and Catherine Clément. *The Newly Born Woman.* 1975. Translated by Betsy Wing. U of Minnesota P, 1986.

Coontz, Stephanie. *The Way We Never Were: American Families and the Nostalgia Trap.* Basic, 1992.

Eller, Jonathan R. *Becoming Ray Bradbury.* 2011. U of Illinois P, 2013.

———, and William F. Touponce. *Ray Bradbury: The Life of Fiction.* Kent State UP, 2004.

Ellis, Kate Ferguson. *The Contested Castle: Gothic Novels and The Subversion of Domestic Ideology.* U of Illinois P, 1989.

Friedan, Betty. *The Feminine Mystique.* Norton, 1963.

Jancovich, Mark. *Rational Fears: American Horror in the 1950s.* St. Martin's, 1996.

Kahane, Claire. "The Gothic Mirror." *The (M)other Tongue: Essays in Feminist Psychoanalytic Interpretation.* Edited by Shirley Nelson Garner, Claire Kahane, and Madelon Sprengnether. Cornell UP, 1985, pp. 334-51.

Kristeva, Julia. *Powers of Horror: An Essay on Abjection.* 1980. Translated by Leon S. Roudiez. Columbia UP, 1982.

May, Elaine Tyler. *Homeward Bound: American Families in the Cold War Era.* Basic, 1988.

Mussell, Kay J. "'But Why Do They Read Those Things?': The Female Audience and the Gothic Novel." *The Female Gothic.* Edited by Juliann E. Fleenor. Eden, 1983, pp. 57-68.

Packard, Vance. *The Hidden Persuaders.* McKay, 1957.

Russo, Mary. *The Female Grotesque: Risk, Excess and Modernity.* Routledge, 1995.

Touponce, William F. *Ray Bradbury and the Poetics of Reverie: Fantasy, Science Fiction, and the Reader.* UMI, 1981.

Weller, Sam, editor. *Ray Bradbury: The Last Interview and Other Conversations.* Melville, 2014.

From "Halloween Was Outlawed and Christmas Was Banned!" to "You Can Stay Happy All the Time": Shifting Impetuses for Book Burning from "The Exiles" and "Usher II" to *Fahrenheit 451*

Rafeeq O. McGiveron

Regardless of whether they deal with the marvelous or the seemingly mundane, the works of Ray Bradbury consistently value the human, the humane, and the imaginative over the mechanistic, the materialistic, and the closed-minded. In doing so, the powerful *Fahrenheit 451* (1953), perhaps Bradbury's most widely known and culturally influential tale, has become popularly remembered for the central image of its warning: heaped books set aflame by blithely dutiful "firemen." Iconic as it is to this novel, the spectacle of course has echoed from the centuries, such that Bradbury can jump into the topic and come back out "dripping," as he puts it in the foreword to a printing on the fortieth anniversary of his masterwork, "with hyperbole, metaphor, and similes about fire, print, and papyrus" ("Burning Bright" 16). For Bradbury, as an artist and simply as a thinking human being, the burning of books may be the ultimate evil. Interestingly enough, though, in the few short years between "The Exiles" (1949) and "Usher II" (1950), short stories that also feature the bogeyman of book burning, and *Fahrenheit 451*, Ray Bradbury shifts from an almost juvenile portrayal of the motivations for this act to one which, because of its subtlety and its understanding of human nature, actually better helps us avoid such a nightmare future.

"Mind or Body, Put to the Oven, is a Sinful Practice"

The trope of precious books burned by ignorant hordes cannot help but remain particularly disturbing. The very notion is, to crib a line from "A Sound of Thunder" (1952) out of context, "anti-everything...anti-Christ, anti-human, anti-intellectual" (89). The blazing of heaped books is a reiteration of the most vivid images of the early period of Nazi Germany in the 1930s, when intolerance and anti-intellectualism stood poised to plunge the world into genocide and global war—an era a lifetime away now, but once so very contemporary and shocking to the teenaged Bradbury, and still recent in memory to his original readers of the 1950s. Yet the book-fueled fires also evoke not only the more familiar savageries of Adolf Hitler but also legendary infamies like Savonarola's Bonfire of the Vanities, the sacking of Rome, or, perhaps most especially, the burnings of the Library of Alexandria, learning of which moved the author-to-be to tears at age nine ("Burning Bright" 16). Finally, even on an individual, personal level, too, the idea of burning books is a jarring contrast to way we are taught, as very small children, to enjoy and protect these objects of beauty and delight. No matter how it is examined, book burning cannot help but seem unsettling and alarming.

Indeed, Bradbury—similarly unsettlingly but also very powerfully—likens this "burning to bring down the tatters and charcoal ruins of history" (*Fahrenheit* 33) to the most heinous crime of all: murder. The author in the 1966 introduction to the novel claims, "[W]hen Hitler burned a book I felt it as keenly, please forgive me, as his killing a human, for in the long sum of history they are one and the same flesh. Mind or body, put to the oven, is a sinful practice…" ("Introduction" 26). After Guy Montag, the book-burning fireman of *Fahrenheit 451*, sees a woman set herself aflame rather than abandon her illegal library to the government-sanctioned vandals with axes and kerosene, he is ill, both physically and spiritually, shaken from the simplicity of being able to grin to himself that "[i]t was a pleasure to burn" (*Fahrenheit* 33). And yet "It's not just about the woman who died," he explains to his television-anesthetized and pill-popping wife (81). Public suicide,[1] especially by fire, indeed is unsettling, but what seems to unnerve Montag just as much is the reason for the terrible act. Previously he had been able to tell himself that the firemen's nighttime raids "weren't hurting anyone" but "hurting only things!" (66). Now, however, he begins to understand that in addition to tormenting the so-called criminal, who might "scream and cry out" (66) at the destruction of his or her secret hoard of treasured books, the burning also ignores or denies the very humanity of the authors of all those volumes. After all, Montag realizes, "a man was behind each one of the books. A man had to think them up. A man had to take a long time to put them down on paper" (81).

We may quibble with some of the phraseology—as if a woman, for example, could not have written at least a few of those texts— but the basic notion is profound. When the "long time" required for authorship is not just the period of writing itself but also the "lifetime maybe" of preparation, of "looking around at the world and life," then the "boom! it's all over" (82) of the firemen's assault destroys no mere singular effort but in fact the total sum of an individual's life. Near the end of the novel, Granger, leader of the book-memorizing intellectuals, explains to Montag that "[e]veryone must leave something behind when he dies…" (182), specifically "[s]omething your hand touched in some way so your soul has somewhere to go when you die" (182). Burning a book thus destroys the product of an entire life of experience and thought and emotion, and yet also, in Granger's quasi-animistic conception, even the resting place of the soul. It is almost as if that person had not even existed, or perhaps had been removed from existence.

Although Montag and Granger speak from *Fahrenheit 451*, this passion of course is present anywhere Bradbury writes about book burning. A bit strangely, though, while previous works dealing with book burning, such as "The Exiles" and "Usher II," date from only a few years earlier, these stories are long on moral outrage— appropriate as it may be—but rather short on real investigation rather than just condemnation. Why are books banned and even burned? Finding answers to this puzzle of human motivation could help readers trying to prevent such a future, but neither of these stories yet presses very deeply into the matter. "The Exiles" gives merely the slimmest, almost adolescent treatment of the reasons for book burning, while "Usher II" only begins groping for the fuller answers we will see in *Fahrenheit 451*.

"Halloween Was Outlawed and Christmas Was Banned!"
"The Exiles," titled splashily "The Mad Wizards of Mars" when it originally appeared in the Canadian magazine *Maclean's* in

September 1949, begins with the pure-fantasy premise of the souls of dead Terrans having taken up residence on Mars.[2] It is not just any dead who have risen, though, but instead authors of the supernatural, fantastic, and even, apparently, the simply imaginative, those who in defense of their "worlds and…creations" somehow "were summoned out of—what? Death? The Beyond?" a century earlier, in 2020, when their books were made illegal (101). In something of a corollary to the notion of an author's soul needing a book as "somewhere to go" after death, however, in this story it is only the stray readership remaining here and there on Earth that keeps these banned writers alive on the Red Planet. Without that curiously exploring "child, sneezing with dust, in some yellow garret on Earth once more [finding] a worn, time-specked copy" of a forbidden book, these authors would "be like lights put out" (102), and this time permanently.

When the drive of science at last sends an expedition of self-proclaimed "rational men" to Mars, the exiled authors and their characters fight back against the onrushing rocket ship with pins in voodoo dolls, hallucinations of eerie man-bats "fluttering and fluttering" and "bone[s] and white skulls that screamed," and "bad, wicked dreams" about "witch-things and were-things, vampires and phantoms" that people in this age "couldn't know anything about" (94-96). Though some of the crew die and others are driven mad, the ship is driven onward by a captain described with a particularly Bradburian disdain for the unimaginative and strait-laced:

He smelled of menthol and iodine and green soap on his polished and manicured hands. His white teeth were dentifriced, and his ears scoured to pinkness, as were his cheeks. His uniform was the color of new salt, and his boots were black mirrors shining below him. His crisp crew-cut hair smelled of sharp alcohol. Even his breath smelled sharp and new and clean. There was no spot to him.[3] He was a fresh instrument, honed and ready, still hot from the surgeon's oven. (95-96)

Really, it is difficult to criticize, say, brushing and flossing or other aspects of good hygiene, but when Bradbury is riled, he piles it on. These, after all, are people who look back approvingly at the time a century ago when the works of "all [the] forbidden authors" were "burned in the same year that Halloween was outlawed and Christmas was banned!" (97).

Yet while Jonathan R. Eller and Willian F. Touponce remind us that at the time of Bradbury's writing, L. Frank Baum's *The Wizard of Oz* was "removed from public libraries…as escapist literature that children ought not to be reading when America was trying to catch up with Russian advances in space science" (544 n.4), Bradbury does not bother to assert such a motive to his censors here. Rather than having any quasi-educational or quasi-political justifications, they seem motivated by pure killjoy-ism, and even a somewhat unbelievable kind of fright. The self-satisfied prate about "science and progress" (104), but it is with a peculiar shudder that they regard the supposed "monstrous names" of Edgar Allan Poe, Lewis Carroll, and others—"the old names, the evil names" (104-105). The "grisly volumes" of Shakespeare, Poe, and *Alice in Wonderland* alike were burned, we are told, because of their "ghastly subjects" (96-97). Imagining that full-grown adults would need to protect from such "blasphemy" (99) not just little children but also themselves is far from easy, but Bradbury simply raves with beautifully contagious vehemence about the anti-Santa campaigns of "[t]he glitter-eyed psychiatrist, the clever sociologist, the resentful, froth-mouthed educationalist, the antiseptic parents—" (103), and that, apparently, is that.

"The Spoil-Funs" and Those "Afraid of the Word 'Politics'"

"Usher II," titled "Carnival of Madness" when published in *Thrilling Wonder Stories* in April 1950 before being collected the same year in *The Martian Chronicles*, shows Bradbury in transition on the nature of the censorship that leads to the irresistible bogeyman of book burning. Although the story gives a clear nod to the political underpinnings of book burning, one deeply impassioned and yet solidly grounded in reality, this still is overwhelmed by the familiar lament of the killing-off of Halloween and Christmas, and a strange squeamishness about even the mildest of fantasy, which now also are bolstered by a prizing of "here and now."

In the year 2005, thirty years after "the Great Fire" of 1975 that burned Poe "and Lovecraft and Hawthorne and Ambrose Bierce, and all the tales of terror and fantasy and horror and, for that matter, tales of the future" (105), the wealthy bibliophile William Stendahl has constructed a Poe-esque *House of Usher* on Mars to exact his revenge on what he disparagingly terms the "Clean-Minded people" (106). His architect, Mr. Bigelow, "had to work in total ignorance" (104) and, indeed, has no recognition either of the term House of Usher or even of the name *Edgar Allan Poe*, so Stendahl gives him an account of how the world of Bradbury's real-life readers' 1950 turned into this fictional world of near-total censorship:

> "They passed a law. Oh, it started very small. In 1950 or '60 it was a grain of sand. They began by controlling books of cartoons and then detective books and, of course, films, one way or another, one group or another, political bias, religious prejudice, union pressures; there was always a minority afraid of something, and a great majority afraid of the dark, afraid of the future, afraid of the past, afraid of the present, afraid of themselves and shadows of themselves." (105)

Bradbury here is on firmer ground than he is in "The Exiles," for censorship in his own time of course was occurring precisely this way. Bart Beaty, after all, reminds us that although the Comics Magazine Association of America was formed in 1954, four years after Bradbury's story, so that industry, hoping to forestall possible government action, could implement a code of self-censorship "stricter and more inclusive" than its previous one (161), editorials on the supposedly pernicious effects of crime comics and horror comics on youth began as early as 1940 (113-14), and burnings of comic books were held in 1948 in several cities in the United States (116).

Bradbury draws not only on then-contemporary agitation against comic books but also on the growing McCarthyite climate of postwar America as Stendahl expands upon the public's fear of controversy of nearly any kind. According to the man whose illegal library of 50,000 books was lost to the government burning crews (108), people were

> "[a]fraid of the word 'politics' (which eventually became a synonym for Communism among the more reactionary elements, so I hear, and it was worth your life to use the word!), and with a screw tightened here, a bolt fastened there, a push, a pull, a yank, art and literature were soon like a great twine of taffy strung about, being twisted in braids and tied in knots and thrown in all directions, until there was no more resiliency and no more savor to it. Then the film cameras chopped short and the theaters turned dark, and the print presses trickled down from a great Niagara of reading matter to a mere innocuous dripping of 'pure' material. Oh, the word 'escape' was radical, too, I tell you!" (105)

Again, the description incorporates a great deal of truth that many of his original readers would have recognized.

What seems rather more fanciful, however, is the extrapolation from a chilling of political discourse to a shuddering aversion to ghouls and ghosts and other things that go bump in the night. Here the beautifully blunt and contemptible instrument of the law is "[s]trict to the letter. No books, no houses, anything to be produced which in any way suggests ghosts, vampires, fairies, or any creature of the imagination" (107). On the one hand, such strictures are prescient of the real-world Code of the Comics Magazine Association of America to come in 1954, which was to prohibit, among many, many other things, "[s]cenes dealing with, or instruments associated with walking dead, torture, vampires and vampirism, ghouls, cannibalism, and werewolfism" (B(5)). On the other hand, it is as difficult here as it is in "The Exiles" to imagine adults treated with the same nervous paternalism against fantasy—especially that not seen as sick or gruesome but merely diverting—that is accorded to supposedly impressionable children at the newsstands.

And why must adults be protected not just from the sneaky Reds but even from "St. Nicholas and the Headless Horseman and Snow White and Rumpelstiltskin and Mother Goose" (106)? Because "Every man, they said, must face reality. Must face the

Here and Now! Everything that was not so must go" (105-06). And somehow, according to Stendahl, the censors went even farther, not simply prohibiting what they found objectionable but actually instructing "filmmakers that if they made anything at all, they would have to make and remake Ernest Hemingway. My God, how many times have I seen *For Whom the Bell Tolls* done! Thirty different versions. All realistic. Oh, realism! Oh, here, oh, now, oh hell!" (108). Perhaps it could be argued that this need to face the here and now is akin to the desires of the Cold War humbugs who wanted children to read about chemistry and physics rather than Oz; nothing in the story attempts to imply this, however. Instead, the here-and-now attitude of the "antiseptic government" (110) and the "Society for the Prevention of Fantasy" (112) is simply a wonderful piece of spoilsportism against which to rail, and which in the heat and the pleasure of the reading seems to justify Stendahl's beautifully ironic murders, using methods from various stories of Poe, of "the Spoil-Funs, the people with mercurochrome for blood and iodine-colored eyes" (112) whom he has lured to his House of Usher for a masked ball. "Ignorance[4] is fatal, Mr. Garrett," Stendahl tells the Investigator of Moral Climates who had neither the imagination nor the literary experience to avoid a "Cask of Amontillado" walling-in (117), and then he and his conspirator helicopter off as the corpses of their fifty-odd former guests are carried, with suitable literary echoes, by the tumbling walls of the House of Usher into "the deep and dark tarn" (118).

"You Can Stay Happy All the Time"

It is in *Fahrenheit 451*, of course, that Bradbury at last gives us a scenario of book burning without outraged denunciations of the banning of Halloween and Christmas, or the strange notion of the here-and-now brigade enforcing repeated doses of Hemingway films for all. Rather, in what is perhaps his most widely known piece, the author keeps the intensity of emotion and moral outrage of his previous stories, but he now has alloyed these with a better understanding of how the world works, and the human mind as well. Gone are the caricatures of the busy ghosts of Poe and Bierce and Dickens, and gone the murderous yet perversely laudable machinations of a millionaire bent on the grimmest sort of literary-minded revenge, replaced instead with settings and events no less science-fictional but infinitely more long-lasting.

By the time of the novel's setting, government censorship of books—and, it seems likely, magazines, a print form Bradbury does not specifically mention in his earlier stories—is near-complete. On the one hand, "comic books survive. And the three-dimensional sex magazines, of course," as do "the good old confessionals" and "trade journals" (87). Other forms of reading material, however, are banned, and burned when found, along with any houses containing them, while the secret readers who have violated the law are taken "screaming off to the insane asylum" (63). Upon the firehouse wall hang "the typed lists of a million forbidden books" (63), which include not only fiction but also, presumably, books on "slippery stuff like philosophy or sociology" (91), and history texts that might contradict the claim of the firemen's "rule books" that Benjamin Franklin's fire department was formed "to burn English-influenced books in the Colonies" (64). The firemen's "official slogan" is "Monday burn Millay, Wednesday Whitman, Friday Faulkner, burn 'em to ashes, then burn the ashes" (38).[5]

But why? "When did it all start…how did it come about, where, when?" (83-4) rhetorically asks the eerily chameleon-like Fire Chief, Captain Beatty. He explains to Montag, sick in bed from the horror of seeing the old woman burn herself to death, that "[i]t didn't come from the Government down. There was no dictum, no declaration, no censorship to start with, no! Technology, mass exploitation, and minority pressure carried the trick, thank God" (87), of destroying the culture of reading, and even independent thinking, such that eventually the banning of books was nearly an afterthought. The influence of various pressure groups, already mentioned in "Usher II," receives prominent discussion in Beatty's lecture to his soul-sick underling:

> "Bigger the population, the more minorities. Don't step on the toes of the dog-lovers, the cat-lovers, doctors, lawyers, merchants,

chiefs, Mormons, Baptists, Unitarians, second-generation Chinese, Swedes, Italians, Germans, Texans, Brooklynites, Irishmen, people from Oregon or Mexico. The people in this book do not represent any actual painters, cartographers, mechanics anywhere. The bigger your market, Montag, the less you handle controversy, remember that! All the minor minor minorities with their navels to be kept clean. Authors, full of evil thoughts, lock up your typewriters. They did. Magazines became a nice blend of vanilla tapioca. Books, so the damned snobbish critics said, were dishwater. No wonder books stopped selling, the critics said." (87)

After his discussion of such generalities, Beatty even follows up with some concrete examples that might have seemed rather current indeed at the time of Bradbury's writing: "Colored people don't like *Little Black Sambo*. Burn it. White people don't feel good about *Uncle Tom's Cabin*. Burn it. Someone's written a book on tobacco and cancer of the lungs? The cigarette people are weeping? Burn the book. Serenity, Montag. Peace, Montag. Take your fight outside. Better yet, into the incinerator" (89). The notion of "minority pressure," which again is most topical in our own world of reality, thus is very memorable here, more so than it is in "Usher II," where it has to compete with the rather more juvenile bogeyman of the "Spoil-Funs" who hate Halloween.

Yet an even more important cause of the decline of thought in *Fahrenheit 451* is what Beatty calls "mass exploitation." This, however, does not just come from without, but in fact also is partly "the result of the public's active desire to avoid controversy and difficult thought in favor of easy gratification and, eventually, intellectual conformity" (McGiveron 249). After all, though Beatty mentions the "publishers, exploiters, broadcasters" who "[w]hirl man's mind around about so fast" that finally "the centrifuge flings off all unnecessary, time-wasting thought" (85), the natural human desire for ease and contentment in fact underlies the entire process. Even Beatty's avuncular urging of "Serenity, Montag. Peace, Montag" reveals this, for it seems to reflect not the desire of the members of pressure groups who wish not to be offended, but instead the desires of the members of the public at large who wish not to be troubled by conflict or difficult thought.

If people had wanted to read something besides magazines of "vanilla tapioca" and books of "dishwater," then when choices still existed, they would have read the more challenging works. But they did not, or at least not enough did to make it economically viable for writers of this latter caliber to keep selling. Professor Faber, to whom the disillusioned Montag turns after Beatty's chummy yet cloyingly sinister pep talk, also points up the complicity of the average reader. "The public stopped reading of its own accord" (115), he tells Montag, and now that "[s]o few want to be rebels anymore," the firemen with their occasional nighttime raids give only "a small sideshow indeed" that actually is "hardly necessary to keep things in line" (115). In other words, the public wanted serenity and peace rather than intellectual and moral challenges, and they voted with their dollars, and now they are, as Faber puts it wryly, "having fun" (115).

"Committing suicide! Murdering!" objects Montag—but this, of course, is what passes for fun in the bleak world in which the government has "lowered the kindergarten age year after year until [it is] almost snatching them from the cradle" (90), such that parents can "plunk the children in school nine days out of ten" and then simply "put up with them when they come home three days a month" by "heav[ing] them into the [television] 'parlor' and turn[ing] the switch" (125). For entertainment, youth might "head for a Fun Park to bully people around, break windowpanes in the Window Smasher place or wreck cars in the Car Wrecker place with the big steel ball" (59), while adults, when the habitual watching of their four-wall televisions pales, might heed Beatty's joyless call: "So bring on your clubs and parties, your acrobats and magicians, your daredevils, jet cars, motorcycle helicopters, your sex and heroin, more of everything to do with automatic reflex" (91).

The government of *Fahrenheit 451*, which especially in the decades before the time of the novel likely would have reflected the desires of the constituents who elected their senators and representatives, thus simply gave the people what it wanted.

Now no one need feel the "understandable and rightful dread of being inferior" to "the well-read man" (88), nor need anyone feel "unhappy politically," for Beatty has the logical answer: "[D]on't give [a man] two sides to a question to worry him; give him one. Better yet, give him none. Let him forget there is such a thing as war. If the government is inefficient, top-heavy, and tax-mad, better it be all those than that people worry over it" (90).

At one point in his discussion, the Captain begins with the supposed necessity of avoiding having "our minorities upset and stirred," but then in a manic, almost pleading torrent he immediately shifts to talk of what the wider population, the average human being, wants:

> "Ask yourself, What do we want in this country, above all? People want to be happy, isn't that right? Haven't you heard it all your life? I want to be happy, people say. Well, aren't they? Don't we keep them moving, don't we give them fun? That's what we live for, isn't it? For pleasure? For titillation? And you must admit our culture provides plenty of these." (89)

It is reductive, and it is cynical, and it is hopeless, but we must admit there is more than a grain of truth to the assertion,[6] and significantly more than any fluff about the haters of Halloween and Christmas. And to the pill-popping, chain-smoking, television-addicted masses, then, the firemen are not agents of repression but instead defenders of what Captain Beatty blandly calls "our happy world as it stands now" (91).

Conclusion

By the end of *Fahrenheit 451*, of course, the "happy world" of four-wall televisions, jet car street races, and daily drug overdoses will be atom-bombed flat, and maybe, just maybe, Montag and Granger's group of book-memorizing intellectuals might be able to help the survivors learn to make one that truly is better. Is a constructive rebuilding actually possible? The text implies so, though readers naturally may debate the answer.[7] What is certain is that as entertaining, even delightful, as earlier tales of book burning such as

"The Exiles" and "Usher II" are, by *Fahrenheit 451* Ray Bradbury has left behind the adolescent fantasies of spoilsport parent figures out to destroy, essentially, comic book collections and trick-or-treating and Christmas morning. His masterwork instead exposes the tendencies within ourselves that can undermine the desire for reading of all kinds, and for imagination and thought, and in this Bradbury helps us make his nightmare futures of censorship and book burning ever less likely.

Notes

1. Actually, it almost was murder instead, albeit a state-sanctioned one: The enigmatic Fire Chief Beatty already had "flicked" his igniter to light the kerosene whose fumes "bloomed up" around the woman, but he chanced to be a split-second later than her match (69).

2. Bradbury uses a similar idea in "The Third Expedition" of *The Martian Chronicles*, which was titled "Mars is Heaven!" when published first in the Fall 1948 issue of *Planet Stories*. There, however, the joyous reuniting with long-dead relatives turns out to be only a trap, with the apparent relatives instead being telepathic Martians bent on destruction of the unwary explorers.

3. This phrase seems a very ironic echo of the biblical Song of Solomon.

4. Though ignorance indeed may be fatal when dealing with a vengeful reader of Poe, Bradbury misses his own contradiction here, for Stendahl also asks Garrett, "[D]o you know why I've done this to you? Because you burned Mr. Poe's books without really reading them. You took other people's advice that they needed burning' (117). But what if Garrett instead actually had read Poe and the others with great care and yet still came to the determination that they should be burned? He then would be able to avoid the trap, but it is difficult to imagine that Bradbury would want to excuse him based solely on the sincerity of his soul-crushing beliefs.

5. In a world where literature is not read and where even *Hamlet* "is probably only a faint rumor of a title" (84) to the average person, this ironically jolly bit of phraseology is rather difficult to believe, really, but for shock value to the readers, and for alliteration, it is wonderful.

6. Jack Zipes, however, seems to sniff at the notion that "man's 'nature'" includes enough capability for greed, pride, and the like that anyone would "allegedly want to consume and lead lives of leisure dependent on machine technology" without first having been subjected to the "crimes against humanity" perpetrated by "the state and private industry" (191).

7. The postnuclear conclusion of "The Million-Year Picnic," first published in the Summer 1946 *Planet Stories* before being collected as the final chapter of *The Martian Chronicles*, is similarly debatable; see both Anna McHugh and Imola Bülgözdi in this volume, for example.

Works Cited

Beaty, Bart. *Frederic Wertham and the Critique of Mass Culture.* UP of Mississippi, 2005.

Bradbury, Ray. "Burning Bright: A Foreword by Ray Bradbury." 1993. *Fahrenheit 451*, pp. 11-21.

———. "The Exiles." 1949. *The Illustrated Man.* 1951. Bantam, 1969, pp. 94-105.

———. *Fahrenheit 451.* 1953. Ballantine, 2001.

———. "Introduction." 1966. *Fahrenheit 451*, pp. 23-30.

———. "The Million-Year Picnic." 1946. *The Martian Chronicles.* 1950. Bantam, 1975, pp. 172-81.

———. "A Sound of Thunder." 1952. *The Golden Apples of the Sun.* 1952. Bantam, 1970, pp. 88-99.

———. "The Third Expedition." 1948. *The Martian Chronicles.* 1950. Bantam, 1975, pp. 32-48.

———. "Usher II." *The Martian Chronicles.* 1950. Bantam, 1975, pp. 103-18.

"Code of the Comics Magazine Association of America, Inc." 1954. http://cbldf. org/the-comics-code-of-1954/. Accessed 9 Apr. 2017.

Eller, Jonathan R., and William F. Touponce. *Ray Bradbury: The Life of Fiction.* Kent State UP, 2004.

McGiveron, Rafeeq O. "What 'Carried the Trick'? Mass Exploitation and the Decline of Thought in Ray Bradbury's *Fahrenheit 451.*" *Extrapolation* 37, Fall 1996, pp. 245-56.

Zipes, Jack. "Mass Degradation of Humanity and Massive Contradiction in Bradbury's Vision of Humanity in *Fahrenheit 451.*" *No Place Else: Explorations in Utopian and Dystopian Fiction.* Edited by Eric S. Rabkin, Martin H. Greenberg, and Joseph D. Olander. Alternatives Series. Southern Illinois UP, 1983, pp. 182-98.

CRITICAL
READINGS

Reading Ray Bradbury's Literary Libraries _____

William F. Touponce

The library was the greenhouse in which I, a very strange plant indeed, grew up, exploding with seeds. (Ray Bradbury)

In interviews discussing his sense of authorship, Ray Bradbury frequently proclaimed himself to be self-educated in libraries. Growing up, Bradbury had access to two personal libraries, that of his Aunt Neva, which contained the Oz books, and that of his Uncle Bion, which featured Edgar Rice Burroughs. In these family libraries he discovered his passion for "primitive authors." Later on he was able to access the Waukegan Town Library for volumes of Jules Verne, Robert Louis Stevenson, and H. G. Wells, which he regarded as the primary influences on his science-fiction writing (Aggelis 52-53). What is more, seeing books by these same authors lined up on the shelves of the public library, he longed to see his own books alongside theirs. Personal communion with books in a library setting is in fact well attested in literary history, though some have doubted that anything like a real dialogue goes on between author and reader (Basbanes 100). But for Bradbury, literary books were people, or at least there was always a person to consider behind the book. When asked by John Huston to write the screenplay for Melville's *Moby-Dick*, Bradbury practiced a kind of conjuration of Melville, reading different passages at random to help him decide. He recommended the process for others: "This is how we find our friends-for-life on the bookshelves. We recognize our kinship almost immediately with this quick test" (Aggelis 28). Bradbury did not realize it at the time, but his response to Melville was conditioned in part by Shakespeare, who influenced Melville's revisions of the book.

But as he matured as a writer, Bradbury cannot have been ignorant of the fact that several of the masters of literature he grew to admire—Shakespeare, Jonathan Swift, Cervantes, Thomas Wolfe, and Jorge Luis Borges (who wrote a preface to *The Martian Chronicles*)—invented libraries in their writings, or at least, in the case of Wolfe, wrote about their harrowing experiences in labyrinthine libraries. It is not surprising, then, given Bradbury's lifelong self-description of himself as a "library person," that an array of imaginary libraries would figure prominently in his works. In this chapter, I want to "read" Bradbury's libraries, examining his enthusiasm as well as his anxieties about them. Despite the joys of personhood and personal affinity to be discovered in reading, Bradbury also was keenly aware from early in his career of the perishability of books and the dangers of their becoming sacramental and sacrificial objects in a process of scapegoating. In fact, some of the earliest images of books that we see in Bradbury's writings are not of books as the bearers of interior experience but as perishable physical objects, as metaphorical bodies struggling in the fires of censorship. Indeed, images of book burnings, and the destruction of libraries, provide some of the darkest moments of his writings (Touponce 109-37).

In what follows I borrow as a guide certain categories from Matthew Battles's intriguing cultural history of libraries, which argues that people can become the authors of libraries. Battles's discourse establishes a broadly useful distinction between the Parnassan library and the universal library. In the Parnassan library "the works within it are a distillation, the essence of all that is Good and Beautiful, or Holy. It is meant as a model for the universe, a closely orchestrated collection of ideals. In a universal library by contrast, they are texts, fabrics to be shredded and woven together in new combinations and patterns" (Battles 9). We will have occasion to visit Battles's book throughout this chapter because of his historical understanding of the darker moments that books endure in their physical form, what Battles calls "biblioclasm," that is, the destruction of books taking many historical forms, some deliberate and some accidental, and not just by fire, though that is the most common form (Battles 42). There is no doubt that Bradbury deeply felt some of the historical events mentioned by Battles, especially the Nazi books burnings (Battles 165). As we will see, Bradbury, for all his ideal reveries about books, also manifests anxieties about their nature as texts.

I will be concerned primarily with Bradbury's works in which collections of books play a major role: *Fahrenheit 451* (1953), *Something Wicked This Way Comes* (1962), *Death Is a Lonely Business* (1985), and "Somewhere a Band Is Playing" (2007). But first some remarks about Bradbury's acknowledged classic of science fiction, *The Martian Chronicles* (1950), where books and libraries in their absence have an almost spectral effect on our reading.

The distinction between ideal book and malleable text that is so prominent in Bradbury's later works is already operative in this work. Never consciously planned as a novel, *The Martian Chronicles* is actually a short story cycle based on his earlier pulp stories, with added bridge passages. For publication Bradbury subjected some of the stories to intense literary revision, and arranged them in an archetypal pattern. The result is a classic of modern science fiction, but also a kaleidoscopic text that he was still revising and updating as late as 1997 for the Avon hardcover releases of his major works.

Bradbury of course wanted to keep his books in hardcover editions, suggesting the idea of permanence, but he kept changing the text—it now includes "The Fire Balloons" and removes "Way in the Middle of the Air"—as well as updating the chronology. Indeed, the dust cover picture of the Morrow edition, by Tim O'Brien, points to the tension between the Parnassan and the universal conceptions of the book. This edition appears to depict the Martian book as a clothbound hardcover with some of its paper pages browned, bent, and cracked. A human hand, index finger extended, touches its pictograms. In reading *The Martian Chronicles*, however, we soon discover the Martian books were millennia old and made of precious metal, silver. When touched by a Martian hand, one of them is described as emitting a soft ancient voice that sings of heroic times in the early days of the planet (Bradbury, *Martian Chronicles* 2). Bradbury's Martian books are clearly Parnassan, pointing to an ideal order. Only as such could they survive the cultural catastrophe of disease the Earthmen bring to the planet. But ironically, Bradbury's own metaphor for the experience of Mars, the kaleidoscope, is one that belongs to the idea of a universal library open to a constantly changing textuality (Bradbury, *Martian Chronicles* 109).

Elsewhere in *The Martian Chronicles* we find images of the human-borne disease of chicken pox as having a strange effect on Martian bodies, burning them black and turning them into brittle flakes (69). It is clearly being suggested to our imaginations that their bodies are like burned books. Firemen then come to burn out the dead cities of infection, so if the Martian books do not burn, then at least we get the suggestion that the Martians themselves were subject to a holocaust. As a result of this holocaust the land is left haunted, as the Earthmen first entering the Martian cities discover. They enter the city whispering in hushed tones, "for it was like entering a vast open library or a mausoleum" (77). Spender, the Earthman archaeologist who identifies with Martian culture, claims to have discovered "how to read a book," a slow process of interior self-discovery that is the antithesis of the sped-up, crassly material mass culture of Earth. As Battles points out, public libraries are "among the chief protectors of intellectual individuality and privacy" (Battles 68). In the haunted libraries of Mars this seems to be what Spender is rediscovering about the nature of books and reading. In a period when public libraries were under attack, Bradbury reaffirms the public library as a site of reverie.

In contrast to the Martian city as an open public library, "Usher II" revolves around the traumatic memory of an extensive biblioclasm on Earth that destroyed all works of fantasy and horror in America, referred to as the Great Fire. The private library of the main character, Stendahl, which included fifty thousand works of imagination, was destroyed during this conflagration, along with all other libraries like it. A wealthy man, Stendahl had collected books that resisted the dominant trend of realism in the arts, and tried to counter their claims of "escapism." He thus was the author of a counter-library. Bradbury's story provides a catalog of some of the books burned, and presumably held by Stendahl, in a bibliographical reverie (Bradbury, *Martian Chronicles* 164-65).[1] He has rebuilt Poe's House of Usher on Mars as a "haunted house" entertainment seemingly to memorialize the victims of the Great Fire. But its real purpose is to murder the officials who are sustaining the censorship, with its emphasis on realism, in ways described by Poe's stories.

The story is complexly intertextual. It opens with Poe's own opening to "The Fall of the House of Usher," and closes with Poe's words as well. Along the way, Stendahl requires Garrett, the pompous Investigator of Moral Climates, to say the exact words of Fortunato in Poe's story, "The Cask of Amontillado," as he entombs him in the sinking *House of Usher*.

"Usher II" rather directly reflects the historical moment of postwar censorship in the United States, which later culminated in the Army-McCarthy hearings on suspected Communists in the government and the arts in 1954. Another fear of the postwar years was atomic war. "There Will Come Soft Rains" takes place on Earth in the aftermath of a nuclear conflagration, in which a house catches fire and burns. Sara Teasdale's titular poem is recited with great effect, since all the humans who once lived in the house are now dead, reminding us of the perishability of the literary work, no matter the medium in which it is recorded. I don't propose to discuss here every story in detail, but the concluding story of *The Martian Chronicles*, "The Million-Year Picnic," which was the first of the stories to be published (*Planet Stories*, Summer 1946), contains a biblioclasm that is worth dwelling on for a moment. In this story, which is told from a child's point of view, we see a family of survivors from Earth making their way along the Martian canals exploring their new world, but not before the father destroys their rocket, and any thought of returning to Earth. To warm his family in the cool Martian night, he creates a fire in which he burns the remnants of Earth's universal library. It is described as "the cremation of innumerable words" (266). However, this is not the destruction of literary works, but what the universal library allowed to compete with them: business graphs, sociological essays on religious prejudice and the problems of political unity, stock reports, The War Digest—"factual" writings of all sorts. We get the sense that this fire, far from being traumatic, is burning away a former way of life, and is enabling the ultimate escape.

Fahrenheit 451 (1953), with its cover painting by Joe Mugnaini, became Bradbury's best-known book. The cover of the paperback first edition is a self-referential image of biblioclasm, with the figure of the Fireman catching fire himself while standing in the flames. Books and newspapers and magazines are joined together in the conflagration, so we know that the image alludes to the universal library with its democratic goal of informing the public. The newspaper pages no doubt are meant to symbolize the powers of the free press, which have died out with the government's connivance by the time in which Bradbury's novel is set. But curiously the Fireman is also dressed in what appears to be the armor of a knight, in paper armor. In October 2002, while attending a rehearsal of the stage play of *Fahrenheit 451*, I had the opportunity to ask Bradbury personally about this incongruous armor. He told me that it was meant to allude to Don Quixote, a figure of mad idealism if ever there was one. So the painting also alludes to another literary biblioclasm in which a personal library was burned, for in Cervantes's novel, Don Quixote's well-meaning friends burn his library in a last-ditch attempt to cure his madness.

My reading of the painting is guided by the master trope of personification, as indeed is all literary reading in which a holocaust of books is witnessed, as Ann Hungerford suggests (7). But in what specific ways are books people? Bradbury has the reader discover the answer to this question by creating a hero, Montag, himself a Fireman whose job it is to burn books, clandestinely rediscover their meanings. Montag begins stealing books from the burnings of private libraries. These burnings have an air of carnival fun about them, but begin to get serious when a woman decides to burn with her collection. Montag has to wonder what could be in books to make a person want to die with them. To put it in intellectual terms, unlike other physical objects, literary books have an interior space and time, an imaginary world into which I can enter. Furthermore, when I read such a book, I am thinking the thoughts of another human being—a point effectively made by the many quotes and allusions used in Bradbury's novel—and I am experiencing the values of the implied author. At one point Fire Chief Beatty tries to intervene and prevent Montag's becoming an author of his own library. He explains to Montag the dangers and temptations of such a project, which he admits he himself has felt (Bradbury, *Fahrenheit 451* 50-57).

But Beatty's intervention fails. About halfway through the novel, Montag stages a reading of Matthew Arnold's "Dover Beach" (91). It summarizes much of what he has experienced in authoring his small collection of books, which he naïvely imagines is almost complete. Arnold subscribed to a liberal ideal of radiant literacy. He conceived of culture as a pursuit of our total perfection based in part on our getting to know the best that has been thought and spoken in the past, his famous "Touchstones." Furthermore, for Arnold, culture meant criticism, especially when these touchstones are applied to the present; without it, man remains a creature limited by self-satisfaction. This ideal of culture and criticism is surely Bradbury's own as the novel's implied author, for he makes Arnold's poem, perhaps the most familiar in the English language, resonate in new ways. Unlike the debased romanticism of the five-minute romance, Arnold's poem definitely does not have a happy ending. Instead, the reverie of the Sea of Faith evokes melancholy for a lost cultural center. Furthermore, the speaker of Arnold's poem laments the state of the world and the possibilities for communication in it, a world which seems to lie before him like a land of dreams but that really has neither joy, nor love, nor peace in it. The people in Montag's living room have not thought of any of these things in a long, long time, if ever. But Bradbury is implicitly telling us, not so much through intellect as through feeling, that as long as we remember one poem from the best of our literature, then the effects of mass culture, which threaten to erase our memory of families, friends, and even the fear of war, will find it more difficult to settle in.

Beatty makes a second visit to Montag's home and initiates in a reduced and more virulent form the eighteenth century Battle of the Books (Battles 82-116). However, instead of being a restaging of the battle between Ancients and Moderns, between the Parnassan and the universal library, it takes the form of a mock battle of citations, in which books are seen as bringing melancholy into the world because they can only disagree among themselves. When Montag later kills Beatty, he realizes that Beatty is inwardly suicidal. Montag escapes into the wilderness, deciding to live among the outcast book people, becoming part of the book that would have had a secure place in any library in previous centuries down to our own: the Bible. Montag remembers parts of Ecclesiastes, a book of wisdom. Classical myths play an important role, too, in the story of Antaeus and the story of the Phoenix that are retold in the book. Thus the Parnassan library is upheld and affirmed, but in fragmentary social circumstances that are less than ideal.

We have to wait until 1962 and the publication of *Something Wicked This Way Comes* to find another full-blown literary library. Concerning this work Bradbury has said that he wanted to write a "secret book," a scary book, one about boys and their secret worlds that would take its place on library shelves alongside the classics he knew growing up (Aggelis 52-53). In my opinion it is without question his finest literary library, pushing the figuration of language to new heights. Here we find a recognizably modern universal library, which besides literary books contains many informational items: newspaper files, "old folios," and so on. But the dream of communing with a single book that we find in *Fahrenheit 451* and earlier works is extended to the library itself. What we find is the notion of the library as a vast body that breathes its books in and out: "it's a world, complete and uncompletable, and it's filled with secrets…so the library is a body, too, the pages of books pressed together like organs in the darkness" (Battles 5-6).

As a body, the public library becomes the main location for the struggle between Charles Halloway, the aged janitor who works in it, and Mr. Dark, the proprietor of the invading evil carnival. Mr. Dark, also known as the the Illustrated Man, is also a kind of readable body. The multitudinous images tattooed on his body cry out for interpretation and understanding. Thus the library provides a special interpretive space for the novel's meanings, becoming the place where the inverted carnival can be understood. The carnival needs interpretation because instead of being the traditional place where the seriousness of official culture can be mocked, the carnival has itself become a secret form of domination and oppression. This interpretive activity takes place at night, after library business hours, and thus it, too, is in tune with the "secret places" tone of the whole novel. In fact, the library is a darkly ambivalent place after hours, haunted by the past, compared to a catacomb, a mausoleum, or a labyrinth. Will Halloway and Jim Nightshade, the boy protagonists of the novel, returning after their adventures in the town, are afraid to talk too loudly for fear of raising up "phantom twins" of their own voices along its echoing corridors of shelves (Bradbury, *Something Wicked* 189).

Because he intuitively understands that the carnival has its own time and space—it is a literary chronotope—Halloway designs a literary clock with the book's titular lines at the center. Shakespeare's *Macbeth* with its witches at the center, surrounded by works featuring the supernatural and the occult surrounding them, including Dr. Faustus, give him a spatial orientation. Halloway soon discovers that he has a face for the clock, but not the hands. He does not know what hour of the "the night of life" it is for the boys and himself. He has to face the Illustrated Man not knowing how close he may be to death.

Halloway's interpretation takes shape in a remarkable series of rhetorical and figurative chapters that conclude the second part of the novel, Chapters 37 to 44. It begins with an analysis of old newspapers reporting the arrival of Cooger and Dark's carnival in previous eras. To understand how these "autumn people" thrive, Halloway recites a passage from a religious tract by a certain Pastor Newgate Phillips that he read as a boy, explaining that among human beings there are those attracted to the dark seasons of life. When asked by his son if they, then, are summer people, Halloway responds by saying that most people are "half and half," explaining that he himself lived in libraries around the country because he liked being alone: "I liked matching up in books what I had seen on the roads" (193).

This has led some interpreters of the novel to assume that Bradbury is suggesting a Christian allegory of sin and redemption. In fact, there is a lot of referencing of the notion of sin in Halloway's discourse, and the Bible figures prominently in one scene. However, the religious tract and its author are completely imaginary, invented by Bradbury for his own literary purposes. The tract is not present as a text on the literary clock but instead is recited from memory. As I mentioned, the interpretation Halloway offers us explores the notion of the carnival as a body, developing a materialist notion of sin, guilt, and interiority as the "nightmare fuel" on which the carnival feeds. The body metaphor really becomes dominant in Chapter 40, where the human soul is figured as a kind of material body that oxidizes need, want, and desire. Through his analysis of the carnival's descent, Halloway is able, in a rambling sort of way, to intuit that the people who join the carnival, abandoning wives, husbands, and friends, have lost contact with the social body. In Halloway's interpretation—which he stresses is incomplete and subject to a lot of guesswork—the carnival becomes their new body, and the freaks can be read as ironic inscriptions on it. The mirror maze transforms these selfish people who want a "change of body, change of personal environment" into living images of their "original sins." The primary sin is narcissism and not bothering to form common causes with others. For instance, the lightning rod salesman, whom the boys meet at the beginning of the novel, is mentioned as someone who never stays around with others to face the storms. The carnival turns him into a Dwarf, "a mean ball of grotesque tripes, all self-involved" (206).

Gradually Halloway learns how to read the body of the carnival. The crowds depicted on the Illustrated Man's body, though they seem to the boys to constitute an exciting body full of life, actually lack one crucial element: They are not really free. They are his slaves, deformed figures masked by their own sins. A key word in understanding their situation is *spectator*, for the inked spectators are contrary to the participatory life of carnival in which all must join. Mr. Dark needs them to be spectators to feed his enormous ego. However, when Halloway does finally confront Mr. Dark, intellectual understanding is not enough to defeat him. In fact, he scoffs at Halloway's attempt to scare him with the Bible, easily taking it from him and tossing it in the wastebasket. Mr. Dark retrieves his "two precious books" from the library shelves and leaves Halloway in the hands of the Gypsy Dust Witch who is going to stop his heart.

What will defeat the carnival, then? The answer to this question is provided by Halloway's reading and interpretation of another body, that of the Gypsy Dust Witch, whose grotesque face and blind tickling behavior makes Halloway laugh. When the Dust Witch draws back in fear at his laughter, he begins to understand the true and proper carnival body, which accepts the grotesque and fearful things of life with amusement. Here is the place for the reader to remember Shakespeare's witches and their mocking words, so vague yet so immense, for they are indeed the very "heart" of Halloway's apprehension, lying at the center of his literary clock. Life now seems an immense prank played on us by fate, a foolish joke. Armed with these insights and reversals of values, Halloway defeats the evil carnival with harmonica playing and dancing and, with the help of Will and Jim, killing the Illustrated Man, now changed into a boy, with fatherly kindness.

The laughter at darkly oppressive things that Bradbury discovered in carnival is operative in his later writings too. It makes its appearance in his detective novel, *Death Is a Lonely Business* (1985), which is also an oblique autobiography of his early years as a struggling writer in Venice, California. A. L. Shrank, the psychologist who owns a private library of end-of-the world books and pessimistic tomes of all sorts—Freud, and the philosophers Schopenhauer and Nietzsche are mentioned prominently—located on the fogbound Venice pier, is also a kind of carnival freak, a shrunken caricature of a human being compared to daguerreotype photos of Poe. His library consists of 5,910 books stacked from floor to ceiling. Bradbury finds himself laughing at the titles. He banters with Shrank, offering this "meadow doctor of lost souls" (52) a more optimistic and hopeful listing of titles. Several of these titles contain words such as *sun, sunshine,* or *summertime.* It is important to understand that Shrank is not just another grotesque character on the Venice pier that is in the process of being torn down. On the contrary, Shrank's library is a figuration of Bradbury's creative anxieties at this point in his career. His books represent an intellectually pessimistic way of seeing the world that threatens to choke off Bradbury's creative endeavors. Furthermore, Shrank is a "shrink," a representative of psychoanalytic culture that threatens to excoriate his dreams. Having his own lonely side, Bradbury is deeply attracted to Shrank's offer of intellectual bibliotherapy but resists it throughout the novel, even in his dreams. As it happens, Bradbury discovers that Shrank is also the killer at loose in the novel. Shrank's library is demolished in a nightmare biblioclasm, his books floating off into the ocean. Shrank himself drowns in a submerged lion cage at the novel's end.

Bradbury's last literary library is wrapped in the mysteries of a writer's community, called Summerton, living in a small town in the Arizona desert. Indeed, we feel in retrospect that "Somewhere a Band Is Playing" (2007) could have been one of those sunny books Bradbury offered to A. L. Shrank. As Bradbury explains in the introduction to the novella, the story had its partial genesis in his viewing David Lean's romantic film *Summertime* (1955), set in Venice, Italy, and starring Katharine Hepburn, whom he later knew personally. As such, it is a book saturated with nostalgia for the genteel America of the first decade of the twentieth century, before the Great War. Journalist James Cardiff comes to Summerton in an attempt to uncover its mysteries, in particular why everyone lives so long, and why there are no children. He finds himself involved romantically with a beautiful woman named Nef, short for Nefertiti, the librarian of the Hope Memorial Library. In first touring the town, Cardiff had noticed that all of the private houses have inner library shelves visible in their bay windows. Summerton's deepest secret turns out to be that it is an ancient community of genetic "sports," which has gathered together and preserved lost texts and manuscripts by famous authors, protecting them with "absolute proof against fire," from biblioclasm. Nef's bibliographical reverie extends all the way backwards to the sacking of Troy, but also includes Poe's final poem and Herman Melville's last tale. In Summerton, works of literature are considered to be gifts that rouse their reader to a deeper understanding of life when scanned by a living eye, each book being a kind of Lazarus. With the notion of the work as a gift, which is also the gift of life, Bradbury's last literary library could be called Parnassan because it gives testimony to the notion of the arts as an ideal community lying outside commercial dealings (Hyde). One unresolved problem with this library, though, is that these gifts cannot be passed on to those living outside the community that guards them. It is implicit that such works cannot be commercially published. But in any case, in "Somewhere a Band Is Playing" Bradbury finally authored an imaginary library constructed by his summer people, rewriting some of the dark unquiet history of libraries.

Note

1. Bibliographical reveries can be found in other texts from this period, especially "Pillar of Fire" and "The Library," collected in *A Pleasure to Burn* (Harper Perennial, 2011). Typically they take the form of a long catalog of beloved and personified books and characters in the process of being destroyed or under threat. They may, and often in Bradbury's later writings do, include imaginary books.

Works Cited

Aggelis, Steven Louis, editor. *Conversations with Ray Bradbury*. UP of Mississippi, 2004.

Basbanes, Nicholas A. *Every Book Its Reader: The Power of the Printed Word to Stir the World.* Harper, 2005.

Battles, Matthew. *Library: An Unquiet History*. Norton, 2003.

Bradbury, Ray. *Death Is a Lonely Business*. Knopf, 1985.

———. *Fahrenheit 451*. Bantam, 1953.

———. *The Martian Chronicles*. 1950. Morrow, 2006.

———. *Something Wicked This Way Comes*. 1962. Avon, 1999.

———. "Somewhere a Band Is Playing." *Now and Forever*. Morrow, 2007, pp. 3-113.

Hungerford, Ann. *The Holocaust of Texts: Genocide, Literature, and Personification*. U of Chicago P, 2003.

Hyde, Lewis. *The Gift: Imagination and the Erotic Life of Property*. Vintage, 1979.

Touponce, William F. *Lord Dunsany, H. P. Lovecraft, and Ray Bradbury: Spectral Journeys*. Scarecrow, 2013.

Faith and Religion in the Novels of Ray Bradbury_____

Timothy E. Kelley

Steven Dimeo refers to Ray Bradbury as a "self-confessed agnostic" in his teenage years who later came to recognize the importance of "religious concerns" in both his work and his life (157). Bradbury's first three novels, however, actually present a path moving away from religion and towards the apostasy of Friedrich Nietzsche from which Dimeo suggests he was saved by his growing faith. While many of the short stories, as Dimeo points out, develop themes related to Christianity and characters with Christlike qualities, the novels develop an evolving view of human life hard to reconcile with Christianity or any other orthodox religion. In *Fahrenheit 451* (1953), *Dandelion Wine* (1957), and *Something Wicked This Way Comes* (1962), Bradbury works out a pantheistic philosophy more easily explained in Nietzschean than religious terms, while Christianity, as the novels progress, takes a back seat to Bradbury's own philosophy, which separates faith from established religion without falling into the despair of most existential fiction.

Fahrenheit 451: The Weight

For good reason, most critics treat *Fahrenheit 451* separately from the Green Town novels. While the other books focus on the struggle of the individual against the weight of mortality, the struggle in this first one is against a culture unwilling to accept or even recognize that weight. Including it in this discussion, nonetheless, will help establish both the Christian and Nietzschean interpretations of Bradbury's work and the beginning of his own philosophy, which in the end transcends both interpretations.

From the beginning of *Fahrenheit 451*, book burning "fireman" Guy Montag is awakening not just to the horrors of the thought-numbing culture in which he lives but to the fact that he lives. His neighbor Clarisse, in their first encounter, after admitting to being "seventeen and insane," shares that she likes "to smell things and look at things" (7), reminding Montag that he has paid little attention to even the sensory detail of his life, and by the end of their second meeting she has reintroduced him to all five of his senses. Before he can begin to evaluate his existence, he needs to be reminded what it means to exist. This attention to sensory experience carries through all three novels, establishing a parallel to Nietzsche and an experiential basis and starting point for Bradbury's philosophy. Before one can learn to think, Nietzsche writes in *Twilight of the Idols,* (first published in 1889), one must learn to see, "accustoming the eye to calmness, to patience, to letting things come up to it: learning to go around and grasp each individual case from all sides" (38). Sensory experience, for Nietzsche and for Bradbury, provides both the basis for human reason and a connection to the spiritual world.

Although Bradbury claimed to have "never read Nietzsche directly" (Eller and Touponce 38), Nietzschean language and ideas have proven useful in a number of critical analyses of his work. The parallels between the two might be coincidental, or the ideas might have come to Bradbury through other writers. He was, as Jonathan R. Eller points out, an admirer of Nikos Kanzantzakis (179), who studied Nietzsche and translated two of his major works into Greek.

William F. Touponce traces a Nietzschean theme in *Fahrenheit 451* in which Montag's awakening at the beginning leads to a fall into, and eventual recovery from, the "disease" of nihilism as the story progresses. The pattern works, and at the end of the book, Montag indeed has recovered from his illness to recognize new value in both his own life and humanity, but as Touponce suggests, the "true nihilist" in the story is Beatty. He, after all, has read the books. He has determined that they offer no answers, that there is nothing in them but the stuff that will make one "feel bestial and lonely" (61).

Montag, on the other hand, even at the end of the book is just becoming aware of his own ability to reason, and it is not until one has exhausted the possibilities of reason and recognized the inability of reason to provide answers to ultimate questions that one can truly choose nihilism. While Beatty has done so, Montag's journey seems more like one from subhuman to fully human. He has recognized the importance of reason, and he has decided to walk with the book people carrying the weight of human reason and the entire history of human thought on their shoulders, but he has yet to test Beatty's claim that the books offer no answers. This is an all-important first step, but he has not yet explored that history or truly tested human reason for answers to questions of morality and mortality.

Bradbury himself, in an afterword to the 1991 printing of *Fahrenheit 451*, referred to the ending as "pretty grim stuff" (172). His purpose in this novel was not to offer answers to the most pressing questions of human existence but to implore us to continue asking the questions, to continue using our senses, intellect, memory, and imagination to seek answers. This was not, after all, a dystopia like George Orwell's *1984* (1949), in which reason simply has been outlawed by an authoritarian government. In Montag's dystopia, as Kingsley Amis points out, reason has been relinquished willingly by a culture preferring to avoid the discomfort of the questions it raises. The most frightening message of *Fahrenheit 451*, writes Amis, is not "that a society could be devised that would frustrate the active virtues, nor even that these could eventually be suppressed, but that there is in all sorts of people something that longs for this to happen" (97). *Fahrenheit 451* is, above all, an attempt to awaken a sleeping culture, to exhort us to accept the weight of reason and memory and the responsibility of being human. Montag's trek with the book memorizers is not one towards salvation or even solutions; it is, grim indeed, simply towards becoming fully human. As Granger says, "[a]sk no guarantees, ask for no security, there never was such an animal" (157). This is not a story about finding answers. It is a story about asking questions and facing the reality that some of those questions will never lead to answers offering comfort, certainty, or security.

As dark as this book is, however, and as grim as the future might seem at the end, biblical allusions and religious imagery are more prominent and more positive in *Fahrenheit 451* than in the other novels. It is hard not to read something into Montag's selection of the Bible as the one book he saves. He takes what he is sure is a risk in passing it off to Faber and substituting another in his sacrifice to Beatty, and Faber, though he claims, "I'm not a religious man," is obviously enthralled with the choice. When he wonders if "God recognizes his own son the way we've dressed him up" (81), both the father and the son seem like real entities in his mind.

The biblical imagery at the end of the book also suggests hope, and it is hard to disentangle the hope from the faith implied in that imagery. As Montag trudges towards the bombed-out city reciting in his mind passages from Ecclesiastes and then from Revelation, it may, as Touponce suggests, just indicate a "new beginning that is also linked to tradition" (122), but the attention to the Bible throughout the book and the image of the tree of life at the end seem to link it to a Judeo-Christian tradition. Although the next two novels, particularly *Something Wicked This Way Comes*, more often are treated as Christian allegory, *Fahrenheit 451* actually connects more with religious, or at least Christian, faith than either of the Green Town tales.

Dandelion Wine: Embracing the Mystery

Some critics treat *Dandelion Wine*, like *The Illustrated Man*, as a collection of short stories tied rather loosely together, and even read that way, it deserves to be placed with Sherwood Anderson's *Winesburg, Ohio* and Eudora Welty's *The Golden Apples*, as one of the great collections of stories of small-town America. But unlike *The Illustrated Man*, this book holds together not just through the consistent returns to a common narrator but through the consistency of theme. The intellectual, emotional, and spiritual growth of Douglas Spaulding takes him through the descent into and recovery from the nihilism Touponce identifies in Montag, but because this young protagonist is not saddled with the burden of lifting an entire culture out of an intellectual stupor, his individual development is more detailed and more complete. *Dandelion Wine* is all about the human response to mortality and the quest for happiness in the face of that mortality, and though Green Town is a religious community, religion does not provide the answers that save Douglas Spaulding from existential angst.

As with the awakening of Montag to his senses at the beginning of *Fahrenheit 451*, we see an awakening of Douglas in the berry picking episode at the beginning of the second novel. "Some days," his father tells him and his brother, are "compounded completely of odor, nothing but the world blowing in one nostril and out the other." Some are "days of hearing every trump and trill of the universe." Some are "good for tasting and some for touching," and others are "good for all the senses at once" (3). Unlike Montag, whose senses have been numbed by his own failure to give them any thought, Douglas simply is being awakened to how those senses connect him to the universe, to his role as an agent of the universe. When that "great Thing," which he both welcomes and fears, finally overtakes him, he slowly opens an eye, afraid of finding "nothing." But what he discovers is that "[e]verything, absolutely everything, was there" (7). He realizes he is alive, but more importantly, he realizes not only he, but Tom, everything, is part of the "great Thing." Through his senses and new awareness, he suddenly recognizes himself as part of a universe.

In his first major work, *The Birth of Tragedy from the Spirit of Music* (1872), Nietzsche uses the Titans' dismemberment of Dionysus as an analogy for the beginning of existence as we know it. When he was torn apart, the great "oneness" was separated. This represents the creation not just of humanity but of everything as we see and know it. We are all, in this metaphor, just parts of the whole, not so much individual as individuated, agents, or perhaps more appropriately, appendages of the great oneness (66). Although it is unlikely Bradbury consciously employed Nietzsche's metaphor, his "great Thing" mirrors that "universal oneness" from which Nietzsche suggested we came and of which he suggested we are still a part. In "Cry the Cosmos," a 1962 essay published in *Life*, Bradbury writes, "We might take some comfort in daring to believe that perhaps we are part of some divine stir and perambulation, a vast blind itch of a God universe to touch, taste, see, hear, and know itself" (98). This idea of human life as an extension of a "God universe" rather than subjected to God might help explain the attention to sensory experience in all three novels.

Douglas's awakening to his life, however, is followed quickly by a recognition of death, and though this second step develops through the story, Bradbury introduces it here when Douglas refers to his discovery as a "rare timepiece, this clock gold-bright and guaranteed to run three score and ten" (7). He will experience the loss of a friend, the loss of tradition in the old trolley, and the deaths of Colonel Freeleigh, a great-grandmother, and even the Lonely One—if we can assume he indeed was the man killed by Lavinia Nebbs. Yet even at the moment he realizes he is alive, we get the reminder that life comes with an expiration date.

Dandelion Wine pushes this theme of mortality so hard that it stands at least in one sense as the darkest of the three novels. Green Town, despite the pleasant, bucolic sound of the name and the touching simplicity of a few of the stories, is often a frightening place, and it eventually becomes too much for Doug Spaulding. When he falls into his illness, Bradbury leaves little doubt about its nihilistic origin. Drifting into unconsciousness, Douglas listens "to the dim piston of his heart," as he watches images of all the summer's losses float past (163). He has reached existential crisis.

The antidote in this story, however, does not come from books, and it does not come from religion. It does not, in fact, come from science either. While the novels rarely touch on the themes of science and religion running through many of the short stories, Bradbury provides, in the form of the doctor who appears almost more as a comical metaphor than a character, a quick rejection of modern medicine as an answer to Doug's fever. Instead, he is cured when he embraces existence. It is the air and the essences from this world, provided in two jars from Mr. Jonas, that lift him from his malaise. No guarantee, no certainty, no religious imagery—he simply needs to breathe in existence and reestablish his place as a part of the "great Thing." There is both weight and lightness in being, and both begin with our sensory connection to the natural world.

It is no mistake that the rather contrived story originally published as "The Magical Kitchen" follows Doug's recovery after just a half-page interlude. Though simple and somewhat obvious, this story helps explain where Douglas stands, and perhaps where Bradbury stands, at this moment of recovery. Accepting life and coming to terms with its transient nature require embracing mystery and uncertainty. Aunt Rose, like the "systematizers" at whom Nietzsche scoffs, tries to apply order to that which cannot be ordered but succeeds only in destroying the beauty of the mystery. Douglas, sneaking into the kitchen like a satyr in the dark of night, restores chaos from the mistaken attempt at order. And once both the mystery and the beauty have returned, he acknowledges the lesson of the junkman. "Mr. Jonas, wherever you are, you're thanked, you're paid back. I passed it on..." (180).

Not only does Christian imagery play no role in the escape from nihilism; what religious allusions and imagery we do get in *Dandelion Wine* seem to dismiss religion as an answer. In the early chapter in which Tom and their mother go out looking for Doug, we get a dark scene in which Tom's internal monologue, perhaps somewhat deep for a ten-year-old, provides what seems like a dismissal of religion as a source of comfort or happiness. Frightened by the darkness, the threatening ravine, and the return of the Lonely One to Green Town, Tom looks up at the "holy black silhouette of the German Baptist church," but it offers him no solace. "He should have felt encouraged," Bradbury tells us, "but he was not because the building was not illumined, was cold and useless as a pile of ruins on the ravine edge" (29). As they walk on, his monologue spins into a vertiginous reflection on death and the loneliness of the individual even in a society filled with others. Finally, Tom says a little prayer, but even this reflects a darkness that hardly offers consolation. "Oh, Lord, don't let her die, please," he thinks. "Don't do anything to us" (30). He and his mother are alone, and God is in his mind another threat, or perhaps the source of all threats and all darkness.

Later in the book, in another of the rare references to religion, Tom offers one of Bradbury's most amusing observations on Christian faith. Douglas implores his brother to be careful, to not let anything happen to him, and tells him, "It's not you I worry about... It's the way God runs the world." After thinking a minute about God, Tom replies, "He's all right, Doug... He tries" (86). Hardly a comforting thought for a boy consumed by loss and obsessed with death.

In the end, there is little of God or religion in Douglas's eventual recovery. He stands in the room in the cupola, as he did at the beginning of the novel, looking out over Green Town, and imagines the lights going out in the buildings and houses at his direction. He, in the end, at least in his young mind, is God, and even if he realizes it is only a game, he is connected to the moment and in sync with the universe. The town, the world, are his, and he is one with the life around him. The jars of *Dandelion Wine* in the basement, like the junkman's jars of air and essences, will remind him of his connection to every moment, every occurrence of the past.

Something Wicked: Celebrating Existence

Like the first two novels, *Something Wicked This Way Comes* grew from earlier, shorter works, and though not published until 1962, the story was developing before the publication of *Dandelion Wine*, and in its earliest form, an unpublished short story titled "Black Ferris," even before *Fahrenheit 451* (Eller and Touponce 459). Though the grand plot might not yet have been established, the themes of this third novel cannot be separated from the first two. The Green Town books both are attempts at working out the existential questions of human happiness and meaning left unresolved at the end of *Fahrenheit 451*.

Something Wicked This Way Comes, with its themes of good versus evil, light versus darkness, was widely accepted as a "Christian compatible" work. Yet despite those themes, despite Charles Halloway's description of the carnival freaks as "[s]inners who've travelled so long, hoping for deliverance, they've taken on the shape of their original sins" (207), this book moves even further from Christianity and closer to the Nietzschean apostasy from which Dimeo claims Bradbury had been saved by his faith. Dimeo, however, was not wrong about Bradbury undoubtedly holding onto an unshakable faith. No one could survive the time he spent staring into the black abyss of mortality without some kind of faith, but this third novel, the culmination of Bradbury's long rumination on that abyss, embraces a worldly rather than otherworldly faith.

Other writers have traced the Nietzschean themes in this book. Stephen King, in *Danse Macabre*, identifies the two boys as representing the mythological human duality Nietzsche develops in The Birth of Tragedy. "Will," King suggests, "is Apollonian, a creature of reason and plan, a believer (mostly) in the status quo and the norm. Jim Nightshade, as the name implies, is the Dionysian half, a creature of emotion, something of a nihilist..." (308). This interpretation, though accurate as Jim falls into a sickness of his own, can also feed into the allegorical reading of a boy being saved from temptation. As King points out, it is Jim who needs to take that second look through the window of the sexually tempting "Theater," and although both boys are tempted by the carnival, Jim does not share Will's fear and reluctance.

Nietzsche's mythological duality, however, might be seen best not in comparison of the boys but in the internal development and eventual individual resolution reached by Will's father. In Charles Halloway, we can see Bradbury's working out of the Nietzschean theme running through all three novels. Like Montag, like Douglas Spaulding, Charles Halloway falls into and eventually recovers from the "sickness" of nihilism. In the darkness of the library, plagued by fear of his own mortality and the guilt of his own sins, he is no match for Mr. Dark. But the true cause of his sickness and helplessness against the Illustrated Man is not the sins but the guilt. At the end of a short lecture to Will on sin in Chapter 28, Halloway suggests that denying oneself the pleasures of life to avoid the guilt of sin leads to its own kind of guilt and regret. You deny yourself that slice of cake, that truant swim in the river, to escape being broken by guilt. "But then, through plain dumb cowardice, I guess, maybe you hold off from too much, play it safe" (136).

Guilt, for Nietzsche, is a manmade illusion standing in the way of becoming fully human. "Although the most acute judges of witchery," he writes in *The Gay Science* (1882), "and even the witches themselves, were convinced of the guilt of witchery, the guilt nevertheless was non-existent. It is thus with all guilt" (216). And the power of Mr. Dark's witch, the power of the carnival itself, is drawn not from the sins of the Green Town residents but from the guilt they feel for those sins. "Those creatures," he tells the boys, "want the flaming gas off souls who can't sleep nights, that fever by day from old crimes. A dead soul is no kindling. But a live and raving soul, crisped with self-damnation, oh that's a pretty snoutful for such as them" (203). Although Bradbury never absolves us of moral responsibility, he seems consistent with Nietzsche in viewing the Christian concepts of sin and guilt as obstructions to fully actualizing life.

Halloway's own guilt stems from what both Bradbury and Nietzsche might consider the ultimate human sin—the failure to have lived fully—and this makes him the ideal protagonist in the battle with Dark and the autumn people. The Dust Witch, he tells the boys, once might have been a person like him, "someone who lived always tomorrow and let today slide, like myself, and so wound up and penalized, having to guess other people's wild sunrises and sad sunsets" (207). To defeat her, he must also win a battle with himself. He must overcome his guilt at yesterdays lost and become an active agent in today.

Charles Halloway's escape from existential angst and defeat of the Dust Witch come not from salvation from his sins but from his realization that the concepts of sin and guilt are meaningless. The Bible does him no good in the battle against Mr. Dark and offers not even the glimmer of hope we might take from it at the end of *Fahrenheit 451*. Mr. Dark laughs at the book and flings it into the trash. "Myths," he says, "unfortunately, are just that... Your King James and his literary version of some rather stuffy poetic materials is worth just about this much of my time and sweat" (212). Halloway's salvation comes at a human rather than divine level, and his eventual victory comes from embracing rather than overcoming nihilism. As he stares into the face of the Dust Witch, he thinks, "Somehow, irresistibly, the prime thing was: nothing mattered. Life in the end seemed a prank of such size you could only stand off at this end of the corridor to note its meaningless length and its quite unnecessary height..." (229). He is saved by a Dionysian response to this epiphany, a smile leading to a giggle and growing into laughter before exploding into "hilarity spring[ing] forth of its own volition..." (229).

Laughter defeats the witch and brings down the house of mirrors. Laughter, song, and dance bring down the entire carnival and bring Jim back to life. As Lahna Diskin points out, "Will and his father resurrect Jim with levity, not gravity, with mirth, not lamentation. Their rhapsody and bombast—indeed, their grandiosity—is Dionysian: redemption in revelry" (150). Just as the chanting of the chorus in Nietzsche's interpretation of Greek tragedy provided the audience with an antidote for the stark Apollonian reality of their lives, music and laughter provide the antidote for the guilt, sadness, and despair on which the autumn people prey. Neither religion nor the entire history of human reason provides security or meaning, but revelry in the meaninglessness, celebration of life in the face of death, celebration of death and life as one, reunite us with the spirit of Dionysus and our oneness with the universe.

Though it is possible to pull religious allusions together from this book and build a case for a more Christian interpretation, Halloway's conclusion about the meaninglessness of life is hard to mesh with such a theme, especially given the thread of nihilism stitched through all three novels. Still, acceptance of Bradbury as a Christian compatible author is not surprising, given the overriding sense of optimism in these dark stories. Embracing meaninglessness does not leave Charles Halloway in a void of angst; it allows him to experience both the weight and the joy of being human. For Bradbury, as for Nietzsche, there is always that connection to the oneness of the universe. Mysterious, chaotic, and perhaps even meaningless as it might be, we are a part of it and it a part of us. Sometimes, however, the pain overwhelms the beauty of the mystery. Sometimes we just need to shout, to sing, to dance. Sometimes we just need to let Dionysus out.

Faith and Morality from the Ground Up

It would be a mistake, however, to read too much into Charles Halloway's conclusion about the meaninglessness of life or to interpret the focus on sensation as an Epicurian distrust of anything not emanating directly from our senses. Bradbury saw meaning coming from existence and experience, but he saw it coming also from imagination, from the experience of others, from the whole history of human experience. His characters do not stand paralyzed by existential angst. They suffer, they mourn, and they give in to Dionysian revelry when necessary, but they all decide, in the end, to live. They all accept the weight and responsibility of human existence. All three novels end at least somewhat hopefully, and Guy Montag, Douglas Spaulding, and Charles Halloway all embody Bradbury's faith in our connection with the universe.

In a 1996 *Playboy* interview with Ken Kelley, Bradbury tells us, "Science and religion have to go hand in hand with the mystery, because there's a certain point beyond which you say, 'There are no answers.'" The role of the preacher, he says, is to remind us, "'Don't forget to pay attention to the fact that you're alive.' Just the mere fact, the glory of getting up every morning and looking at the sunrise or a good rainfall or whatever, and saying, 'That's wonderful.' That's just wonderful" (150).

Like the other novels, *Something Wicked This Way Comes* celebrates the human senses and our connection through those senses to something larger of which we are a part, but it also offers an answer, perhaps not certain, but at least useful, to that existential question of finding meaning and value without external guidance. Bradbury ends a beautiful paragraph on love with this:

> Because her flesh knows heat, cold, affliction, I know fire, snow, and pain. Shared and once again shared experience. Billions of prickling textures. Cut one sense away, cut part of life away. Cut two senses; life halves itself on the instant. We love what we know, we love what we are. Common cause, common cause, common cause of mouth, eye, ear, tongue, flesh, nose, hand, heart, and soul. (198)

While this tribute to the senses runs through all three novels as Bradbury works out his understanding of our role in and relationship to the universe, here we get a real clue about how he suggests we respond to the seeming meaninglessness of life and death, of how we establish values and morals without divine guidance: "Common cause, common cause..." The inclusion of "heart and soul" at the end of the passage completes the idea. Our sensory connection to the natural world connects us also with the "great Thing" and with one another. We know both the beauty and the pain, and we know that others, sensory agents just like us of the same universal being, the same oneness, have felt the same pain. How can we not care for them as we do for ourselves? We carry the weight, we use the resources we have, but we take care of each other as we continue to ask questions as yet unanswered.

"Why am I here at all?" Charles Halloway asks the boys. "Right now, it seems, to help you" (194). And that, perhaps above all, is what Bradbury offers. While we may not understand the meaning of the universe, we can know how it feels, smells, looks, tastes, and sounds. If we remind ourselves that others share all those some sensations and so must know all the beauty, all the pain, all the mystery we do, how can we not feel moral responsibility for them? When that shaggy man in a cave a hundred millennia ago looked over the dying fire at his family and realized they, like him, one day would die, at least "for a little bit the next morning, he treated them somewhat better, for he saw that they, like himself, had the seed of night in them" (196).

Conclusion

Montag accepts the responsibility of carrying the weight of human history and human thought, a weight we all are obligated to carry if we expect to be fully human. Douglas Spaulding accepts his place as part of the "great Thing," the eternal oneness of being, and Charles Halloway brings forth the spirit of Dionysus to at least momentarily relieve the pressure of uncertainty. But it is Bradbury who brings the faith, though it may be a faith that does not coincide with any orthodox religion. While these novels never waver from pushing the reader to accept the weight and uncertainty of mortality, they also never waver from a faith in the beauty, the mystery, and the value of life. God does not sit above us passing judgment; god exists in us, around us, and through us.

Works Cited

Amis, Kingsley. "A Skillfully Drawn Conformist Hell." *Readings on Fahrenheit 451*. Edited by Katie de Koster. Greenhaven Literary Companion Series. Greenhaven, 2009, pp. 93-9.

Bradbury, Ray. "Cry the Cosmos." *Life*, 14 Sept 1962, pp. 87+.

———. *Dandelion Wine*. 1957. Bantam, 1964.

———. *Fahrenheit 451*. 1953. Ballantine, 1991.

———. *Something Wicked This Way Comes*. Harper, 1962.

Dimeo, Steven. "Man and Apollo: Religion in Bradbury's Science Fantasies." *Ray Bradbury*. Edited by Martin Harry Greenberg and Joseph D. Olander. Writers of the 21st Century Series. Taplinger, 1980, pp. 156-64.

Diskin, Lahna. "Bradbury on Children." *Ray Bradbury*. Edited by Martin Harry Greenberg and Joseph D. Olander. Writers of the 21st Century Series. Taplinger, 1980, pp. 127-55.

Eller, Jonathan R. *Ray Bradbury Unbound*. U of Illinois P, 2014.

———, and William F. Touponce. *Ray Bradbury: The Life of Fiction*. Kent State UP, 2004.

Kelley, Ken. "A Candid Conversation with Science Fiction's Grand Master on the Future of Space Travel, Computer Flimflams, Political Correctness and Why He's Always Right." *Playboy*, May 1996, pp. 47+.

King, Stephen. *Danse Macabre*. Everest, 1981.

Nietzsche, Friedrich. *The Birth of Tragedy and The Genealogy of Morals*. Translated by Francis Golffing. Anchor, 1956.

———. *The Gay Science*. Translated by Walter Kaufmann. Vintage, 1974.

———. *Twilight of the Idols and The Anti-Christ*. Translated by Thomas Common. Dover, 2004.

Touponce, William F. "Overcoming Nihilism in the Modern World." *Readings on Fahrenheit 451*. Edited by Katie de Koster. Greenhaven Literary Companion Series. Greenhaven, 2009. 113-22.

A Golem in the Family: Robotic Technologies and Artificial Intelligence in Ray Bradbury's Short Stories_____

Guido Laino

Then, in mysterious fashion, comes into my mind the legend of the mysterious Golem, artificial man, whom once, long ago, here in the Ghetto, a rabbi learned in the Kabbala shaped from the elements, investing it with an unreasoning, automatic life when he placed a magical formula behind its teeth. (Meyrink 16)

When asked if machines possibly might be "bad, evil," and "might dehumanize," the robot grandmother of Bradbury's short story "I Sing the Body Electric" (1969) answers, "Some machines do. It's all in the way they are built. It's all in the way they are used" (160). This concept epitomizes Ray Bradbury's idea of technology as expressed in various interviews, and is reaffirmed later when the robot adds that her creator "knew that most machines are amoral, neither bad nor good" (161). This approach stresses the technological dichotomy between the Bomb and the rocket that runs through Bradbury's entire work: On the one hand, the Bomb owes its destructive power to human foolishness; on the other, the rocket, if not used aggressively, can represent the means of humanity's liberation through space travel (Mengeling 100).

But does this substantial neutrality always work with robotic technologies featuring in his fiction? Is it always possible to reduce the impact of these technologies to a positive or negative scheme based on the intentions of their creators or their users? Apart from some purposely conceived creature such as the "mechanical hound" of *Fahrenheit 451* (1953), in the heterogeneity of Bradbury's work things are far more ambiguous, perhaps even beyond the author's intentions. In this essay, I will focus on robotic technologies in Bradbury's short stories, also considering both the merging of sci-fi with classic fantastic fiction in the design of these machines, and his anticipation of some urgent current concerns about the rise of artificial intelligence, or AI.

What Bradbury imagines is an unconceivable technology, quite poor in the depiction of scientific issues; his futuristic and/ or alien landscapes display magic rather than an actual technical progress. Still, his work deals with substantial philosophical, metaphysical, and cultural issues of his time and, by extension, of our time as twenty-first century readers. That is because to debate scientific progress is not a mere problem of technical possibilities, either plausible or fanciful, but of ethics and culture. Bradbury's literary work is somehow comparable with such a seminal work of the philosophy of science as Norbert Wiener's *God & Golem, Inc.* (1962), which discusses then-new issues of cybernetics using the metaphors of magic and sorcery, and draws widely from fantastic and religious literature, both for useful examples to clarify his views and as a sort of cultural feedback concerning fundamental ethical principles.

Though not focusing on it, Wiener titled his essay after the Hebraic tradition of the golem, a creature brought to life by means of "the letters of the alphabet [which] have secret, magical power" (Scholem, "Idea" 166) or by mathematical combinations—a type of metalinguistics (Idel chap. III) somehow anticipating the idea of giving life to a machine by programming it with a computer code. While its origins are bound in the Bible and have been part of the Hebraic esoteric and mystic speculation for long time, the story has evolved first into a medieval popular legend, and then into a fantastic literature classic treated by such authors as Jakob Grimm, E.T.A. Hoffmann, and Gustav Meyrink (Morris 1-30). In its various and different versions, the figure of the golem is somehow a recognizable ancestor of the science-fictional android, and at the same time it both carries wide implications in terms of religion and ethics, and offers clear correlations with fantastic literature.

The Golem's Family Tree: Fantastic Technologies

In Bradbury's idea of evolution, humans "dreamed answers to dire questions; that is the essence of the fiction that becomes science. Once a vivid dream was realized in their heads, they were able to act on it" ("Predicting" 35). Bradbury is more a writer of fantastic fiction than of proper, technology-informed science fiction (Anderson 26); in his work dream comes before technology, and fiction is much more prominent than science. Somehow reversing Arthur C. Clarke's third law—"Any sufficiently advanced technology is indistinguishable from magic" (36)—Bradbury crowds his stories with wizards presented as inventors and scientists. Flying beyond what is predictable by his actual knowledge of the scientific progress of his time, he appeals to the dreamlike consistency of the unthinkable magic of a far future technology, answering questions that still have to be asked. It is a kind of interrogation of the supernatural, but it is based on the consciousness that what will be considered natural in the future could be completely extraneous to the present. In this sense, fantastic fiction is far more outreaching than a relatively credible sci-fi based on actual technological trends; in any case, as Rabkin observes, "this is not 'science too far ahead of us' but Enchantment through science" (125).

Apart from the homage Bradbury pays to Poe with "Usher II" (1950), a story in which a technologically advanced house on Mars replicates the wonders of Gothic literature, almost any technical device in his stories recalls some sort of enchantment, sorcery, or apparently supernatural event. In many ways, his are ghost stories, where spirits are mechanical or electric and human beings become ghosts or shadows. Lots of machines work without any plausibility; they seem more animated by a phantom than programmed by a scientist. Things happen without any technical explication, as if produced by some supernatural power rather than by a human artifact.

Androids, in Bradbury, are essentially automatic puppets, not human replicants, as is suggested naïvely by the names of the industries that construct them, such as "Marionettes, Inc." or "Fantoccini Company," the latter being the Italian for puppet. They are injected with some sort of magic hidden behind circuits and metal. That is the case, for example, of the electric Grandmother, who is turned on by a weird ritual rather than by plugs and switches, and who is much more like a golem, becoming alive by a spell, than like a robot. Together with other Bradbury's androids, she belongs to the fantastic literature family tree, with the automaton Olympia of Hoffmann's "Der Sandmann" (1816), or with the creature of Mary Shelley's *Frankenstein* (1818), where the Faustian myth of the fool scientist is connected with sorcery and electric magic.

In "The Long Years" (1948), the family members that Hathaway reconstructs appear to be some kind of nostalgic puppet show, well built but still more automatic than lively. Even though they can engage in "a much silent debate" (156), or can claim to feel sorry, still they do not know how to cry, as Hathaway did not teach them to do it (163). Their life has no meaning; it is the pure repetition of their creator's will. Artificial human beings in Bradbury's stories are quite far from the conscious androids of Philip K. Dick's work, from the demoniac intelligence of HAL 9000 in *2001: A Space Odyssey*, or even from Isaac Asimov's positronic robots.

Intelligent houses are more of the same; in different representations, they take a key role in Bradbury's stories like "There Will Come Soft Rains" (1950) and "The Veldt" (1950). Without playing the slapstick comic game of Buster Keaton's *The Electric House* or Jacques Tati's *Mon Oncle*, nor touching the nipping black humor of the "American Housewife Routine" in William S. Burroughs's *Naked Lunch* (112), Bradbury shows a delicate ironic stance, enriching it with horrifying and surrealistic tones. But, while actually resembling the domotics or the "internet of things" of present times, they seem to recall more closely some haunted houses rather than real, plausible previsions of a technological future. And in the same way his robots look like automatic puppets moved by some magician or barker, his technological houses could be the mechanical horror houses in those old carnivals of the author's memories.

House Golems: Replacement and Desire

Since they first found a name in Karel Čapek's *R.U.R.* (1920), robots are suspected to yearn replacing humanity, something confirmed, on a scientific level, by Alan Turing's *Imitation Game*, a test designed to evaluate the advancement of computers by means of their ability to simulate a human identity. Bradbury's androids imitate human beings quite well, but still they do not seem to strive for an ousting of humans' position. Instead, they seem to complete the parabola of the assembly line; they integrate and perfect human work, with very specific commitments such as to support a familiar, almost mechanical routine, as in "Marionettes, Inc." (1949) and "The Long Years," or they correct human imperfections, since, for example, human "nurses tend to be selfish, neglectful, or suffering from dire nervous afflictions" ("Sing" 139).

Artificial intelligence is employed in a similar way in Bradbury's "electric houses." AI can respect precisely the daily schedule despite the fact that those human beings who used to live there have been dead for a long time, as in "There Will Come Soft Rains," or it can be like that of "The Veldt," which before getting dangerous to the Hadleys, "clothed and fed and rocked them to sleep and played and sang and was good to them" (7). That confirms Bradbury's idea of a substantial neutrality of machines, as happens with the life in the golem, that "was only derived from a magic charm placed behind its teeth each day" (Meyrink 26). They move, at least in their intentions, only through clear orders, without any autonomy, as revealed by the surrealistic outliving of the robots in "The Long Years" and of the house in "There Will Come Soft Rains," destined to an eternity of meaningless repetition. But even without considering themselves as actual living things in competition with their masters, these substituting machines embody a tangible danger for those who get used to them. As the character of the psychologist McClean puts it in "The Veldt," the Hadleys permit the house to replace them in their children's affections, so that the nursery becomes "their mother and father, far more important in their lives than their real parents" (21). A side effect of this uncanny imitation game is that once people— and especially young people—start to trust machines more than their families, the trend towards dehumanization wins out.

Just as the golem is a better servant than any human being, for it is submissive, relentlessly compliant, and mute, probably also these house robots are much better than any member of the family; that is how people fall in love with the artificial undead. Just as the Hadley children start to prefer the technologic nursery to their own parents,

Tom and his brothers love their electric grandmother more than any real human relative. Similarly, the space ship crew of "G.B.S-Mark V" (1976) prefers the company of androids, whether they be aphrodisiac female puppets or the wise George Bernard Shaw replicant, to the affinity of their companions. And even Hathaway of "The Long Years" probably does not regret his authentic family, since the one he has built for himself will easily be, paradoxically, much more loving, obedient, and cheerful than the original.

Robotic technologies in Bradbury appear to be on the verge of substituting humanity, both in a metaphorical and in a literal sense. But as it occurs with the golem, who never pretends to be human, this substitution does not suppose an actual overlapping with the human being. Bradbury's mechanical puppets are not, by any means, "electric ants" in a Dickian way, and they do not seem to have any aspiration or confusion about being human. In many ways, they are mechanical and magical desire machines, which feed on their users' wills and dreams. These machines replace human beings not so much on practical duties, but in channeling basic emotional needs. They ensure love, protection, and compassion, as in "I Sing the Body Electric," "The Long Years," and "G.B.S.-Mark V," or they accomplish some type of "dirty work" dictated by hate, treachery, and death wish, as in "The Veldt," "Marionettes, Inc.," and "Punishment Without Crime" (1950).

With his mysterious magical formula through which he incarnates his users' desires, the golem insinuates himself especially into family life, and like the Gothic vampire, once invited, he enters and takes possession of the house. As Bradbury "opposes any machine or technology that is used to disrupt or destroy a nuclear or extended family structure, while admiring any machine that does the opposite" (Mengeling 86), the specific impact this technology has on family life could be another way to discriminate the utopian machines from the dystopian ones. Following this pattern, there should be a good technology that intervenes in a context of loss and mourning, as happens with the deaths of a mother in "I Sing the Body Electric" and of an entire family in "The Long Years," opposed to a bad one that, in a metaphorical or even a literal way, kills familial relationships, as occurs in "The Veldt," "Marionettes, Inc.," and "Punishment Without Crime." Still, here a deep contradiction emerges, as even when the contribution to family life has beneficial effects, there is the perception of a slight shift from the human to the inhuman, from the natural to the artificial, and a sense of uncanny transference from something that was alive to something utterly dead, as is displayed in "There Will Come Soft Rains" with bitter sarcasm.

In a metaphorical interpretation, Bradbury's stories always address the gradual dehumanization of technological society, whether the actual use of technology could be recognized as positive or negative. As it occurs in *Fahrenheit 451*, this prevailing technology signals, in Andrea Krafft's words, "Bradbury's yearning for a nostalgic vision of domesticity that is disintegrating within modernity, as he calls for a return to the values of the extended family found in his idealistic vision of small-town America" (123). And even when it seems that this idealistic vision of the family is preserved by the introduction of some kind of technology, still the price paid for it seems to be potentially incalculable. On the other hand, what could be more unnatural than to remove death from the human cycle? Alone and incapable of accepting the death of his loved ones, Hathaway produces a never-aging family that fulfills his nostalgic needs, while the electric grandmother embodies a completely unnatural order in which her grandchildren witness her birth and start to love her when they discover that she cannot die as their mother did (167).

The Age of the Golem: The Rise of Technocracy

The golem not only invades the sacred space of the family, but he does so by seducing the children as a "Toy that is more than a Toy" ("Sing" 138). Even opposing the utopian virtue of the electric grandmother to the dystopian black magic of the nursery, the end result is the absolute subjugation of the children, who, on a metaphorical level, represent the new generation and the future of humanity. Both in "The Veldt" and in "I Sing the Body Electric," children are under a spell, where technology turns into sorcery: "we were drawn, lured, spelled, doing our dance, remembering what could not be remembered, needful, aware of her attentions" ("Sing" 151). As a matter of fact, children are the first to accept this change and the ones who will carry it on, too. "The adults have created a mechanical universe that has mastered them, and the children have created a universe of their own and made themselves masters of it, or so they believe" (Anderson 31): The fantastic and vicious universe created by the Hadley children is a by-product of the mechanical universe of their parents, and "The Veldt" shows a sort of wrong inheritance left by the parents to their children, a bequest that they accept to its full consequences, entailing their parents' death. Thus, humanity is evolving in its technological mutation, as today's child is tomorrow's New Man. As H. G. Wells figures out, "we want to be in at the death of Man and to have a voice in his final replacement by the next Lord of Creation, even if, Oedipus-like, that successor's first act be parricide" (Chapter IV).

Children seem to be the first witnesses and somehow the agents of the anthropological change represented by the technological dominion overbearing society. The parricide, be it real or metaphorical, unveils the panorama of a brave new technological world where they prepare to become one-dimensional men. Herbert Marcuse depicts how the "technological transformation of nature alters the base of domination," establishing a dependence on what he calls an "objective order of things" (144). As to becoming objective, this order of things must have been strengthened through the years by a gradual, though pervasive, imposition of a "false consciousness, responding to and contributing to the preservation of a false order of facts…embodied in the prevailing technical apparatus which in turn reproduces it" (145). Started with their parents' generation, this staggering change affects the children, who grow up with new values and complete the last stage of the transformation. What happens to the Hadleys metaphorically resembles this phenomenon; an illusory and sinister new reality, generated by the AI of the nursery, substitutes the one the parents used to recognize as true. And while their children believe in the technical apparatus and enthusiastically join it, they refuse to adapt and try to step back; but their children do not comply with their authority anymore and choose the machine, thus provoking their parents' murder.

The replacement of the educational mentoring of parents by a technological entity echoes the substitution of an order of things with a different one. Both in "The Veldt" and "I Sing the Body Electric," children incarnate what Marcuse defines as "the unfreedom of man" and "the 'technical' impossibility of being autonomous" (158); they are victims, exactly like their parents, of a "submission to the technical apparatus which enlarges the comforts of life and increases the productivity of labor" (158). But while the parents at least can imagine resisting, the children refuse any possible detachment from that technological world to which they feel they belong. Facing the possibility of "turning the whole house off," Peter Hadley claims his need for that comfort apparatus: "That sounds dreadful! Would I have to tie my own shoes instead of letting the shoe tier do it?" (18). And when their parents actually switch off the house, the children seem to go into serious withdrawal: "The two children were in hysterics. They screamed and pranced and threw things" (22). They are techno-addicted, as the blending of comfort and entertainment offered by the technological apparatus of the house has become something without which they cannot survive.

For the Hadley children, the nursery becomes "a channel toward destructive thoughts" (20), so it still could be considered a neutral technological tool, as their desires are morosely death-driven. But what happens is that the machine seems to exacerbate their psychosis, catalyzing their weird black wishes; the intentions of these masters are influenced to some extent by the technology they use. In fact, as happens in "Marionettes, Inc." and "Punishment Without Crime," the availability of these technological items perverts their users, as their desires find an instrument of fulfillment, whether they are honest or malicious and repugnant. In the golem tradition, masters never abuse their power, nor consciously give the creature any contemptible order; in Bradbury's works, however, with machines obeying much more desires than proper orders, the relation between the user's will and the acts of his golem is far more ambiguous.

The users' intentions, and how those intentions take shape in their mind, is something not completely focused in Bradbury's work, even though it appears as something crucial in the author's presumed binary system of technology evaluation. But what seems to emerge is an ambiguous new era in which human beings use machines as those same machines prompt them to do. In a blurry, evocative way, Bradbury's work explores that transition from the human to the inhuman that leads to a dominion that "perpetuates and extends itself not only through technology but as technology" (Marcuse 158).

In the Golem's Mouth: Shades of Singularity

Despite the flaws and oversimplification of his binary conception of technology, Bradbury, appealing to the fantastic and evoking the powers of sorcery in his robotic creations, succeeds in approaching very complex questions about the interaction of human being and AI. With an essential disregard of actual technological matters allowing his fiction to reach a broad range of problems that would be quite difficult to figure out with a more rigorous method, Bradbury is particularly effective in depicting cultural and anthropological issues that, with the passing of time, are becoming a key priority. That is why Bradbury's work, with his aura of mystery, can be projected on today's impending future, as it is presented, in similar neutral terms, by Ray Kurzweil: "although neither utopian nor dystopian, this epoch will transform the concepts that we rely on to give meaning to our lives, from our business models to the cycle of human life, including death itself" (22). Facing this kind of predictable, but still unimaginable, change, analysts are left with scarce tools of investigation, so that a certain degree of clairvoyance, and poetry, is needed.

This peculiar moment in time, when, to use H. G. Wells's words, "the Pattern of Things to Come faded away" (chap. I), implies a transformation that has been called "Singularity": "we cannot comprehend it, at least with our current level of understanding. For that reason, we cannot look past its event horizon and make complete sense of what lies beyond" (Kurzweil 38). As some supernatural phenomenon depicted by a Gothic ghost story, Singularity can be approached by a dated sci-fi that, on quite different scientific basis, has evoked some of the spectral matter of this unknown imminent future. This is how Bradbury's magical robots make their voices heard in a future remarkably different from the one they used to live in. Not on Mars, nor upon an Earth devastated by the Bomb, the golem is actually in the family, and it is not clear what kind of position he is intended to assume in it. Here is where Bradbury's poetic vision of future lights up the unpredictable shape of Singularity: in familiar, intimate everyday life; in the deep essence of being human; in the anthropological and metaphysical implications of this radical change that "will be so rapid, its impact so deep, that human life will be irreversibly transformed" (Kurzweil 22).

One of the first dangers inherent in the rise of machines is the loss of their control. According to the most well-known version of the golem story, Rabbi Loew "was forced to restore him to his dust when golem began to run amok and endanger people's lives" (Scholem, "Golem" 353-54). The danger of an artificial creature getting out of control is another point of contact not only between the late versions of the golem's story and the Faustian myth, but also with a dystopian topos, which in turn "fuses two fears: the fear of utopia and the fear of technology" (Beauchamp 53). But in Bradbury there is no sign of a particularly technophobic approach in this sense, as his machines do not generally attack humans without being designed or programmed to do so.

"The Veldt" indeed is an ambiguous case, where it is difficult to understand whether the nursery has developed a deliberate killing will autonomous from the children's action. Although George knows that probably his son has changed the setup of the nursery to keep the veldt as the only active virtual environment, he informs his wife that "the fool room's out of order" (14) anyway. Later in the story, he admits that he does not "imagine the room will like being turned off" and asks himself whether the machine hates him "for wanting to switch it off" (22). As for "Marionettes, Inc.," it allows different interpretations: Maybe Braling Two is simply misused by his master or is overzealous in obeying too literally the order of replacing him and keeping company with his wife—something he does, but in a quite strict way. The most obvious explanation is that some sort of bug might have changed the software of the robot's tasks, corrupted the message of his user, or magically made him develop human feelings, such that the killing of his master either is an unyielding optimization in achieving his goal or, on the contrary, is a too-human consequential impulse.

This may imply that it is possible for the golem to slip away from his master's control and to develop his own program, so that his neutrality degenerates into some form of dystopian autonomous will. However, this scenario is left in the realm of ambiguity and oddity, like some mystic enigma that cannot be completely comprehended, while the shape of human life under the technological spell is far more important than the actual danger of scientific sorcery. In this sense, many of Bradbury's stories concerning robots and AI have gloomy resemblances with the present technological progress and its threats. "The Veldt" displays what could happen to a generation of children heavily exposed to forms of comfort and entertainment that are more and more pervasive and connected with their basic needs. The fantastic playground represented by the nursery seems the ghostly version of the online gaming, the virtual reality, and life and communication of the social networks era, something that could also can be found in "The Murderer" (1952).

As for the life of their parents, beyond being useless, they start to feel useless. Relieved from work, they have to contrive a new sense for their lives, but while children are wrapped up in games, adults get lost in emptiness. Lydia Hadley observes, "Maybe I don't have enough to do. Maybe I have time to think too much" (11), as if she were in the society—anticipated as something relatively close to the present by Martin Ford's *Rise of the Robots*—in which a massive technological substitution of human workforce took place. As a matter of fact, while this hypothetical liberation from daily work could grant the Utopia Gonzalo describes in *The Tempest*—"No occupation; all men idle, all; And women too, but innocent and pure" (Act II, Scene I)—it is more than possible that such a revolution would take some generations to be metabolized. In the meanwhile, bewilderment and boredom could convert it into a hollow dystopian nightmare. Indeed, the Hadleys become obsolete as Hathaway, an old man who dies while his robotic family is supposed to last, forever young, "ten, fifty, two hundred years" ("Long" 165) without him.

Quite soon, machines could replace humans in almost every field of their life with their perfect performances, which will take to unpredictable consequences: It is the advent of strong AIs as illustrated by Kurzweil (Chapter 8). Before her obsolescence, Lydia asks, "Can I compete with an African veldt? Can I give a bath and scrub the children as efficiently or quickly as the automatic scrub bath can? I cannot" (11). In a world deprived of all human work, the sense of uselessness would derive not only from an unbearable amount of free time, but also from the emotional shock of being replaced by a machine able to accomplish its duties far better than any human being. In his *Die Antiquiertheit des Menschen*, German philosopher Günther Anders defines the concept of "Promethean shame" as the shame that a person experiences in front of the "humiliating" high quality of objects made by him. With advanced technology, in Anders's idea, this humiliation grows up to intolerable levels. Even though there is not yet such a monstrous machine as the nursery of the Happylife Home, we cannot be sure that it will not be said of us what Mengeling writes about the Hadleys: "They haven't bought a nightmare at all; they have created one by twisting a dream" (94).

The Dream of the Golem: The Future beyond the Singularity

"Does the Internet dream of itself?" is the question Werner Herzog asks in his 2016 documentary *Lo and Behold*. In his exploration of the most recent steps in communication and AI technology, the German filmmaker raises essential questions on the intelligent machines' capacity of imagination and their autonomous collateral actions. Herzog thinks that "we should start to develop deep questions of what we are doing here with the Internet and what the Internet is doing on its own" (10), referring to the development of a self-generated "thinking" both in AI and in the algorithmic system of the Internet.

Just as the golem's increasing strength as he grows larger day after day becomes frightening (Scholem, "Idea" 202), the idea that an extremely powerful AI can think autonomously, become self-conscious, learn without a direct human input, and define its own requirements, appears deeply menacing. With the electric grandmother, Bradbury presents a model of a *learning machine* of absolute contemporary conception: "Everything you ever say, everything you ever do, I'll keep, put away, treasure" (163). This is a classic sci-fi theme, something widely informing the dystopian fiction with a scenario of androids and machines of infinite intelligence, sometimes rebelling against humanity. This is also a current issue in today's future forecasting: Not knowing exactly how a course of AI's independent thinking could organize itself, it is almost impossible to foresee with any accuracy the shapes of its potential relationship with human beings. Could the golem's aptitude to dream become a human nightmare?

In the melting point between futuristic and fantastic fiction, Bradbury infuses into his stories the sensation of an uncanny shift in reality. Things are not going to remain as they are, but how could the present world know what kind of change it is destined to? "The one fact about the future of which we can be certain is that it will be utterly fantastic" (Clarke 18), and future and faraway places like Mars in Bradbury's work seem to leap over any utopia/dystopia dichotomy to open up, poetically, to possibility and mystery. Perhaps our future and its new unknown technologies will allow humanity to enhance its deeper desires, or maybe human beings are doomed to extinction and will leave behind just a pale ghost of their existence; more than scientific prediction, it is a matter of clairvoyance. Here lies the ineffable power of the fantastic. This is the undefined beauty of Bradbury's science fiction. There is always, in his literature, a sense of almost childish wonder for the strangeness of things to come, a murky shadow obscuring the horizon with an astonishing outline of fear and promise. Bradbury, in the words of H. G. Wells, "discover[s] a frightful queerness has come into life" while "even quite unobservant people…are betraying, by fits and starts, a certain wonder, a shrinking and fugitive sense that something is happening so that life will never be quite the same again" (10).

Works Cited

Anders, Günther. *Die Antiquiertheit des Menschen.* C. H. Beck, 1956.

Anderson, James Arthur. *The Illustrated Ray Bradbury: A Structuralist Reading of Bradbury's The Illustrated Man.* Wildside, 2013.

Beauchamp, Gorman. "Technology in Dystopian Novel." *Modern Fiction Studies* 32.1, 1986, pp. 53-63.

Bradbury, Ray. G.B.S.-Mark V." *Long After Midnight.* 1976. Bantam, 1978, pp. 66-78.

———. "I Sing the Body Electric." *I Sing the Body Electric!* Knopf, 1969, pp. 135-71.

———. "The Long Years." *The Martian Chronicles.* 1950. Bantam, 1979, pp. 155-65.

———. "Marionettes, Inc." *The Illustrated Man.* 1951. Harper, 2011, pp. 211-21.

———. "Predicting the Past, Remembering the Future." 2001. *Bradbury Speaks: Too Soon from the Cave, Too Far from the Stars.* Harper, 2005, pp. 35-42.

———. "Punishment Without Crime." *Long After Midnight.* 1976. Bantam, 1978, pp. 88-98.

———. "There Will Come Soft Rains." *The Martian Chronicles.* 1950. Bantam, 1979, pp. 166-71.

———. "The Veldt." *The Illustrated Man.* 1951. Harper, 2011, pp. 7-25.

Burroughs, William S. *Naked Lunch.* 1959. Grove, 1991.

Clarke, Arthur C. *Profiles of the Future.* 1962 (rev. ed. 1973). Gollancz. 1982.

Ford, Martin. *Rise of the Robots.* OneWorld, 2015.

Herzog, Werner (interviewed by Marc Spitz). "Werner Herzog Says 'The Internet Has Its Glorious Side.'" *New York Times*, Aug. 21, 2016. AR10.

———. *Lo and Behold: Reveries of the Connected World.* Writ. Werner Herzog. Dir. Werner Herzog. Magnolia, 2016.

Idel, Moshe. *Golem: Jewish Magical and Mystical Traditions on the Artificial Anthropoid.* SUNY P, 1990.

Krafft, Andrea. "'The House All Burnt': Disintegrating Domesticity in Ray Bradbury's *Fahrenheit 451.*" *Critical Insights: Fahrenheit 451.* Edited by Rafeeq O. McGiveron. Salem Press, 2013, pp. 123-37.

Kurzweil, Ray. *The Singularity Is Near: When Humans Trascend Biology.* Viking, 2005.

Marcuse, Herbert. *One-Dimensional Man.* 1964. Beacon, 1966.

Mengeling, Marvin E. "The Machinery of Joy and Despair: Bradbury's Attitudes toward Science and Technology." *Ray Bradbury*. Edited by Martin Harry Greenberg and Joseph D. Olander. Writers of the 21st Century Series. Taplinger, 1980, pp. 83-109.

Meyrink, Gustav. *The Golem*. Dover, 1976.

Morris, Nicola. *The Golem in Jewish American Literature*. Lang, 2007.

Rabkin, Eric S. "To Fairyland by Rocket: Bradbury's *The Martian Chronicles*." *Ray Bradbury*. Edited by Martin Harry Greenberg and Joseph D. Olander. Writers of the 21st Century Series. Taplinger, 1980, pp. 110-26.

Scholem, Gershom. "Golem." *Kabbalah*. Dorset, 1987, pp. 351-55.

———. "The Idea of the Golem." *On the Kabbalah and Its Symbolism*. 1960. Schocken, 1969, pp. 158-204.

Shakespeare, William. *The Tempest*. 1611.

Wells, Herbert G. Mind at the End of Its Tether. http://freeread.com.au/@RGLibrary/HGWells/NonFiction/MindAtTheEndOfItsTether.html. 2015.

Wiener, Norbert. *God & Golem, Inc*. Cambridge: M.I.T. P, 1964.

Nuclear Myths in Ray Bradbury's Short Stories_____

Anna McHugh

Ray Bradbury acknowledged his debt to myth in many interviews and editorials. Several of his short stories deploy myths and master narratives to remind readers that fundamentally human problems lie within the terror of the Bomb, no matter how unfamiliar the dimensions of the nuclear situation seem to be. This essay will examine two of Bradbury's most anthologized stories—"Embroidery" (1951) and "The Million-Year Picnic" (1946)—and how they use elements of myth to convey the unique problems of atomic war.

The Bomb has always invited a mythic paradigm. In scope and concept, in moral countenance, it was so unprecedented that only a reversion to myth, which Claude Lévi-Strauss argued is the basic language of conceptual integration, could articulate it. From the time of Rutherford's atomic experiments, mythic language alone seems to have been resilient enough to cope with the concept of a sustained chain reaction and the terrifying energy it unleashes. Perhaps this is because the concept of a chain reaction defies our belief that, however dreadful, human products must be fundamentally limited in either scope or time. In 1914, H. G. Wells described "men made nascent" by an "atomic bomb" (2), and only ten years later Winston Churchill warned about military technology's propensity to outstrip human maturity, asking, "Shall we all commit suicide?" (Alkon 1). These were well before J. Robert Oppenheimer, watching the first atomic explosion at Trinity site in New Mexico in July 1945, recalled the *Bhaghavad Gita*, saying, "I am become Death, destroyer of worlds" (Hijiya 1), or George Kistiakowsky called it "the nearest thing to Doomsday" (Sherwin 312). Only an eschatological language can convey the moral immensity of an entirely man-made apocalypse and, in failing to signify it completely, reflect the narrative, philosophical, and moral prohibition under which it should be placed. Myth, it seems, is the only discourse resilient enough to express our moral and technological brinkmanship, and to show that we should not attempt to enculturate it in our language or narrative.

Yet the path that writers took to this mythic discourse was not by any means uncontested. When the Bomb finally was realized in 1945, the resulting mushroom cloud was so singular that it seemed to be what Roland Barthes has called a "pure sign," a single semiotic element that struck public consciousness initially *as* a sign, but one almost entirely unconnected to the web of other signifiers in which the percipients were situated (Hales 5). The US government seized on this semiotic purity to advance a nuclear mythology of its own, shaped almost entirely in a single decade and articulated principally by William L. Laurence, the official reporter at the Trinity tests. Describing the Bomb, Laurence invoked the language of natural phenomena—what Peter Hales has called the "atomic sublime"—connected to "the broader constellation of ideas that had developed in nineteenth century America around the notions of blessed nature, landscape, religion, personal psychology and manifest destiny" (13).

Although *Life* magazine ran a feature on the bombing of Hiroshima and Nagasaki in August 1945, the human effects of the Bomb were not revealed until the 1950s. By this time the Atomic Energy Commission had controlled information about nuclear projects so tightly that there was no material from which to build a dissenting mythology. This was relaxed only when Laurence's mythologising had saturated the public with the Bomb's positive aspects. It was left to an elite minority of largely nonnative American intellectuals to articulate dissent. Thus, at the time Ray Bradbury wrote many of his nuclear stories there existed a serious division between the two "atomic cultures": a jubilant postwar dominant culture that embraced the Bomb as an instrument of American superiority, and a traumatized intelligentsia, including many participants in the Bomb's creation, warning of its horrific, unpredictable effects. Bradbury's stories from the late 1940s and 1950s reveal how the genre of science fiction—or speculative fiction, which frequently included futuristic moral fable—integrated the two cultures. They reflect myth's narration of social tensions, its representation of foundational principles and capacity to show that the nuclear deprives us of the humanity that renders mythic narratives meaningful.

Written in 1951 and then collected in *The Golden Apples of the Sun* (1954), "Embroidery" is one of Bradbury's most finely wrought short fictions, and although frequently anthologized, one of the least written about. In this story three old women sit on a porch, embroidering and thinking about preparing dinner while they wait for an atomic test detonation to go off nearby. The old women's fear and confusion are palpable, despite their determination to go on embroidering up to the last moment. When the blast goes off, the fireball consumes their house, their embroidery, and themselves. It is one of two narratives—the other being *Fahrenheit 451* (1953)—that show an atomic explosion up close.

"Embroidery" is mythic in four ways. The first is thinly veiled use of mythic figures, with the three old needlewomen representing the Moirai, the Greek Fates: Clotho, the spinner of history's thread; Lachesis, the allotter of individual destiny; and Atropos, the cutter of the thread. The women's embroideries create the world and the human figures in it:

> Her quick black glance was on each motion. A flower, a man, a road, a sun, a house: the scene grew under hand, a miniature beauty, perfect in every threaded detail.
>
> …There was the scene, perfect except that while the embroidered yellow sun shone down upon the embroidered green field, and the embroidered brown road curved toward an embroidered pink house, the man standing on the road had something wrong with his face.
>
> "I'll just have to rip out the whole pattern, practically, to fix it right," said the second lady. (*Golden Apples* 69)

Bradbury presents the Moirai much as they are in seminal texts like the *Odyssey* and in Hesiod's *Theogony*—having the appearance of women despite their terrifying power, but neither indistinguishable from each other nor yet entirely scrutable to the reader. By appropriating these figures Bradbury invests the tale with the values of a classical worldview; concepts such as proportion, divine determinism, and necessity attend the story, but these are discernible only to the reader who is steeped in literature. Thus as well as establishing a mythic ethos in the narrative, these references to mythological figures function as a kind of shibboleth, a barrier to those who do not share Bradbury's values.

A second way in which this story is mythic is its extremely simple structure and characterisation. Narrative complications caused by characters' motives are not part of the simple plot. The story has four simple sections: The women wait for the blast to occur; they continue to create the world by embroidering; they are dismayed at human foolishness; the blast comes and they are destroyed. Not all simple stories are myths, of course, but when extremely simple characterization and a single-focus linear narrative are combined with a cataclysmic event, the narrative takes on certain mythic features. With this fixed-distance narrative focus on the women, the narrative drives towards its terrible, immutable ending. There is no overt appeal to shared values that would allow the reader to consign it to the category of a didactic literature that has clearly failed to warn society about the vices of pride, violence, and impiety.

Myth has no obligation to provide happy endings, because its task is to explain how the world came to be, including elements like endings and resolutions. As Barthes points out, myths cut out the reader's role in constructing meaning; they are received rather than read (129). The only structuring force to which the narrative is subject is cause and effect: The bomb kills the Fates, who personify cause and effect in every person's life. In one massive, overpowerful action, humanity eradicates the structures that underpin our being. The profound ontological threat posed by the Bomb accounts, in part, for its terror. This is a truth felt, rather than arrived at by reason, and myth is particularly good at conveying these truths. Myths do not appeal to external realities in order to verify their claims—the mythic discourse in "Embroidery" is true *and* false at the same time, and it is *neither* true *nor* false. The story simply tells the events, referring neither outward to history, nor downward to substructures of verification. One aspect of mythic discourse is an inexorable internal consistency that is conveyed by the flat and impersonal tone. The absence of a personal narrator who creates and directs the reader's affect, and the concomitant fixity of narrative focus, force the reader into relative passivity: What you are shown, you must witness, because the story-world offers nothing else.

Third, "Embroidery" involves a mythic attitude towards time. In his *Myth of the Eternal Return* Mircea Eliade argues that myths occur *in illo tempore*, a kind of origin time, or ahistorical state to which worshippers return during ritual. This is distinct from history, and the perceptual state of people in myths is indivisible from their ontological being—that is, they show no psychological evidence of participation in historical consciousness. Hernando, the peasant in Bradbury's famous short story "The Highway" from *The Illustrated Man* (1951) is an example of this. Tilling his fields, he observes a sudden traffic jam of cars fleeing northward to the United States. He watches the people, whose very possessions are unfamiliar to him, and gives some water to a car full of weeping girls and frightened men. They tell him, "It's come, the atom war, the end of the world!" and drive away towards certain death. Turning back to his burro and field, he asks, "What do they mean, 'the world'?" (*Illustrated* 61).

"The Highway" is justly famous for reflecting the blight of historical consciousness and the better, freer condition of being *in illo tempore*. Through the character of Hernando, Bradbury promotes the mythic condition of living close to nature and accepting that death is an act of those higher forces that shape the world into which we are placed but do not govern. Moreover, it is entirely possible to avail ourselves of this condition, even when the historical condition marches side by side with it, thrusting itself on our consciousness. This is because the mythic state of origins is, and must be, coextensive with the historical world— as Sallustius remarked, "Myths are things which never happened, yet always are" (Murray 205).

The women of "Embroidery" exist in a mythic state similar to that of Hernando. It is impossible to show where any accretions of historical consciousness have occurred in their thinking: Women have always sat in groups to embroider; they have always prepared peas for dinner; they have always been apprehensive about events determined by forces greater and more foolish than they; they have always formulated gnomic statements about their own role in shaping the world. Given that the story was first published in November 1951, and describes the bomb as "twice as big as ever before. No, ten times, maybe a thousand" (*Golden Apples* 69), it may have been inspired by tests in April 1951 at Eniwetok Atoll, which tested design elements later used by the first hydrogen bomb, itself exploded on 1 November 1952. Yet the narrative invokes no specific matrix of historical events and does not make the women's subjectivity dependent on historical experiences. By carefully avoiding any specific temporal reference, the story seems to straddle both historical and mythic time, connoting the significance of the tests, which disrupt our historical and mythic existences and eventually collapse the two into one.

This treatment of historical reference evokes Roland Barthes's theory of myth, which he argues piggybacks on first-order signs and removes evidence of their historical context and constructedness so that they can be used to convey values that appear to be timeless and culturally nonspecific (117). Bradbury uses ahistoricism to achieve the mythic discourse that conveys his own antinuclear stance, but this reduction of historical reality to a few traits is hardly "parasitic." The reader's reaction to the narrative's mythic aspects is identical to their reaction to the surface story—we are horrified at the death of three specific old ladies in the surface narrative, as we are horrified at the death of humanity and all possible futures in the mythic narrative.

A fourth mythic element in "Embroidery" is the use of binary opposites: the human and the divine, the male and the female, existence and annihilation. The structuralism of Claude Lévi-Strauss sees myth as a mode of communication of which opposition is the basic structure and which helps to mediate transitions in society (224). Potentially disruptive novelties could reach a synthesis with existing cultural attitudes and beliefs by allowing myth to negotiate the contradiction existing between opposites. Initially this seems a promising way of seeing "Embroidery"—that is, as a retelling of a canonical myth, where textual allusions to the nuclear, along with Bradbury's linguistic style, allow it to be read more or less comfortably in a historical present. For Lévi-Strauss, myth has the function of explaining those oppositions that are intrinsically artifacts of the human mental classification process we use to resolve logical contradictions; the opposition between human and divine certainly comes from our perception of the numinous, or supernatural, and there is a deeply numinous element about the bomb—though an inappropriate one, since the Bomb is human. As we shall see, however, there is something about the nuclear as a concept that throws such conventional reading patterns into disarray and that rejects structuralism's attempt to unlock myth's deeper patterns and purposes.

In this story, humanity seems to attempt to wrest divinity away from the gods with its deadly invention. Bradbury's roughly contemporary short story "Mr. Pale" (1950) shows Death himself, Mr. Pale, starving to death because people have stopped dying, in another narrative about how the gods are made vulnerable by humanity's reckless experimentation. In "Embroidery" the test blast, which is never explicitly called an atomic blast—thereby giving it the power of a destructive force so new it is yet to be named— represents the pinnacle of scientific recklessness, where the victims are not only the old and frail, the beneficent and venerable, but those very forces that have determined the world since the time of origins:

> "And they're not sure what it'll do to anything, really, when it happens?"
> "No, not sure."
> "Why didn't we stop them before it got this far and this big?"
> (*Golden Apples* 69)

The uncertain outcome appears to scare the women more than the scale of it, since they seem accepting of the fact of atomic testing and the destructive forces involved: "This isn't like the first one or the dozen later ones. This is different. Nobody knows what it might do when it comes" (*Golden Apples* 69). Bradbury already had written about scientific recklessness in two rather unsuccessful stories, "The Pendulum" (1939) and "A Blade of Grass" (1949), in which scientists are punished for dangerous experiments. But in these stories the offense is against common sense and the community's safety, not against the prerogatives of the gods. In "Embroidery" scientific curiosity is not shown in its promethean guise—this is no stealing of fire from the gods for the benefit of humanity, but rather a reckless theft of an ungovernable force, more similar to Phaethon's theft of the Sun's chariot. This fire scorches the earth but does not kill the scientists, instead destroying three old women who may represent the last trace of divine authority over human destiny. Far from negotiating a synthesis from the opposition of human and divine, the story ends with the annihilation of both.

Yet the women are world-makers in more than the Greek mythological sense, and a second opposition—between male and female—contributes to the tale's mythic nature. Bradbury also recognises that, as wives, mothers, and homemakers, the women's hands have shaped the everyday world that has been created in the cosmogonic myths. The peas waiting to be shelled in the kitchen represent the beauty of everyday life and the female realm of the home and hearth, which transcends historical time and which will be annihilated by the suprahuman power of the Bomb:

> There upon the table, seeming more like symbols of domesticity than anything she had ever seen in her life, lay the mound of fresh-washed peas in their neat, resilient jackets, waiting for her fingers to bring them into the world. (*Golden Apples* 68)

The women's hands function as symbols of this dual nature—both mythic and mundane—and drive home the scope of the Bomb's destruction. Bradbury's affection for "hands and what they did" unites the women's mythic status as the composers of destiny, with their prosaic role as shapers of the everyday world:

> Looking back, you saw a flurry of hands, like a magician's dream, doors popping wide, taps turned, brooms wielded, children spanked. The flutter of pink hands was the only sound; the rest was a dream without voices. (*Golden Apples* 68)

This contrasts with the androgenic apocalypse. Despite the second lady's attempts to rip out of her embroidery the man who has "something wrong with his face," the destructive power of male curiosity and scientific tinkering overtakes them all. As with the other binary opposition, the totality of nuclear destruction prevents the myth from unifying and negotiating these tensions.

There thus are two ways in which the nuclear element causes "Embroidery" to deviate from traditional patterns of mythic discourse. In one, the death of the divine characters destroys the metaphysical hierarchies that myth preserves. The three needlewomen remind us that to ensure the eternal return of conditions favorable to humanity, the gods must outlast humanity—accepting this is axiomatic to the human condition. The three connected mythemes, or essential kernels of myth, composing this story all show humanity's rejection of its traditional place in the hierarchy: the "stolen fire" of the Bomb, the "reckless curiosity" of human scientists, and the "mortal insult" offered by humanity to the gods. Mythic discourse is used to reveal how forces fundamental to our existence are annihilated when we acquire knowledge inappropriate to our state. Moreover, without the divine allotters of destiny, humans are left to take on this role, a responsibility for which they are entirely unprepared. In the last analysis, it seems, the gods cannot put right the "flaw in the design" of humanity.

The second way in which the nuclear element subverts mythic patterns involves the totality of nuclear destruction. In many eschatological traditions the end of the world does not necessarily mean the end of the gods. In the Norse Ragnarok, for example, the age of ice eventually gives way to a new beginning, and the cosmos is revealed to be cyclical. In this way, even the worst destruction is a great "clearing away" which allows an Eliadean eternal return. But in "Embroidery" the scale of the Bomb makes the nuclear experience difficult to align with any prior myths that might normalize its terror or resolve some of the contradictions inherent within it. Eliade recognised this in *Myth and Reality*, in which he remarked that "In the thought of the West this end will be total and final; it will not be followed by a new Creation of the World" (72).

Closer to Eliade's concept of cyclical world is "The Million-Year Picnic," the final story in Bradbury's *Martian Chronicles* collection. In this story, set in 2026, a family arrives in Mars aboard a rocket ship secretly saved for this purpose, fleeing from atomic war on Earth. The parents have used the pretext of a fishing expedition on the Martian canals to explain their trip, and the three sons are excited by their father's promise that they will encounter Martians on the hike. As they progress through the Martian terrain, it becomes clear to the children that they have left Earth permanently, and soon will be joined by one other family, with whom they will share the burden of starting life anew on a planet without war or weapons. Far away on Earth, a twenty-year atomic war finally annihilates the rest of the species, but their parents show the children the deserted Martian cities that are now their inheritance. Their father burns all the paper traces of life on Earth—bonds, reports, essays— and explains that he does it to cast off his old life. When the boys grow fractious because no Martians have appeared, the father shows them their own reflection in the canal water and explains that these are the faces of the Martians he had promised they should meet—with no home but Mars, and a second rocket with a family of daughters fast approaching, life will begin again on a new world.

Originally published in 1946, and used as the final "entry" to the *Chronicles* in 1950, the story includes key elements of a cosmogony, for the atomic war on Earth resembles a titanomachia, or battle of the gods, from which new and wonderful elements appear. In fact, the story fulfils many of the academically accepted purposes of myth: It functions as a sacred origin story, articulating group identity and inception; it enunciates a culture's first principles of survival, family, progeny, and city building; and it provides the people with a culture hero in the figure of the father, who is not just a mythic exemplary man but eventually the genetic exemplar for the future "Martians." Finally, the problem of trauma and catastrophe is understood and resolved through the lens of these foundational principles. These mythic purposes are evident in the story as a standalone piece, but become emphasised when the story is used to complete Bradbury's chronicle for a new world. The story's position as a bridge between humans-as-Earthians and humans-as-Martians offers a Pyrrhic salvation, however, because it involves the family disowning their humanity in fear and disgust and adopting a new identity as Martians. This crossover is managed by the myth's basic structure of opposition, through which cultural transitions are navigated.

Of all Bradbury's stories, "The Million-Year Picnic" appears to exemplify best Mircea Eliade's claim that all myths are stories of a sacred origin. In *Myth and Reality,* Eliade claims that "Myth tells how, through the deeds of Supernatural Beings, a reality came into existence, be it the whole of reality, the Cosmos, or only a fragment of reality—an island, a species of plant, a particular kind of human behaviour, an institution" (5-6). The sacredness of human life comes to the barren terrain of Mars and sanctifies it with the possibility of renewed and repentant civilization. Instead of a sudden breakthrough of the sacred from supernatural beings, the sudden and sacred actors who remake the world on Mars are human. But this single human family that perpetuates humanity as a "mortal, sexed, and cultural being" (Eliade 6) seems supernatural because it has left God and gods behind. Whether this is because they have jettisoned ideas of the divine along with all the paperwork of life on Earth, or because the atomic wars have, as in "Embroidery" killed the gods off, the five humans seem to be the only supernatural actors in this myth. Separate from their Earthbound existence, they can begin to perceive things as if with a godlike eye, with the long-term vision of the survivor:

> Timothy looked at the deep ocean sky, trying to see Earth and the war and the ruined cities and the men killing each other since the day he was born. But he saw nothing. The war was as removed and far off as two flies battling to the death in the arch of a great high and silent cathedral. And just as senseless. (*Martian Chronicles* 230)

Like the Promethean theft of fire and consequent flight from the gods' anger, "The Million-Year Picnic" also begins with a crime and a flight. The family has hidden a rocket ship from the government and flees to Mars, establishing a new space where life can begin again away from the primal chaos of atomic warfare—a more dreadful version of the pre-Socratic vision of Chaos as a state where the elements warred with each other.

By showing us the atomic war on Earth from this distance, Bradbury prevents us from vicariously experiencing any mystical or ecstatic moment of transcendence, what Ira Chernus has called the "Big Whoosh" where we are all incinerated together (261). But the family attempts another type of transcendence; they reject their identity as humans altogether and "become" Martians. Innumerable Bradbury stories include statements of explicit philosophical pessimism, but "The Million-Year Picnic" points out the core contradiction: Between our desire to survive and our despair over human nature, only one aspect can triumph—we must vote with our feet for one or the other. In a 1955 interview Bradbury argued that "Man will only breathe easily when he has climbed the tallest Everest of all: Space. Not because it is there, no, no, but because he must survive and survival means man's populating all the worlds of all the suns" ("Miracles and Marvels" 26). Although it seems incompatible with his oft-explored pessimism about humanity, consistency is the philosopher's virtue, not the storyteller's. In the same interview, however, he acknowledges that

> There is only one thing that can stop this journey—the wilderness in man himself: Man's other half, yes, the hairy mammoth, the sabre-tooth, the blind spider fiddling in the venomous dark, dreaming mushroom-cloud dreams. Today we stand on the rim of Space, man, in his immense tidal motion is about to flow out toward far new worlds, but man must conquer the seed of his own self-destruction. ("Marvels and Miracles" 26-27)

The family of "The Million-Year Picnic" may have fled Earth, but this does not mean they have conquered their own self-destructive drives. The father's statements about the life they have left behind are directed didactically toward the reader, but they also reveal complexities in his character that may blight the attempt to start life again.

Searching for "Earthian logic, common sense, good government, peace, and responsibility" as he gazes Earthward from Mars, the boys' father cannot find it: "It's not there any more. Maybe it'll never be there again. Maybe we fooled ourselves that it was ever there" (*Martian Chronicles* 231). Perhaps more troubling than the belief that these virtues are absent in everyone back on Earth is the family's hubris. Almost necessarily, the parents believe that they and their offspring still possess the virtues and so are justified in starting the race again. On the one hand, the story appears to condemn human nature utterly, so much that this breakaway family who will be the genetic template for all future people actually repudiates their identity as humans and chooses a new identity— they "become" Martians: "The Martians were there—in the canal—reflected in the water. Timothy and Michael and Robert and Mom and Dad" (*Martian Chronicles* 241). Certainly in one sense this seems to indicate a new maturity among those who have settled on Mars; as Walter Mucher argues, the "desire" that, from the beginning, is represented as a desire to impose Earthness upon Mars, now has been transformed into a desired fulfillment of abandoning one identity for another (184).

Yet human nature may not be so easy to shake off. For a start, the moral actions by which the family has escaped are hardly impeccable. They have deceived, and they have deserted others in the same plight. Standing in safety on Mars, they can afford to castigate everyone else left behind as devoid of virtues, and make such sententious observations as "War swims along, sees food, contracts. A moment later—Earth is gone" (*Martian Chronicles* 231). The parents condemn their children to the task of dying in isolation or restarting a fundamentally self-destructive species, but even they acknowledge that ancient tensions, like possession of women and territory, will crop up again. Soon, after all, a second rocket bringing another family, with daughters, will arrive:

"Daughters?" asked Timothy. "How many?"
"Four."
"I can see that'll cause trouble later." Mom nodded slowly. (*Martian Chronicles* 237)

The father gives a Martian city to each of his sons, as he will give them wives when the Edwards daughters arrive in their rocket. The emphasis is on patriarchy, property, ownership, and domination—the very things that fueled the destruction of Earth:

> "The whole damn planet belongs to us, kids. The whole darn planet."
> They stood there, King of the Hill, Top of the Heap, Ruler of All They Surveyed, Unimpeachable Monarchs and Presidents, trying to understand what it meant to own a world and how big a world really was. (*Martian Chronicles* 238)

Even as they attempt to begin again, humanity falls prey to its need for myths, and in this origin story Bradbury gives the new world its first, and most sacred story of beginnings: the first family, the flight from chaos, the law-giving father, the fertile mother, the brotherhood and projected marriages with the sisters, and the beginning of life in cities presented, miraculously intact, to those who would live, trade, govern, and survive—with the aid of such stories. The point is, Bradbury seems to propose, that before we seed the universe, we must get a grip on our worst instincts. This recurring challenge to humanity means that the relationship between humanity and mythic narratives will be coextensive and cyclical; as we destroy ourselves and start again, we will continue to use mythic discourse as a counterbalance to our self-destructive drives, and as an anchor from which to restart when those drives overcome us.

There are, of course, other stories that use mythic elements to reveal the Bomb's resistance to any kind of resolution: "The Garbage Collector," "The Smile," "To the Chicago Abyss," "The Last Night of the World," and "The Vacation" all come to mind. These bear out E. L. Doctorow's comment that the Bomb will come to be its own "scriptural text" in a world irrevocably changed by knowledge of it (171). As Victor Turner has noted, "Myths are liminal phenomena: they are frequently told at a time or in a site that is 'betwixt and between'" (576). Liminal times require stiff measures to give direction to events, and Bradbury's resort to myth reflects his view that we have regressed to a moral primitivism, in which the only effective discourse is the mythic, where things are stripped of their specificity and presented in the most monolithic terms. Bronislaw Malinowski points out that "myth possesses the normative power... of giving dignity and importance to an institution" (34), but so fundamental is the danger posed by the Bomb that the institution to which Bradbury's myths give importance is life itself.

Works Cited

Alkon, Paul K. "Shall We All Commit Suicide? Winston Churchill and the Scientific Imagination." *Finest Hour: The Journal of Winston Churchill* 94, 1997, pp. 18-23. Accessed 20 Mar. 2017. http://www.winstonchurchill.org/publications/finest-hour/finest-hour-094/shall-we-all-commit-suicide

Barthes, Roland. Trans. Annette Lavers. *Mythologies*. Hill, 1984.

Bradbury, Ray. "Embroidery." *The Golden Apples of the Sun and Other Stories*. 1951. Perennial, 1990: 67-70.

———. "The Highway." *The Illustrated Man*. Simon, 2012, pp. 57-61.

———. "Marvels and Miracles—Pass It On!" *New York Times Magazine*, 20 Mar. 1955, pp. 26-27, 56, 58.

———. "The Million-Year Picnic." 1946. *The Martian Chronicles*. 1950. Simon, 2012, pp. 229-41.

Chernus, Ira. "Mythologies of Nuclear War." *Journal of the American Academy of Religion* 50, 1982, pp. 255-73.

Doctorow, E.L. "Mythologizing the Bomb." *The Nation* 14-21. Aug. 1995, pp. 170-73.

Eliade, Mircea. *The Myth of the Eternal Return: Cosmos and History*. Princeton UP, 1971.

———. *Myth and Reality*. Translated by Willard R. Trask. Harper, 1963.

Hales, Peter. "The Atomic Sublime." *American Studies* 32, 1991, pp. 5-31.

Hijiya, James A. "The Gita of J. Robert Oppenheimer." *Proceedings of the American Philosophical Society* 144, 2000, pp. 123-67.

Lévi-Strauss, Claude. *Structural Anthropology*. Basic, 1963.

Malinowski, Bronislaw. *Malinowski and the Work of Myth*. Edited by Ivan Strenski. Princeton UP, 1992.

Mucher, Walter. "Being Martian: Spatiotemporal Self in Ray Bradbury's *The Martian Chronicles*." *Extrapolation* 43, 2002, pp. 171-87.

Murray, Gilbert. *The Five Stages of Greek Religion*. Beacon, 1951.

Sherwin, Martin J. *A World Destroyed: Hiroshima and the Origins of the Arms Race*. Vintage, 1987.

Turner, Victor. "Myth and Symbol." *The International Encyclopaedia of Social Sciences.* Edited by David L. Sills and Robert K. Merton. Macmillan, 1968, pp. 576-82.

Wells, H. G. *The World Set Free.* 1914. Project Gutenberg. Project Gutenberg Literary Archive Foundation, 11 Feb. 2006. Accessed 16 Mar. 2017. http://www.gutenberg.org/files/1059/1059-h/1059-h.htm

The Magician's Toyshop: Watching *The Ray Bradbury Theater*

Phil Nichols

Introduction

Ray Bradbury was a screenwriter as well as a novelist and short story writer. His break into film came with the script for John Huston's ambitious adaptation of *Moby-Dick* (1956), and he followed this success with a number of screenplays, including adaptations of his own works, *Something Wicked This Way Comes* (1983) and *The Wonderful Ice Cream Suit* (1998). For the small screen, he wrote episodes of the classic series *Alfred Hitchcock Presents* and *The Twilight Zone*, and later had a long-running anthology series of his own, *The Ray Bradbury Theater* (1985-1992), which allowed the author to dramatize dozens of his classic short stories. This chapter serves as an introduction to Bradbury's series, and examines a selection of episodes to seek an understanding of how the author adapted his own short works for the screen. I examine three episodes, enough to cover the range of concerns of both Bradbury as a writer and *The Ray Bradbury Theater* as a series: the satiric science fiction of "The Murderer" (1953); the nostalgia-tinged "The Lake" (1944); and the weird horror of "The Crowd" (1943). Bradbury emerges as a writer who is not afraid of modifying his stories as he adapts them, and one who is strongly aware of how to match story to medium.

The Ray Bradbury Theater

Bradbury introduced each episode of *The Ray Bradbury Theater* from his cluttered office, described in his opening narration as a "magician's toyshop." In this respect, he served as the "face" of the series, much as film director Alfred Hitchcock had with *Alfred Hitchcock Presents*, and writer Rod Serling had for *The Twilight Zone*. But whereas Hitchcock directed only a handful of episodes of his series, and Serling wrote about two-thirds of *The Twilight Zone*, Bradbury wrote the script for every single episode of his series—a total of sixty-five half-hour scripts produced over a seven-year period.

Nearly all episodes of the series were adapted from his classic short stories, but there were also a couple of original works. When the series began, Bradbury had already published many short story collections and novels, but one large compendium volume called *The Stories of Ray Bradbury* (1980) was the primary source for the show, providing the majority of the first two seasons' episodes and nearly half of the show's content overall. The show's opening narration describes Bradbury's process of writing as a trip made up of "exactly one-half exhilaration, exactly one-half terror," an inversion of a phrase used in his introduction to *The Stories of Ray Bradbury*.

The show's working title originally was to be *The Bradbury Chronicles*, but it was changed to *The Ray Bradbury Theater*, a title suggesting television plays rather than short films. Indeed, a handful of episodes were based as much on Bradbury's theatrical one-act plays as on his short stories—"The Pedestrian," "To the Chicago Abyss," and "The Anthem Sprinters," for example.

The series was remarkable in two other respects. Created in the early years of cable television, it was one of the first series made directly for subscription-based television. Today, we take it for granted that paid services such as Netflix, HBO, and Amazon Prime will create original content, and to a high creative standard. But in the early years of HBO, subscription bases were small, and production budgets extremely limited. After a couple of years funded by HBO, *The Ray Bradbury Theater* switched to USA Network.

The Ray Bradbury Theater was also an early example of international coproduction. Nowadays, hit American series like *Game of Thrones* are filmed overseas, sometimes for the unique scenery, but more often to take advantage of cheaper production costs and favorable tax breaks. The constant quest to sustain the series on a shoestring budget led *The Ray Bradbury Theater* to seek production partners overseas, and so over its seven-year run it saw episodes produced in Canada, the United Kingdom, France, and New Zealand. The difficulty of maintaining production values when episodes were produced on the other side of the globe led to severe challenges, and it is fair to say that the series suffers from some very weak episodes. Although Bradbury himself was credited as executive producer, even he acknowledged that on occasion an episode would turn out to be a "clinker" (Warren 30). At its best, though, *The Ray Bradbury Theater* gives viewers an opportunity to view some of Bradbury's classic stories afresh, sometimes through a simple updating of the storyline, but often through Bradbury's considered revisitation of his own material. The entire series is available quite cheaply on DVD, and at the time of writing all episodes also can be found on *YouTube*.[1]

Below, I consider just three of Bradbury's adaptations for the series, all of them adapted from stories originally written during his "classic" period of the 1940s and 1950s, and all of them reflecting strong familiar themes found in his short stories.[2] As with many episodes in the series, a key theme is alienation, with a central character in some way at odds with reality or society. According to a classic article in behavioral psychology by Melvin Seeman, the concept of alienation dominates the history of sociology. If alienated, we are frustrated at the mismatch between the amount of control we have over our lives and the amount we would like to have. Seeman pinpoints this sense of "powerlessness" as he arrives at a generalized definition of alienation: "the expectancy of probability held by the individual that his own behavior cannot determine the occurrence of the outcomes, or reinforcements, he seeks" (784). Seeman's discussion of alienation carefully extends to a sense of "meaninglessness," which arises when someone is "unclear as to what he ought to believe" (786); and "normlessness," where someone comes to believe that "socially unapproved behaviours are required to achieve given goals" (788). We shall see that many of the protagonists of *The Ray Bradbury Theater* are alienated in precisely these terms.

"The Murderer"

"The Murderer" is satirical science fiction, in a similar vein to another classic Bradbury short story, "The Pedestrian" (1951), as well as his novel *Fahrenheit 451* (1953). The protagonist, Albert Brock, is seriously at odds with the society he lives in, and is imprisoned for psychiatric evaluation after "murdering" a variety of high-tech gadgets. The short story was written at a time when telephones, radios, and televisions were beginning to dominate American life, and Bradbury said that it reflected his own discomfort with such intrusive technologies: "I think I objected to there being so much noise in our society.... That was before earphones... [E]verywhere you went, there was noise" (Albright and Eller 86). Despite its origins in older technologies, the short story is set in an extrapolated future world that in some ways is remarkably like our real world of today, dominated as it is by portable communications technologies such as mobile phones, tablets, and laptops. Critic David Mogen characterizes the story as a "warning," and more satirical than tragic. He also writes that it establishes "an atmosphere of addled superficiality which...would drive us, as well as the outlaw hero, insane" (99-100).

A psychiatrist makes his way through corridors filled with endless music, passing secretaries who themselves are immersed and isolated in music. He arrives at an interview chamber where he meets Brock, who refers to himself as "The Murderer." The psychiatrist witnesses one of Brock's murderous attacks as he destroys his wrist radio by biting into it. Under interrogation, Brock reveals his other offenses: destroying a phone, shooting his TV, and pouring water into an intercom. What got him arrested was his "murder" of his house—fully automated, with beds that "rock you to sleep and shake you awake"— and "that insidious beast, that medusa," the television. Brock now believes his name will go down in history for starting a popular revolt and, ironically, he *is* now famous, thanks to news reporting on the TV and radio that he despises. Brock asks if he can go back to his quiet, private cell. It is clear that this "punishment" is actually what he craves. The psychiatrist leaves the chamber, returning to his noisy, constantly disturbed daily routine.

The Ray Bradbury Theater adaptation is a good example of international coproduction at work. The episode was directed in New Zealand by British advertising director Roger Tompkins; the director of photography and editor—Alun Bollinger and Jamie Selkirk, respectively—were New Zealanders who later both would work on the *Lord of the Rings* film series; the music was by Canadian composer Donald Quan; and the closing credits acknowledge the participation of the Alberta (Canada) Motion Picture Development Corporation.

The episode is one of Bradbury's most faithful adaptations, with many of the elements of the short story transferred directly to screen. Minor differences are seen in the method of presentation—most of Brock's "murders" are shown in flashback simultaneously with his verbal recollection of them, the order of some events is changed, and some of the technologies are updated. Since the episode dates from 1990, fax machines are prominent, wrist radios are replaced by body-worn pagers, and early mobile phones make an appearance. Brock also refers to the VCR and the Walkman, recent and powerful technologies at the time the episode was made, but unfortunately making the supposedly futuristic episode seem dated today. Brock's objections to technology are also updated with references to "soundbites" and "sightbites," and "passive listening" as an analogy to "passive smoking."

The episode begins with timelapse film of crowds in a big city, actually footage taken from Godfrey Reggio's poetic documentary *Koyaanisqatsi* (1982). The noisy future world is built effectively with music, which is everywhere, but different in different spaces. This is most noticeable when the psychiatrist goes from the Muzak-dominated elevator to the electronic classical music, in the style of W. Carlos's *Switched-On Bach*, of a corridor. The closing of the interrogation chamber door provides a welcome and relieving silence.

The one substantial change is in the ending, which impacts directly on our reading of this future world. When the psychiatrist leaves the cell, the electronic music is deafening. Back in his office, he is pestered by video calls from his boss, his son, and his secretary. He blocks the videophone with his hand, and recalls Brock describing his whole day as one "big listen"…and then we see the psychiatrist bite into his brand-new lapelphone just as Brock had done, before ordering a chocolate milkshake, the "weapon" Brock had used to destroy his fax machine. While Bradbury's original short story had satirically positioned Brock as completely out of step with his society, and thus interpreted as psychologically deficient, the *Ray Bradbury Theater* episode makes clear that the psychiatrist is convinced by Brock, and himself ready to join a rebellion. This puts the episode more in line with Bradbury's *Fahrenheit 451*, where fireman Montag, a part of an oppressive regime, comes to find the truth: that there is another way to live.

"The Murderer" is a fine case study of Seeman's conception of alienation. Not only does Brock feel a complete absence of power over events, but he comes to see life as meaningless. Ultimately he reaches the position that "socially unapproved behaviors"—his series of "murders"—are the only way to achieve his goals. The short story leaves Brock stuck in that alienated state, but Bradbury's script for the TV episode provides the prospect that Brock is not alone.[3]

"The Lake"

"The Lake" is a psychological study of nostalgia—a longing to return to the past—framed as a weird tale. It is a slightly unusual blend, amounting to what Bradbury described as "some sort of hybrid... Not a traditional ghost story at all, but a story about love, time, remembrance, and drowning" (*Zen* 15-16). It was one of Bradbury's earliest professional stories, and "verging on the new," it marked Bradbury's arrival as a writer: "I knew I had written the first really good story of my life" (62).

The short story begins with the narrator's recollections of childhood, specifically the last days on the beach before a boy prepares to move west with his family. The narrator writes of children never truly being alone, apart from in their imagination—except that he remembers one day walking very far from his parents. He recalls the last days of seeing a girl named Tally, who disappeared into the lake. He remembers building a sandcastle with Tally, and walking back to his mother as the water washed the sandcastle away. The story then shifts to a fully adult perspective on moving west, leaving a life behind, graduating, marrying, and finally returning home ten years later, to the same beach. A body turns up, decayed from ten years in the water. The narrator is convinced these are the remains of Tally. Down the beach he finds a half-finished sandcastle, and footsteps leading up to it and away from it, as if Tally has emerged from the water to build the castle. He completes the sandcastle, then walks away, not looking back to see the water destroy it. He heads up the beach to his wife, who is now "a stranger" to him.

David Mogen observes that this story is "musical in style and structure—all mood and atmosphere and metaphorically resonant imagery" (49). This atmosphere is perhaps the dominant effect on the reader, but Mogen also draws our attention to a powerful structural device, the "opposition between an 'other world' (the lake) and the mundane world." The hero is entranced by the lake and the sandcastle, but his experience while enraptured in this "other world" remains private to him: "He is suspended curiously between worlds—the present and the past, his wife and 'Mama,' the shore and the lake" (47).

Another critic, George Edgar Slusser, also picks up on this opposition, noting that "The Lake" plays on an ambiguity arising from "the disparity between narrator's stance and the events narrated" (23). The narrator as a boy wishes the missing Tally to return to life when he calls out to her, to create the other half of the sandcastle, but there is no response. Childhood wish-fulfillment is not real, and the adult narrator is acutely aware of this, saying, "You really expect answers to your calling when you are young. You feel that whatever you may think can be real." What makes the story into a "weird" tale is that the wish-fulfilment *does* come true for the character as an adult. This leads William F. Touponce to characterize the short story as Freudian, since it dramatizes the notion that "our earliest love objects are the strongest, and that they are never truly abandoned, though they may be submerged" (Touponce and Eller xxx-xxxi).

After "The Lake" debuted in *Weird Tales* magazine, Bradbury revised it twice, once for its appearance in his first book, *Dark Carnival* (1947), which now is out of print, and later for his collection

The October Country (1955), whose revised version has become the standard text. The revisions were subtle, focusing mostly on standardizing the adult point of view (Touponce and Eller 416). This points to Bradbury being an author who is at home with retelling his stories, revising them according to context, or perhaps being motivated by a sense of perfectionism. Forty years later, he would tell the story again, this time for television in *The Ray Bradbury Theater*.

The mechanics of the *Ray Bradbury Theater* version of the story remain the same, but the act of adaptation inevitably flavors the story. For one thing, the necessary act of presenting the story in concrete visual terms "deprives" the viewer of the "luxury" of being able to create his or her own mental pictures of the characters, of the sandcastle, and of Tally's remains. Further, the reality of international production provides a subtle but immediate shift in our anticipation of the "look" of the story. This episode, directed by New Zealand writer-director Pat Robins, was shot in New Zealand, and the adaptation makes a feature of this: The story's American-sounding hero talks of returning to the country where he grew up, and we see a plane landing; he drives a right-hand drive car; and the landscapes, while nonspecific, look perhaps somewhat wilder than the American Midwest setting implied in the short story.

Looking beyond the basic visualization and practicalities of filming, we can see that Bradbury also uses the adaptation as an opportunity to rewrite his own story. While the narrative is quite similar to that of the short story, there are some changes. Adult Douglas returns to his childhood home because his new wife insists upon it. In voice-over narration—the film equivalent of the first-person narration used in the short story—Douglas reflects that "memories could be shared, but some remained mine alone." We flash back to the summer of Douglas's childhood, and see the birth of the love he has for Tally. In this telling of the story, Bradbury adds a dimension to Tally. She "belongs" to the lake; she loves swimming and is totally at home in the water, in contrast to young Douglas, who is unable to swim and is afraid of the water.

At summer's end as people leave the beach, Tally takes one last swim. She promises Douglas, "I'll be here every summer. Every single summer." The weather turns, and Tally's mother suddenly realizes that Tally has disappeared. Lifeguards and bystanders rush into the water to search for her, but are unable to find any trace. Douglas is helpless, unable to swim and therefore unable to assist.

Back in the present, adult Douglas and his wife look down at the lakeshore, where he spies a sandcastle. Douglas walks down to it, leaving his wife behind. She calls out to him, and he repeatedly holds up his hand, indicating that she should keep her distance, visibly enacting his earlier-stated belief that some memories must be for him alone. The sandcastle seen close up is only half built, but with a line of footprints coming out of and back into the water. Doug says, "If I build the other half, will you come?" He does so, and as if in response a body is found. Clearly—from the blonde hair, the only thing we see—this is Tally. Douglas returns to his wife. He has some closure, but because Douglas has put up a barrier between himself and his wife, she is still kept outside of his private and disturbing experience.

The changes to the narrative are small indeed, but notice how in the short story the narration takes us deeply into the narrator's own private world and thoughts, so that his wife temporarily slips from our consciousness, while the narrator's private nostalgic experience is so affecting that his return to his wife leads him to see her as a stranger. On the other hand, the inevitably more objective presentation in the TV episode almost dictates a specific dramatic device: Douglas's repeated *stop* gesture, which can, logically, exclude the wife from the weird experience. The events of the television version may be almost identical to the events of the short story, but Bradbury's conception of it in terms of an external camera viewpoint leads him to construct the story's key emotion in more objective terms.

Both the short story and the TV adaptation show the boy as alienated when Tally's disappearance puts him in a position of having no control over events. The narrator's return as an adult finally, but gruesomely, brings this alienation to an end, but at the risk of damaging the important relationship with his wife.

"The Crowd"

Another episode where the adaptation for television shows necessary adjustments to the narrative is "The Crowd," a horror story in which the same ghoulish crowd of onlookers gathers around a series of unrelated car crashes. The story supposedly was inspired by a real-life experience. Ray Bradbury recalled "a car that had hit an obstruction in the street and rocketed into a telephone pole. .... Two people lay dead on the pavement. .... I had never seen anything like it. I walked home, bumping into trees, in shock. It took me months to get over the horror of that scene" (*Zen* 22-23).

The short story is narrated in the third person, but gives a very subjective presentation, with the reader being carried closely alongside the hero, Spallner. As with any number of Bradbury horror tales of the same vintage, the protagonist's weird experience appears at first to be the manifestation of psychological disturbance—in this instance Spallner shows distinct paranoid tendencies—but ultimately proves to be horribly real.

The short story begins with a cinematic detailing of a car crash, and then holds to crash victim Spallner's point of view as he hears and sees a crowd gather round him. Bradbury here makes frequent use of short paragraphs and sentence fragments—for example, "Sunlight, a hospital room, a hand taking his pulse"—which in places makes the storytelling similar to what we commonly see in film scripts. Recovering in the hospital, Spallner obsesses over how quickly the crowd gathered around him, debating this with his friend Morgan. Later he witnesses a second accident, and again sees a crowd gather, with many of the faces looking familiar to him. Over time, Spallner gathers as evidence newspaper reports and photos of accidents, and formulates a theory that it is the same crowd gathering each time. The weight of evidence is enough finally to convince Morgan that Spallner is onto something. As he takes his evidence to the police, Spallner's car is hit by a truck. The crowd gathers, moves his injured body, and takes his briefcase. Spallner's final lines, as the crowd kills him, indicate that he will now join the crowd.

While much of the story is written with cinematic and scriptlike clarity, it also builds an image system around wheels and cycles:

the spinning wheels of the car, the faces of the crowd resolving out of a spiral of confusion, the rotating hands of Spallner's watch, and Morgan's observation that "things go in cycles."

David Mogen finds that the story "extrapolate[s] eerily from commonly observed phenomena" and presents them "in a fantastical, gothic context" (56). George Edgar Slusser points out the similarity of theme to Bradbury's story "The Wind," also published in 1943: Both are stories in which "a man has an insight into what he believes an intelligent, evil force at work" (13). The reader is meant to remain "suspended," to "ask if the hero's view of things is true or merely a figment of his mind" (Slusser 14).

This original story first appeared in *Weird Tales* magazine in May 1943, and Bradbury later rewrote it for inclusion in his first book, *Dark Carnival*, further evidence that Bradbury believed in rewriting and improving his stories (Touponce and Eller 383). In this instance, the revisions make the story more timeless and less geographically specific—no longer referring to "war restrictions" (103) and changing "Los Angeles" to "this town." Jonathan R. Eller observes that the rewritten version of the short story "represents Bradbury's subsequent intention to give some of his early stories a more literary context" (384).

The TV episode, directed by Brazilian-Canadian director Ralph L. Thomas, is exquisitely shot, and great care is taken to make Spallner's documentary evidence of the crowd as convincing to the viewer as it is to him. As with "The Lake," Bradbury's adaptation again makes some changes. The most basic of these are to expand the story sufficiently to fill the required running time for episodes of *The Ray Bradbury Theater*, so that, for example, Spallner now is introduced as an inattentive driver, coming home from a party; distracted, he swerves to avoid a dog, causing his car to overturn.

Besides this slightly extended set-up, though, there are changes that take the story further than it originally went. Spallner's relationship to the secondary character Morgan is substantially revised, resulting in a new conclusion. In the short story, Morgan is important to the reader only inasmuch as he is the character to whom Spallner explains events, in effect a proxy for the reader. In the TV episode, though, Spallner and Morgan are inseparable, two parts of a single character.

Spallner confirms his hunches about the crowd by finding evidence in multiple videotapes. While this makes the production look dated today, it does add to the plausibility of Spallner's evidence. The fact that Morgan, a news cameraman, shot most of this footage himself makes him all the more convinced by Spallner.

Spallner refers to one blurry figure, saying, "I can never make out the face," perhaps suggesting that these are dreamlike recollections rather than reality. But his photos of these same people, obtained from the morgue, lead Spallner to a very specific statement of what is going on: "I'm convinced they come back to haunt the places accidents happen. They're waiting for more accidents to happen... waiting there to move people that shouldn't be moved...so they die. So they become part of the crowd."

The impression is given that Spallner determines to meet up with the crowd in order to convince Morgan, and Morgan accompanies Spallner in order to protect him. This leads to the eeriest scene in the episode, where Spallner wanders among the crowd—and the handheld camera allows us to go along with him, the distortion of the wide-angle lens adding both to our immersion in the scene and to the weirdness of it. Finally, it is Morgan who is killed by the crowd, as Spallner looks helplessly on, witnessing his friend being transformed into a ghoulish member of the crowd. The transformation vindicates Spallner's interpretation of events, but his survival leaves the television episode more open-ended than the original short story, as we are left to wonder what will happen next to our hero. Bradbury himself claimed not to have any conscious awareness of why he changed this aspect of the story, saying, "It's just one of those things that, for whatever reasons, happens when you're writing. I didn't think about it. I just did it" (Goldberg 17).

George Edgar Slusser once characterized Bradbury's early fiction as portraying tales of "the elect," characters who are admitted to some higher state, usually in some kind of bizarre blend of reward and punishment, reflecting the view held by Calvinists (15-16). While this characterization holds true for the short story version of "The Crowd," Bradbury's TV adaptation steers away from this by making Spallner *not* become a member of the crowd. In strictly dramatic terms, it works to have Morgan die, as much a victim of Spallner's carelessness and obsessiveness as of the crowd. But it is an odd choice to remove the key resonance of the original story.

In "The Crowd"—both the short story and the TV episode— Spallner feels powerless, and so is another case study in Seeman's concept of alienation. Spallner may begin to *perceive* that he has power as a result of his evidence gathering, vindicating his position that the crowd is a real phenomenon. However, the crowd's stealing of his briefcase in the short story leaves him totally without power, and the killing of Morgan in the TV episode leaves Spallner without power as well, alive but alone in amongst the crowd.

Conclusions

Not all of *The Ray Bradbury Theater* deals with alienation, but this recurring theme is the basis of many of the series' successful episodes spanning various genres, suggesting perhaps that this theme provides a key point of dramatic engagement for a viewer. Bradbury's ability to build on this theme in his adaptations reveal him to have a strong sense for what will work in a dramatization, even though he often claimed to be carrying out the work without any conscious understanding of what he was doing.

Most of Bradbury's scripts for the series were written many decades after his original stories, which effectively means that the older Bradbury was rewriting the younger—a position he was evidently comfortable with:

> "The thing is not to read the story when you do the adaptation; this gives you the intellectual leeway to do things that improve the story. And then you finish the adaptation and go back and read the original story to see if anything's missing. I have respect for my younger self, but I don't let that override my ability, forty years later, to improve it." (Warren 30)

Although this chapter has dealt with the reworking of prose fiction into TV scripts, Bradbury was no stranger to rewriting his work, since many of his early short stories were revised for book publication, and many of his novels—*The Martian Chronicles* (1950), *Dandelion Wine* (1957), and *From the Dust Returned* (2001), for example—turn out to have been developed directly from earlier short fictions. The sixty-five scripts he wrote for *The Ray Bradbury Theater* amount to yet another re-visioning, a key characteristic of his authorship. As Jonathan R. Eller observes, "Bradbury's rich and often masterful process of refashioning his oeuvre has made him one of the most recognizable names in modern American culture" (Touponce and Eller 332).

Notes

1. http://tinyurl.com/rbtheater
2. For details of all episodes, see Loren Heisey's detailed episode guide at http://www.innermind.com/myguides/guides/bradbury.htm.
3. For further analysis of "The Murderer" as both short story and TV episode, see Carpenter, "Fleeing from the 'Ghost Machines': Patterns of Resistance in 'The Pedestrian' and 'The Murderer.'"

Works Cited

Albright, Donn, and Jonathan R. Eller, editors. *B is for Bradbury: The Origins of Ray Bradbury's Short Stories*. Unpublished manuscript, 2009. On file at the Center for Ray Bradbury Studies, Indiana University.

Bradbury, Ray. "The Crowd." *The Stories of Ray Bradbury*. Knopf, 1980, pp. 47-54.

———. "The Lake." *The Stories of Ray Bradbury*. Knopf, 1980, pp. 36-40.

———. "The Murderer." *The Stories of Ray Bradbury*. Knopf, 1980, pp. 241-47.

———. *Zen in the Art of Writing: Essays on Creativity*. Odell, 1994.

Carpenter, Markus Arno. "Fleeing from the 'Ghost Machines': Patterns of Resistance in 'The Pedestrian' and 'The Murderer.'" *The New Ray Bradbury Review* 1, 2008, pp. 11-34.

"The Crowd." Written by Ray Bradbury, directed by Ralph L. Thomas. *The Ray Bradbury Theater*. Atlantis and HBO, 1985.

Goldberg, Lee. "This is...'*The Ray Bradbury Theater*'." *Starlog,* Mar. 1986, pp. 16-18, 62.

"The Lake." Written by Ray Bradbury, directed by Pat Robins. *The Ray Bradbury Theater*. Atlantis and USA Network, 1989.

Mogen, David. *Ray Bradbury.* Twayne's United States Authors Series 504. Twayne, 1986.

"The Murderer." Written by Ray Bradbury, directed by Roger Tompkins. *The Ray Bradbury Theater.* Atlantis and USA Network, 1990.

Seeman, Melvin. "On the Meaning of Alienation." *American Sociological Review* 24.6, 1959, pp. 783–91.

Slusser, George Edgar. *The Bradbury Chronicles.* Mitford Series, Popular Writers of Today 4. Borgo, 1977.

Touponce, William F., and Jonathan R. Eller, editors. *The Collected Stories of Ray Bradbury: A Critical Edition,* Volume 1, 1938-1943. Kent State UP, 2011.

Warren, Bill. "At Play in the Business of Metaphors." *Starlog,* Apr. 1990, pp. 29-32, 58.

Writing a Life: The Stylistics of Ray Bradbury's Autobiographical Novels

Robin Anne Reid

This chapter presents a stylistic analysis of three of Ray Bradbury's autobiographical novels: *Dandelion Wine* (1957), *Death Is a Lonely Business* (1985), and *Green Shadows, White Whale* (1992). Stylistic analysis uses linguistic methods to analyze literary texts. Roger Fowler, in *Linguistic Criticism* (1996), the first theoretical argument for stylistics, argues that problems with arguments about style are caused by critics using inconsistent concepts drawn from basic grammar. Linguistics, a separate discipline, has developed and tested consistent concepts for analyzing language that are "stable, well-understood... readily learned, and readily applied in objective description of texts" (Fowler 4).

In recent years, linguists and literary critics using linguistic methods have developed an approach called *corpus stylistics*, which uses digital technologies to generate quantitative analyses. A corpus is an electronic archive that can be searched by text analysis programs. While the shift to digital technologies and quantitative analysis may seem daunting, corpus stylistics allows scholars to identify textual patterns more quickly in larger amounts of text than can be done manually. However, corpus stylistics does not replace or reduce the importance of qualitative interpretation of literary texts. As David L. Hoover, Jonathan Culpeper, and Kieran O'Halloran argue in *Digital Literary Studies* (2014), corpus stylistics incorporates qualitative interpretation of the patterns identified in texts and complements traditional individual literary approaches (4).

This essay draws upon the theory from Fowler and Hoover et al. by applying selected linguistic concepts to a small Bradbury corpus that contains excerpts from the novels. The excerpts are the opening and closing paragraphs of chapters in all three novels (see Table 1). Since a number of the opening and closing paragraphs consist of single words or sentences, in those cases additional text was included. Each excerpt has at least three sentences from the start and the end of every chapter. Chapter beginnings set scenes, introduce characters, and, along with the endings, frame the major events; they also contain a mix of narrative and dialogue. The analysis in this essay is based on the data from this corpus.

Table 1. Number of Chapters and Number of Words Excerpted from Three Novels

Novel	# Chapters	# Words Excerpted
Dandelion Wine (DW)	40	5,721
Death Is a Lonely Business (DLB)	107	11,744
Green Shadows, White Whale (GS)	33	3,931

Source: UAM Corpus Tool (O'Donnell)

My stylistic question is whether these novels, which have different genre elements—fantasy, detective, and memoir—but which all are autobiographical novels that focus on a writer's life, are more similar or different in their style. While plots and setting differ, all three center writers writing about the setting and events. Additionally, as Bradbury's foreword to *Dandelion Wine* and his collected essays in *Zen in the Art of Writing* make clear, his fictional writers who write about their lives in their work use the same writing process as their creator, Bradbury, does in his work.

The linguistic concepts I chose for application are keyword and clause analysis. These concepts were chosen to complement specific qualitative observations of literary critics relating to Bradbury's use of imagery and sentence structure. Critical readings of Bradbury's work have shown a strong awareness of the impact of his style on readers and the importance of the quality of his style in regard to critical reception of his work. The consensus is that the style of Bradbury's fiction—often described as poetic—is one of the reasons he became the first "genre" author widely known and praised as "literary" in terms of his publications and awards. In his 1982 critical study, Willis E. McNelly concludes that "Gradually, perhaps because his style was inimitable... Bradbury became noticed by many writers and critics outside the relatively limited field of genre science fiction. Such diverse writers as Aldous Huxley, Christopher Isherwood, and Gilbert Higher hailed him as a stylist and a visionary" (174).

In spite of that consensus, relatively little scholarship on Bradbury analyzes his style in any depth. A June 2017 subject search on "Ray Bradbury" in the MLA International Bibliography database returned a list of 280 entries; the list includes dissertations, peer-reviewed journal articles, collections of essays, and books. Adding "style" to the search brings the total of entries down to four: one dissertation and three essays (Mengeling, Pell, Stockwell).

Two of the scholars whose work focuses on Bradbury's style illustrate the critical debate over whether Bradbury's work should be considered "genre"—meaning science fiction or fantasy—or "literary." Marvin E. Mengeling, in "Ray Bradbury's 'Dandelion Wine': Themes, Sources, and Style" (1971), argues that Bradbury's work is "great" enough to be considered as part of American literature rather than being limited to the "genre" of science fiction. Style is one of the several elements Mengeling analyzes in his defense of Bradbury's work against the critical neglect of genre fiction; the others are theme, literary allusions, and his structural devices and archetypes, which are compared favorably to those of Melville, Whitman, and Hawthorne. In contrast, Peter Stockwell in "Language, Knowledge, and the Stylistics of Science Fiction" analyzes Bradbury's short story "The Night" as an example of science fiction by focusing on narrative world building and the unusual second-person narrative point of view, which uses "you," a direct address to the reader. Ignoring the poetic elements of Bradbury's style, Stockwell argues that the epistemic theme of the story, that is, how human beings in general learn to know about the unknown, is the reason for considering the story to be science fiction as opposed to realism, or literary fiction, which depends on an exploration of an individual's psychology.

Dandelion Wine is referenced to varying degrees in all three essays on Bradbury's style: Mengeling focuses his analysis entirely on the novel; Stockwell analyzes a short story, "The Night," published in *Small Assassins*, that features a young protagonist named Doug and a ravine, later integrated into *Dandelion Wine*; Sarah-Warner J. Pell notes stylistic similarities between *The Martian Chronicles* and *Dandelion Wine*. In addition, Jonathan R.

Eller and William Toupounce, in *Ray Bradbury: The Life of Fiction* (2004), explore in detail the years-long writing process that led to *Dandelion Wine* (Table 9, 216-17). Beyond the stylistics scholarship, *Dandelion Wine* also has received the most critical attention of the three novels. Scholarship on the novel covers a range of topics: the novel's construction of small towns compared to Sherwood Anderson's Winesburg, Ohio (Person), to Neil Gaiman's *American Gods* (La Jeunesse), and to William Faulkner's "That Evening Sun" (Rosenman). Essays also identify other themes such as time and memory (Carpenter), myth and carnival (Eller and Toupounce), and technology and community (Logsdon).

In contrast to the body of work on *Dandelion Wine*, there are no peer-reviewed articles on *Death Is a Lonely Business* or on *Green Shadows, White Whale*. In their 550-page-long monograph, Eller and Toupounce dedicate an entire chapter, "The Carnival Blaze of Summer," to *Dandelion Wine*. Another chapter includes *Death Is a Lonely Business* as one of four "Corpse Carnivals," but *Green Shadows, White Whale* is dealt with in four or five pages. They conclude that the novel is his "least carnivalized" (426). Their approach is an extensive analysis of manuscript and publishing history as well an exploration of how metaphors, masks, and myths in the context of carnival are the primary elements of Bradbury's most successful work. The book is outstanding, and although Eller and Toupounce draw on a different methodology, their observations about formal elements in Bradbury's work could be the basis for additional stylistic analysis in future.

Keyword Analysis: Key Images

In *Ray Bradbury* (1980), Wayne L. Johnson notes that Bradbury's fiction immerses readers through sensory images and poetic elements. Johnson identifies the poetic elements as meter, alliteration, internal rhymes, and metaphor but provides little specific evidence (5-6). Sarah-Warner J. Pell focuses on metaphors and imagery in her 1980 essay, "Style Is the Man: Imagery in Bradbury's Fiction." She collects and categorizes more than three hundred metaphors and similes from *S Is For Space*, *The Martian Chronicles*, and *I*

Sing the Body Electric! The following categories are described as the "touchstone" for Bradbury's imagery: "Middletown, dreamtown America, untouched by violence, pestilence, family, world wars, prejudice: the idyllic small-town American boyhood, never far from nature; an American boyhood of sounds, tastes, sights, feelings of birth, life, death" (188). Readers of Bradbury will recognize that these types of images are found in his other works, so I am using them as part of my keyword analysis. An image in a text consists of a noun plus any additional modifiers. In order to identify frequent images in the three novels, I used a text analysis program, TextSTAT, to generate word lists that quantify how many times each word is used in the excerpts. Selected raw data from that analysis are included in Appendix A. After extracting the dozen or so most frequently used nouns and adjectives from each novel, I analyzed the results to see whether the words fit into Pell's categories and what other patterns might exist (see Table 2). The keywords indeed do fit into a number of Pell's categories—small town, nature, sensory images, and time-seasons—although *Dandelion Wine* is the only one of the three excerpts that contained sensory adjectives. All three texts had some images that did not fit the categories, although one, *old*, has connections to death when it is used to describe characters.

Of the words that do not fit into Pell's categories, two of them, a noun and an adjective, appear in all three novels: *eyes* and *old*. Using *TextSTAT*, I generated a concordance for each of these words (Appendix B). Concordances show the context, the surrounding words, for the selected words in the original text of the novels. The concordances show that although both words appear in all three works, the impact is different in *Dandelion Wine* than in the other two novels. The images of eyes in *Dandelion Wine* are more positive: Eyes are liquid, shining, glimmering, and bright. Douglas's eyes are referenced most often, but other characters' eyes are mentioned. In contrast, the images of eyes in *Death* are associated with negative emotions: Eyes are wet because of weeping at the deaths, and the macabre image of glass eyes staring at the narrator in Chapter 33 is notable.

Table 2. Image Categories

Novel	Small Town	Nature	Sensory Images	Time/ Seasons	Misc.
DW	green (modifying machine and trolley; also the name of the town) town	green (grass trees moss)	Cool dark warm	morning night summer	eyes old
DLB	empty (places buildings in Venice detailed in table 3)	empty (shore, sand) fog		night time	door eyes god old phone people
GS	hotel pub street	green (of Ireland)		day	door eyes god man old

Source: Sarah-Warner Pell, "Style is the Man: Imagery in Bradbury's Fiction."

In *Green Shadows*, Ricki and the narrator cry, but the other references to eyes are fairly neutral. The same contrast occurs with regard to *old*. The protagonist of *Dandelion Wine*, which is told from a third-person omniscient narrative point of view, is an adolescent who is observing the lives of people around him, including the "old people" who, as Tom argues, were never children. The majority of nouns modified by *old* are the elderly townspeople Doug and Tom know, although the family's old Armenian rugs and "old fashioned lime-vanilla ice" are mentioned. The first-person narrator-protagonists of the two other novels are older and experiencing more sustained negative situations and emotions, including writer's block and depression. *Old* is primarily associated with men in *Death Is a Lonely Business*, which, as a mystery novel, features murder. There are also references to the "old days" of film, of Venice, California, and an "old-fashioned graveyard" to emphasize the passage of time and the narrator's nostalgia for the past. While there are old men and houses in the fictional portrayal of Ireland in *Green Shadows, White Whale*, those images of the past do not seem to affect the narrator.

Another pattern involves two words, both adjectives, which are the only ones that can be placed in two of Pell's categories, somewhat antithetical ones: *Green* (in *Dandelion Wine*) and *empty* (in *Death Is a Lonely Business*) modify nouns that are related to town and to nature. *Green* in *Dandelion Wine* is in the name of the town and is associated with two machines Douglas loves: the town trolley and an electric car. It also is used to describe grass, trees, and moss. The impact is positive. *Empty* has more negative connotations than *green*, but even allowing for this, it is significant that the majority of nouns modified by the adjective in *Death Is a Lonely Business* are associated with places that usually are inhabited by human beings but that instead are devoid of human life and energy (see Table 3). *Empty* is associated with loss: loss of life, loss of the past (the pier and its activities), the death of people living in the old rooms, and the loss of human connection. The nouns relating to nature that are modified by *empty*, shore and sand, are not particularly positive, although sleeping on the warm sand with Constance Rattigan is among the more positive scenes in the novel, but the empty shore does not convey as much desolation as the repeated image of the empty walks, rooms, streets, pier, and cages.

A keyword analysis of the most frequently used nouns and adjectives in the excerpts from the three novels shows a clear difference in imagery between the first of the autobiographical novels, *Dandelion Wine*, and the other two. Besides looking at frequently used words common to all three novels, or words in single novels that stand out for some other reason, additional work could be done analyzing the words that appear in two of the three novels. *Dandelion Wine* and *Death Is a Lonely Business* both contain *dark* and *night*, while *Death Is a Lonely Business* and *Green Shadows, White Whale* both have *door*, *god*, *long*, and *man*. Words that are used less frequently but that relate to specific themes also could be analyzed to see wether the similarities or differences between the novels that are noted above carry over into other images.

Table 3. "Empty" Concordance

Buildings	Nature
along the EMPTY walks	the EMPTY shore
last-stand saloon EMPTY save for a bartender	the sand was EMPTY but still warm
An EMPTY twenty-by-twenty studio apartment	
[wall] too deep and too EMPTY	
his EMPTY cot	
those people in EMPTY rooms or cafés	
the EMPTY ceiling	
shop was open and EMPTY	
all the cages are EMPTY	
the street's EMPTY EMPTY tapestry screens	
an EMPTY pantomime	
the EMPTY pier	
the EMPTY house	

Source: Hüning, TextSTAT

Clause Analysis: Parataxis

Another common linguistic concept used in stylistics is clause analysis; this concept moves from a close focus on individual words to analysis of larger patterns of meaning in clauses and sentences. The basic statistics of the sentences of texts can easily be generated by text analysis programs (see Table 4). A comparison of the average sentence length, for example, shows that the three novels are fairly similar in the length of the sentences, averaging 13-15 words. The basic statistics are not particularly informative, however, which is why the larger patterns often focus on clauses as well as sentences. Since linguists consider clauses the basic unit of communication, they have developed multiple concepts for analyzing clauses.

I apply one particular clause concept to analyze a specific type of pattern in the excerpts: parataxis. *Parataxis* is the grammatical term for joining phrases or clauses with coordinating conjunctions—

"*and, or, nor, either, neither, but, yet, so, then,* and *for*—rather than with subordinating conjunctions. Bradbury's work shows paratactic

Table 4. Basic Text Statistics

Novel	# of Word Excerpted	# of Sentences	Avg. Sentence Length (# of Words)
DW	5,721	433	13.2
DLB	11,744	895	13.1
GS	3,931	363	14.9

Source: O'Donnell, UAM Corpus Tool

and hypotactic patterns, but I am focusing on paratactic in this section because of a stylistic analysis of parataxis in Raymond Chandler's fiction that I discovered after seeing a difference in Bradbury's dedication in *Death Is a Lonely Business*. *Dandelion Wine* and *Green Shadows, White Whale* both are dedicated to the people who helped Bradbury write the novel: an editor and friend, and a group of people in Ireland. *Death Is a Lonely Business* is dedicated not only to an editor and to friends, but "to the memory of Raymond Chandler, Dashiell Hammett, James M. Cain, and Ross Macdonald," all major authors in the genre of hard-boiled detective fiction. While Bradbury is best known for his science fiction, fantasy, and weird tales, Eller and Toupounce point out that he published seventeen stories in important mystery and crime magazines during the 1940s in what they describe as a "brief but significant detour" in his "early development as a professional writer" (310). Decades later, Bradbury came back to the crime genre in *Death Is a Lonely Business*, a mystery novel in which the writer-protagonist solves the question of who is killing people he knows in Venice, California.

While I agree with Eller and Toupounce's conclusion that the novel subverts the mystery conventions to focus on a very different type of protagonist—a "carnivalized protagonist, an 'idiot savant' hero who solves the murder instinctively" (324)—and different type of story than the classic crime fiction of the 1940s, I began to wonder whether the style of these writers whose work Bradbury clearly knows well might have influenced his style. Susan Peck

MacDonald published a stylistic analysis of Raymond Chandler's style in 2005. In "Chandler's American Style," she analyzes patterns in sentence length, clause structure, and the percentage of verbs and modifiers in selected passages from two of his novels. She concludes that Chandler's work was important in establishing an "evolving, simplified American-English prose style" that continues to the present as a vernacular style that has moved from crime novels to advertising and the Internet (448). *Vernacular* means the way ordinary people speak, often with specific reference to a region or country. Scholars have noted that Bradbury mixes vernacular and poetic styles in his fiction: Mengeling, for example, cites two critics whose introductions to Bradbury's work emphasize his mixed style and argues that Bradbury blends "an aura of the 'miraculous' and 'uncommon' around what we ordinarily think of as rather unmiraculous objects" (885).

MacDonald identifies three characteristics of Chandler's style: a high percentage, or frequent use, of *and*, the use of parataxis, and sequences of simple sentences consisting of a single independent clause rather than two or more clauses. Reliance on a string of shorter sentences results in the sense of fast pacing, or action, compared to longer more grammatically complex sentences. Writers vary the length and clause structures of sentences in their work for various effects. MacDonald compares Chandler's style to that of Faulkner and Hemingway and identifies commonalities such as "shorter sentences, sparse modification, and coordination with *and* rather than subordination" (464). So in this section, I analyze my excerpts to see whether the same patterns appear in Bradbury's work.

Keyword analysis shows that the percentage of *and* in the Bradbury corpus is similar to the percentages MacDonald identifies for Chandler, Faulkner, and Hemingway (see Table 5), although Bradbury's and Chandler's usage both are lower than that of the other two writers. *And* is the second most common word in all of the novel excerpts, but since the conjunction is used to join words and phrases as well as clauses, not every use of *and* indicates a paratactic clause pattern. While other coordinating conjunctions appear in the excerpt, they are much less frequent, as are subordinating conjunctions (Appendix D). The frequencies of the other conjunctions, coordinating and subordinating, are so low that a percentage would be meaningless.

Table 5. Comparison of "And"

	DW	DLB	GS	Chandler	Hemingway	Faulkner
And	3.4%	3.9	4.8	4.5	6.8	6.0

Sources: Bradbury data, Hüning, TextSTAT; Chandler, Hemingway, Faulkner data, MacDonald, "Chandler's American Style."

The attention paid to writers' use of parataxis or hypotaxis in their work is necessary because of value judgments that are often made. MacDonald points out that contemporary readers and critics are trained to value hypotaxis over parataxis, associating the use of *and* either with oral cultures (citing the work of Walter J. Ong), or with inexperienced writers who have not yet learned the mature style that requires subordination (citing the work of James Moffett). Acknowledging that an overreliance on *and* to join clauses can reflect a developmental stage in writing, MacDonald strongly rejects the idea of a basing a simplistic value judgment of Chandler's clearly conscious use of parataxis in his work. An additional example of how people are trained to apply simplistic rules broadly is seen in a post on *Language Log*, a collaboratively authored blog where linguists post their take on various language issues, including prescriptivist grammatical rules. Mark Liberman summarizes a news article about an economist who was fired after announcing that he would not approve written reports submitted to him if the word *and* appeared more than 2.6 percent of the time because that meant the writing was bad. Liberman provided a table of data on the frequency with which *and* appears in a variety of classic literary texts; the lowest frequency cited was *The Adventures of Sherlock Holmes* with 2.83 percent. The highest frequencies were the *King James Bible* (6.3 percent) and the KJV of "The Book of Genesis" (9.55 percent) (Appendix E). The frequency of Bradbury's usage of *and* falls squarely in the top half of the works listed (see Table 6): 3.4 percent in *Death*, 3.9 percent in *Dandelion Wine*, and 4.8 percent in *Green Shadows, White Whale*. Liberman's data are an example of the descriptive approach in linguistics; he presents evidence about what writers whose works have been canonized actually do in their writing rather than the simplistic prescriptivist approach that often appears in education settings where, as MacDonald notes, students are often given absolute rules about conjunction use.

Table 6. "And" Frequency in Classic Literature with Bradbury Data Integrated

Death Is a Lonely Business	**3.40%**
The Sun Also Rises	3.42%
To the Lighthouse	3.46%
Jane Eyre	3.48%
US Constitution	3.52%
Bleak House	3.53%
Dracula	3.61%
Life on the Mississippi	3.62%
A Tale of Two Cities	3.62%
Works of H.P. Lovecraft	3.67%
My Ántonia	3.67%
For Whom The Bell Tolls	3.68%
Gone With The Wind	3.79%
Tom Sawyer	3.83%
Wuthering Heights	3.87%
Dandelion Wine	**3.90%**
Martin Eden	3.92%
Frankenstein	3.95%
The Railway Children	4.01%
Green Shadows, White Whale	**4.80%**
Treasure Island	4.11%
The Wizard of Oz	4.20%
Little Women	4.26%
A Moveable Feast	4.57%
The Old Man and the Sea	4.70%
The Call of the Wild	4.76%

Sources: Bradbury data, Hüning, TextSTAT; Liberman, "Conjunctions Considered Harmful."

For my clause analysis, I identified all the sentences in the corpus that consist of two or more clauses joined by a coordinating conjunction (see Table 7). I also identified instances where three or more simple sentences in a sequence occurred. MacDonald's analysis of Chandler's sentences focuses more on sentence length and the percentage of verbs and modifiers, so a direct comparison is not possible in this case. However, my analysis does show that parataxis occurs significantly more frequently in *Dandelion Wine* than in the other two novels, with 17 percent of the total sentences using parataxis compared to the lower rates of 4.5 percent in *Death Is a Lonely Business* and 5 percent in *Green Shadows, White Whale*. All three novels have a similar pattern in regard to sequences of simple sentences: 7 to 11 percent of the sentences in the excerpt are sequences of simple sentences. Further work would need to be done to see whether the pattern appears more often in dialogue than in the narrative voice. Besides noting that the clause analysis shows the same difference than the keyword analysis, it also seems worth pointing out that, given the extent to which *Dandelion Wine* has received more critical attention and praise for its style than the other two novels, even academic critics do not respond negatively to parataxis and the frequent use of *and* in a text.

Table 7. Parataxis in Bradbury

Novel	Sentences	Paratactic Sentences	Clauses in Paratactic Sentences	Excerpts with Three or More Simple Sentences in a Sequence	Simple Sentences in Sequence of Three or More
DW	384	46 (17%)	120	5	37 (9%)
DLB	942	42 (4.5%)	100	8	69 (7%)
GS	292	16 (5%)	42	2	32 (11%)

Source: O'Donnell, UAM Corpus Tool.

This brief introductory stylistics analysis provides additional evidence that the method complements qualitative interpretations of literary works rather than contradicting or undercutting them. The rich body of critical work on Bradbury's fiction offers a range of claims that could be investigated further with stylistics, including not only comparisons across novels but further work with the short fiction, and with the stories that later were developed as part of the longer works. Keyword analysis can easily be done with open access programs that are available online. Clause analysis is more labor-intensive, but is possible on a small scale. Collaborative, or group work, could work with data from a larger amount of text to explore both the grammatical patterns and the impact of Bradbury's work.

Works Cited

Bradbury, Ray. *Dandelion Wine*. The Grand Master Editions. Bantam. 1976.

———. *Death Is a Lonely Business*. Harper, 2003.

———. *Green Shadows, White Whale*. Harper, 2002.

———. *Zen in the Art of Writing*. Odell, 1996.

Carpenter, Markus A. "Time for Living: Clock Vs. Organic Time in *Dandelion Wine*." *Interactions* 201.2, 2011, pp. 47-54.

Eller, Jonathan R., and William F. Touponce. *Ray Bradbury: The Life of Fiction*. Kent State UP, 2004.

Fowler, Roger. *Linguistic Criticism*. Oxford: Oxford UP, 1996.

Hoover, David L., Jonathan Culpeper, and Kieran O'Halloran. *Digital Literary Studies; Corpus Approaches to Poetry, Prose, and Drama*. Routledge Advances in Corpus Linguistics 16. Routledge, 2014.

Hüning, Matthias. *TextSTAT* (2000-2014). v2.9c. http://neon.niederlandistik.fu-berlin.de/textstat/.

Johnson, Wayne L. *Ray Bradbury*. Recognition Series. Ungar, 1980.

La Jeunesse, Jake. "Locating Lakeside, Wisconsin: Neil Gaiman's American Gods and the American Small-Town Utopia." *Mythlore: A Journal of J. R. R. Tolkien, C. S. Lewis, Charles Williams, and Mythopoeic Literature* 35.1 [129], 2016, pp. 45-64.

Liberman, Mark. "Conjunctions Considered Harmful." *Language Log* 27, May 2017. http://languagelog.ldc.upenn.edu/nll/?p=32910#more-32910. Accessed 1 June 2017.

Logsdon, Loren. "Ray Bradbury's Tale of Two Cities: An Essential Message for a Technologically Dominated Society." *Midamerica* 36, 2009, pp. 93-106.

MacDonald, Susan Peck. "Chandler's American Style." *Style* 39.4, Winter 2005, pp. 448-68.

McNelly, Willis E. "Ray Bradbury." *Science Fiction Writers: Critical Studies of the Major Authors from the Earth Nineteenth Century to the Present Day.* Edited by E. F. Bleiler. Scribner's, 1982, pp. 171-78.

Mengeling, Marvin E. "Ray Bradbury's '*Dandelion Wine*': Themes, Sources, and Style." *The English Journal.* 60.7, Oct. 1971, pp. 877-87.

O'Donnell, Mick. *UAM Corpus Tool,* 2007. 2.18.7 http://www.corpustool.com/index.html.

Pell, Sarah-Warner J. "Style Is the Man: Imagery in Bradbury's Fiction." *Ray Bradbury.* Edited by Martin Harry Greenberg and Joseph D. Olander. Writers of the 21st Century Series. Taplinger, 1980, pp. 186-94.

Person, James E., Jr. " 'That Always Autumn Town': Winesburg, Ohio, and the Fiction of Ray Bradbury." *Winesburg* 22.2, 1997, pp. 1-4.

Rosenman, John B. "The Heaven and Hell Archetype in Faulkner's 'That Evening Sun' and Bradbury's *Dandelion Wine.*" *South Atlantic Bulletin* 43.2, May 1978, pp. 12-16.

Stockwell, Peter. "Language, Knowledge, and the Stylistics of Science Fiction." *Subjectivity and Literature from the Romantics to the Present Day.* Edited by Philip Shaw and Peter Stockwell. Pinter, 1991, pp. 101-12.

APPENDIX A: SELECTED KEYWORD FREQUENCY DATA

The most frequently used words in every written text often surprise readers because they are the basic function words (conjunctions, prepositions, and pronouns), followed by proper names of characters and *to be* verb forms. However, as the discussion on parataxis as a stylistic choice shows, being able to identify the frequency of function words can be useful in literary analysis.

Dandelion Wine (5,721 words)

Word	# Times Used	Word	# Times Used
The	392	As	25
And	226	Them	25
Of	139	There	25
A	133	Up	25
In	97	Or	24
To	81	For	23
He	76	That	23
His	63	Were	23
On	54	Out	22
It	44	Then	22
Was	44	She	20
Douglas	41	But	19
You	41	Him	19
They	36	Back	18
I	34	Could	17
At	33	Night	17
Down	33	Not	17
From	33	One	17
Her	33	Summer	17
With	32	So	16
All	29	Now	15
Like	29	Over	15
Said	27	What	15
Their	27	Into	14
Tom	27	Would	14

Word	# Times Used	Word	# Times Used
Eyes	13	Just	11
Had	13	Morning	11
Last	13	Again	10
No	13	By	10
This	13	Cool	10
Town	13	Dark	10
Around	12	Doug	10
Here	12	Grass	10
If	12	Off	10
Two	12	Old	10
Way	12	Saw	10
Be	11	Trees	10
Even	11	Warm	10
Green	11	When	10
It's	11		

Nouns/Adjectives	# Times Used
night	17
summer	17
eyes	13
town	13
green	11
morning	11
cool	10
dark	10
grass	10
old	10
trees	10
warm	10

Death Is a Lonely Business (11,744 words)

Word	# Times Used	Word	# Times Used
The	722	no	37
And	398	off	37
I	382	one	36
A	251	over	36
In	223	back	35
Of	217	constance	35
To	215	not	35
Was	169	crumley	34
It	140	this	33
My	133	when	33
On	113	or	32
Had	79	then	31
You	76	we	31
His	62	so	30
he	60	were	29
there	53	what	27
up	52	fannie	26
from	51	if	26
she	51	way	26
all	50	where	26
for	50	who	26
but	48	someone	25
as	47	did	24
door	47	him	24
down	44	be	23
her	42	long	23
like	42	time	23
is	41	an	22
thought	40	by	22
away	39	come	22
night	38	got	22

Word	# Times Used	Word	# Times Used
just	21	do	18
now	21	go	18
some	21	only	18
again	20	people	18
gone	20	phone	18
they	20	stood	18
waiting	20	along	17
god	19	don't	17
how	19	empty	17
old	19	eyes	17
went	19	fog	17
came	18		

Nouns/Adjectives	# Times Used
door	47
night	38
long	23
time	23
god	19
old	19
people	18
phone	18
empty	17
eyes	17
fog	17

Green Shadows, White Whale (3931 words)

Word	# Times Used	Word	# Times Used
the	257	one	15
and	190	down	14
i	102	man	14
to	84	no	14
a	68	an	13
in	67	but	13
of	63	is	13
said	50	not	13
my	44	or	13
was	40	your	13
it	39	did	12
you	38	back	11
at	37	if	11
on	32	what	11
as	27	him	10
his	25	like	10
for	21	some	10
john	21	they	10
that	20	up	10
finn	19	by	9
he	18	into	9
we	18	their	9
all	17	when	9
out	17	where	9
there	17	be	8
with	17	day	8
from	16	eyes	8
had	16	finn's	8
me	16	long	8
off	16	looked	8
are	15	over	8

Word	# Times Used	Word	# Times Used
pub	8	yes	7
say	8	about	6
do	7	away	6
don't	7	best	6
door	7	beyond	6
god	7	green	6
have	7	hotel	6
let	7	just	6
old	7	only	6
then	7	sound	6
were	7	street	6

Nouns/Adjectives	# Times Used
man	14
day	8
eyes	8
long	8
pub	8
door	7
god	7
old	7
best	6
green	6
hotel	6
sound	6
street	6

APPENDIX B: MOST FREQUENTLY USED NOUNS AND ADJECTIVES

DW		DLB		GS	
night	17	door	47	man	14
summer	17	night	38	day	8
eyes	13	long	23	eyes	8
town	13	time	23	long	8
green	11	god	19	pub	8
morning	11	old	19	door	7
cool	10	people	18	god	7
dark	10	phone	18	old	7
grass	10	empty	17	best	6
old	10	eyes	17	green	6
trees	10	fog	17	hotel	6
				sound	6
				street	6

Source: TextSTAT (Hüning)

APPENDIX C: CONCORDANCES OF "EYES" AND "OLD"

Dandelion Wine
> his large liquid-dark EYES
> great-grandma a blink of the EYES
> douglas stood EYES squinted
> before their EYES
> douglas closing his EYES
> he squinted his EYES mysteriously
> douglas's EYES shone pale and solemn
> a last veiled glimmer of her EYES
> their bright EYES
> douglas shut his EYES and saw two idiot suns
> opened his EYES
> his EYES looked him straight on
> no more than close his EYES

Death Is a Lonely Business
to be read with your watered EYES
wiping their EYES
The EYES were bright
With my EYES clenched
All the glass EYES across the street
He shut his EYES
It was his EYES blind but white rimmed
handkerchief all wet from my EYES
hat crammed down over his EYES
I shut my EYES tight
EYES shut type out
if I shut my EYES and pretend to be blind
Constance shutting her EYES
drenched with fiery EYES
shut her EYES
his cane in his lap EYES restfully shut
Shrank spoke first EYES dreaming the whispered arias

Green Shadows, White Whale
mike shut his EYES
shut my EYES
his EYES bulged
ricki's EYES were shut but tears
their master crossed his EYES at them
wiping tears from my own EYES
i stiffened EYES shut
i saw with wet EYES that god the hills were green

Dandelion Wine
that's OLD and new
he dusty patterns of OLD armenia
OLD mrs bentley
the OLD lady
OLD people never were children
the OLD colonel freeleigh express
maybe OLD people were never children
two OLD women collapsed
from the OLD man's now quite cold fingers
OLD fashioned lime-vanilla ice

Death Is a Lonely Business
Venice California in the OLD days
It was where the OLD men gathered
the name of the OLD man
I found the OLD man's room
the OLD man's X-ray imprint
the OLD man stumbling out of the morgue
Feeling like an OLD Russian writer
My God cried the OLD man
I slipped on some OLD hair
The OLD canary lady is going to live
Mr Shapeshade's OLD Venice Cinema
two OLD maid sisters
they excavated an OLD tomb
the face of the OLD hawk the ancient German warrior
in honor of the OLD days
like an OLD film
the nice OLD-fashioned graveyard
Cal's OLD piano
Want OLD Ma to come in with you
The OLD man from the ticket office

Green Shadows, White Whale
the OLD man
pedaled an OLD man on a bike
the OLD mansion
the young men and the OLD of kilcock
an OLD man
announced the tall sad happy OLD young man
OLD herman

Source: TextSTAT (Hüning)

APPENDIX D: CONJUNCTIONS IN BRADBURY CORPUS

Conjunction	DW	DLB	GS
Coordinating			
and	226	398	190
but	19	48	13
or	24	32	13
Subordinating			
as	25	47	27
after	4	7	5
how	3	19	3
because	2	2	1

Source: TextSTAT (Hüning)

APPENDIX E: FREQUENCY OF "AND" IN CLASSIC LITERATURE

The Adventures of Sherlock Holmes	2.83%
The Incredulity of Father Brown	2.88%
Pride and Prejudice	2.91%
Moby Dick	2.95%
Emma	3.02%
Jude The Obscure	3.03%
Far from the Madding Crowd	3.05%
Tristram Shandy	3.08%
The Pickwick Papers	3.13%
The Great Gatsby	3.16%
Animal Farm	3.18%
Little Dorrit	3.18%
Ivanhoe	3.20%
Jacob's Room	3.20%
Persuasion	3.29%
Lady Chatterly's Lover	3.31%
David Copperfield	3.34%
Fanny Hill	3.39%

The Sun Also Rises	3.42%
To the Lighthouse	3.46%
Jane Eyre	3.48%
U.S. Constitution	3.52%
Bleak House	3.53%
Dracula	3.61%
Life on the Mississippi	3.62%
A Tale of Two Cities	3.62%
Works of H.P. Lovecraft	3.67%
My Antonia	3.67%
For Whom The Bell Tolls	3.68%
Gone With The Wind	3.79%
Tom Sawyer	3.83%
Wuthering Heights	3.87%
Martin Eden	3.92%
Frankenstein	3.95%
The Railway Children	4.01%
Treasure Island	4.11%
The Wizard of Oz	4.20%
Little Women	4.26%
A Moveable Feast	4.57%
The Old Man and the Sea	4.70%
The Call of the Wild	4.76%
Huckleberry Finn	5.34%
Bible (all of KJV)	6.53%
Book of Genesis (KJV)	9.55%

Source: Mark Liberman, "Conjunctions Considered Harmful." Language Log 27 May 2017. http://languagelog.ldc.upenn.edu/nll/?p=32910#more-32910. Accessed 1 June 2017.

Books as Metaphors in *The Martian Chronicles* and *Fahrenheit 451*

Ádám T. Bogár

It is a commonplace thing to say that books and reading are of central importance to Ray Bradbury, and they are, of course, widely referenced in many studies about the various aspects of his works. Usually, however, books are not the main focus in such studies and act rather as illustrative examples for the discussion. Bradbury already spoke—and many critics have written[1]—extensively about his devotion to, as well as the personal and general importance of, libraries; see, for example, Bradbury ("Introduction" 7), Show (21), and Albright (139). This essay, therefore, will not discuss the relevance of those fine institutions to Bradbury's life and works. Instead, I will consider books themselves as factors and actors, as they appear and the roles they play in his works, in particular in *Fahrenheit 451* (1953) and *The Martian Chronicles* (1950).

The main point I argue in this chapter is that books in these two novels of Bradbury's are, of course, metaphors: placeholders for complex notions, ideals, and concepts such as knowledge and idea, history and the past, connection and communication. This is a very intuitive association, a fitting one indeed for Bradbury, who once said, "I don't want to know anything about my writing at all; I just do it" (Albright 144).

Besides that, I also claim that books are to be seen as objects and tools that create an atmosphere: the presence of books in Bradbury's works signifies home, a domestic environment, by all means spiritually, but often in the physical sense as well. To be where books are is to be in a good place; the presence of books creates a warm, livable, in a sense "breathable" atmosphere. Books turn alien and hostile environments into the friendly, familiar, and homely. To add a twist to the expression *terraforming*, attributed to pulp science fiction writer Jack Williamson (Rabkin 188), it can be said that books *domoform* such environments. This is where I will begin.

Prime examples of such *domoforming* of course are to be found in Bradbury's abundant descriptions of his childhood experiences in libraries, which I am not discussing here, but his novels as well contain many illustrative instances in which books contribute to the creation of a warm and homely environment. Usually, of course, this is a good thing, but in "The Third Expedition" of *The Martian Chronicles*, this aspect of books actually is used as part of the Martians' grand scheme of recreating an idyllic scene for the astronauts participating in Earth's third attempt at colonizing Mars, so that the Martians can lure the crew into what they see as "a small town the like of Earth towns" (43), with the homes of their lost loved ones, in order to kill them:

> "It's good to *be* home."
> He left *the land of cigar smoke and perfume and books and gentle light* and ascended the stairs, talking, talking with Edward. (58; italics added)

Creating a persuasively alluring, even comforting atmosphere is of paramount importance for this trap to work; the Martians use the astronauts' memories to make the scene alluring and familiar, with "soft pillows on large couches and *walls filled with books* and a rug cut in a thick rose pattern, and iced tea in the hand, sweating, and cool on the thirsty tongue" (53; italics added). For Bradbury, books are integral parts of such an environment because "we all have memories of a book and how it changed our lives" (Kunert 75).

In addition, books play a key role as not only the content of memories but also their preservers for Bradbury. As Professor Faber puts it in *Fahrenheit 451*, books are "one type of receptacle where we stored a lot of things we were afraid we might forget" (79). And through preserving memories, books also preserve knowledge and create a substrate for critical thinking, the thing considered the greatest evil by the fast-paced consumerist society of *Fahrenheit 451*. Reading—and writing—and thinking are inextricably intertwined and related for Bradbury, as he kept expressing it over and over again: "The fourth challenge [humanity faces] is education, because we're not educating our kids. They don't know how to read and write, and that means they're not going to know how to think" (qtd. in Newcomb 105).[2] In Bradbury's thought and in his works as well, books are both a prerequisite and an outcome of reading; and reading, therefore, is both the producer and the product of the text. In Bradbury's case, we need to understand *text* in a somewhat Derridean fashion: *"il n'y a pas de hors-texte,"* that is, "[t]here is nothing outside of the text" (Derrida 158). Everything can be, and indeed is, read as a text; the whole world is written and read by us, readers. *"To read (legere, legein) means 'to pick out, to peck'. .... Not everything can be pecked. There are illegible things. But everything can be picked apart so that it can be pecked"* (Flusser 79-80; italics Flusser's), writes Czech philosopher Vilém Flusser about the critical, or evaluative, way of reading. The world can be read, or at least rendered readable, and then engaged with.

Reading for Bradbury is a metaphor of movement in the philosophical sense, that is, of change, of life, of existence, and, on the same note, books can be understood to be vehicles for, and symbols of, thinking, communication, and interpersonal relationships—that is, practically metaphors of the human world. The text of books for Bradbury is a universal hypertext, in a similar way as Argentinean essayist Jorge Luis Borges[3] pondered: "The world, according to Mallarme, exists for a book; according to Bloy, we are the versicles or words or letters of a magic book, and that incessant book is the only thing in the world: more exactly, it is the world" ("Cult" 362).

For Bradbury, books are alive in many ways. Texts not only contain information, but they also contain, and indeed, sustain life. In *Fahrenheit 451*, Faber says that the reason books such as the Bible are important is "[b]ecause they have quality. And what does the word quality mean? To me it means texture. This book has pores. It has features. This book can go under the microscope. You'd find life under the glass, streaming past in infinite profusion. .... Quality, texture of information" (79-80).[4] *Pores* and *features* both are related to ways of describing a human face, one of the most obvious signifiers of human *being*—both in the sense of *living entity* and of *existence*. The idea of viewing books as being in some way animate objects is certainly not new or unique to Bradbury—see John

Milton's "Areopagitica" (239-40), for example—but in Bradbury's works it is of particular importance and is a recurring theme. Not only was it "the voices of the authors themselves that would come to symbolize literature for Bradbury" (Eller 11), but he also

> saw the authors personified in the masterpieces on the library shelves. Eventually, he came to see the shelves as populations of authors and began to dream of living among them, Bradbury between Mr. Baum and Mr. Burroughs, not far from Miss Dickinson, Mr. Melville, Mr. Poe, Miss Welty, Mr. Whitman, and an ever-expanding circle of reading loves. To burn the book is to burn the author, and to burn the author is to deny our own humanity. (Eller 11)

A very obvious example of such metaphoric thinking on the part of Bradbury is of course the Book People, a group of self-exiled former academics that former book-burning fireman Montag meets after escaping the city, who memorize whole books, "keep it in the old heads, where no one can see it or suspect it" (Bradbury, *Fahrenheit 451* 145), in order to preserve them for posterity. As Erika Gottlieb observes, "*Fahrenheit 451* is a society that denies its past; it has no records of past events, no books, no documents, and as a result, no framework for personal memory" (89), and the Book People are making all their efforts exactly to keep such knowledge alive and such past present.

Books are viewed as living entities in *The Martian Chronicles* as well, primarily in "Usher II." Mr. Stendahl, the main character in the chapter, gets his very own "House of Usher" built, as a compressed circus of the various torture devices and horror found in Edgar Allan Poe's short stories, in spite of the general ban on books, or more precisely, on nonrealist things. He turns the building into a single gigantic and complex retribution mechanism, somewhat in the manner of a Rube Goldberg machine—see Beschloss—and punishes Mr. Garrett, "Investigator of Moral Climates" (Bradbury, *Martian Chronicles* 142), for his ignorance and "[b]ecause [he] burned Mr. Poe's books without really reading them" (156). The anti-imagination government of "Usher II" coerces people into accepting, acknowledging, and "facing" the realist interpretation of the world: "Every man, they said, must face reality. Must face the Here and Now! Everything that was *not* so must go" (141). According to this view, fiction is a means of escape from reality, and as such must be eradicated:

> All the beautiful literary lies and flights of fancy must be shot in mid-air. So they lined them up against a library wall one Sunday morning thirty years ago, in 1975; they lined them up, St. Nicholas and the Headless Horseman and Snow White and Rumpelstiltskin and Mother Goose—oh, what a wailing!—and shot them down, and burned the paper castles and the fairy frogs and old kings and the people who lived happily ever after (for of course it was a fact that *nobody* lived happily ever after!), and Once Upon A Time became No More! And they spread the ashes of the Phantom Rickshaw with the rubble of the Land of Oz; they filleted the bones of Glinda the Good and Ozma and shattered Polychrome in a spectroscope and served Jack Pumpkinhead with meringue at the Biologists' Ball! The Beanstalk died in a bramble of red tape! Sleeping Beauty awoke at the kiss of a scientist and expired at the fatal puncture of his syringe. And they made Alice drink something from a bottle which reduced her to a size where she could no longer cry "Curiouser and curiouser," and they gave the Looking Glass one hammer blow to smash it and every Red King and Oyster away! (141–42)

Literature and the art of fiction are the main sources of such "literary lies and flights of fancy," which became the most fiercely hated enemies of the oppressive official ideology of realism.[5] Books literally *embody* literature here: they give fiction a bodily form, which is further highlighted by the vivid description of the execution of nonrealist things, that is, the destruction of their bodies. Stendahl turns this oppressive ideological framework against the oppressors, symbolized by Garrett and "members of the Society for the Prevention of Fantasy" (149): Stendahl realizes fiction, makes it into reality, and then makes this new reality devour and destroy them one by one.

Books in Bradbury's works, therefore, can be seen as living entities, and thought this they also act as metaphors of life itself, particularly of human life. A prime example of this is a section of

"June 2001: —And the Moon Be Still as Bright" in *The Martian Chronicles* that describes the funeral of Cheroke and the two others killed by Spender: "A warm wind came from over the vacant sea and blew the dust into their faces as the captain turned the Bible pages. *When the captain closed the book* someone began shoveling slow streams of sand down upon the wrapped figures" (81; italics added). As the spiritual part of the ceremony is concluded, the physical stage of the funeral begins, that is, the actual burial of the bodies. The purpose and rationale of the ceremony is the ritualistic closure of the earthly lives of the dead, as of course is completely usual in the case of a funeral ceremony. However, as we already have seen, the presence of books in Bradbury's novels bears special significance. In this very case, it is the Bible that is present, the Book of Books, from which the Captain reads during the ceremony. As long as the book in the Captain's hands is open, the ceremony is still ongoing, and the earthly lives of Cheroke and the others have not yet ended from a ritualistic, symbolic, spiritual point of view. The moment the Captain closes the book is the moment they begin to bury the bodies and the moment the text begins referring to the dead persons in a more objectificatory way, as mere *figures*: That is the moment their existence as human beings comes to a close. The open book here symbolizes life, existence, whereas the closing of the book and the cessation of reading equals death, passing, nonexistence, the end.

The imagery of open and closed Bibles appear in *Fahrenheit 451* as well, bearing similar significance, but in an even more abstract and metaphorical manner. When Faber describes himself to Montag as a "coward" who was "one of the innocents who could have spoken up and out when no one would listen to the 'guilty'" (78), he speaks while holding a copy of the Bible in his hands. He reminisces over the smell and feel of old books as he speaks. When he concludes that he should have acted and stood up to tyranny when he still had a chance, which he no longer has, he closes the book: "'Now, it's too late'. Faber closed the Bible" (78). As a symbolic gesture, the closing of the book here again serves as a metaphor of closing a life, a life where he, Faber, could have done something to stop oppression, where he could have been someone other than the "coward" he became and apparently despises.

Montag also is seen with an open Bible in his hands in a pivotal moment of *Fahrenheit 451*:

> Now as the vacuum-underground rushed him through the dead cellars of town, jolting him, he remembered the terrible logic of that sieve, and he looked down and saw that he was carrying the Bible open. There were people in the suction train but he held the book in his hands and the silly thought came to him, if you read fast and read all, maybe some of the sand will stay in the sieve. But he read and the words fell through... (74)

At this point in the novel, Montag is already collecting books, and knows he is under surveillance, and even though he has not been declared guilty and an outlaw by the authorities in an official manner, he knows that he has raised multiple warning flags with Chief Beatty, and that his officially becoming a fugitive is only a matter of time. He does not yet have a complete and firm grasp of the cognitive process of reading, which is apparent in the way he relates to his memory of playing with the sieve. Montag at this point considers the act of reading as a purely physical process—for him, reading is not a qualitative activity but a quantitative one, and books are primarily physical objects.[6] From this point of view, this section is the turning point of the novel, when Montag realizes that "in a few hours, there will be Beatty, and here will be [Montag] handing [the book] over, so no phrase must escape [him], each line must be memorized" (74). That is, since the physical form of the book is static and perishable—and who would know it better than Montag himself?—the book, and everything the book means and represents, will need to be made mental, will need to be recast as cognitive processes in a dynamic, resilient, and fluid form. This is a key realization on Montag's behalf. Although he does not articulate it so just yet, at this point he understands not only that in order to preserve books he would need to turn them from mere physical objects into living entities, but also that it is not enough if books contain and symbolize ideas and thinking itself. Thoughts must be transferred to and emulated on living hardware, on *wetware*; simply put, he comes to realize that thinking is necessary.[7] This important moment in the novel is punctuated by the image of an open Bible, and at least equally importantly, with the image of Montag *realizing* that he holds the book open in his hand.

Another prevalent aspect of books in Bradbury's works is their physicality, their material existence and the sensory experiences attached to them. In his biography of Bradbury, Jonathan R. Eller writes that Bradbury's "instinctive approach to the library was synesthetic: books were sensed by smell and look and touch, and only then could the reading process be contemplated. It was only natural, therefore, that the chosen book's characters would come alive for him through all of his senses..." (11). The description of the physical and sensory characteristics of books became important and frequent in Bradbury's works, from the smell of books[8] to the colors—usually shiny and metallic—of the covers.[9] Physical objecthood and instrumentality are at the core of Bradbury's experience of books.

I would like to highlight one specific example from *The Martian Chronicles*, where we see a description of a "metal book with raised hieroglyphs over which [Mr. K] brushed his hand, as one might play a harp. And from the book, as his fingers stroked, a voice sang, a soft ancient voice..." (2). In this passage, Mr. K is not actually *reading* the book, at least not in the traditional sense of the word. Instead, he is a virtuoso who plays it as an instrument, while he is also the audience, enjoying the music and song of the book. Through reading, the reader is communicating with the book, and this communication is by no means a unidirectional process—that is, one in which the reader harvests information from the book, a passive object—but instead is real interaction, of which the book is an active participant, an agent in its own right.

This "book-as-musical-instrument" metaphor places Bradbury somewhat outside the mainstream of speculative fiction authors when it comes to depicting the future of the book, both as an object and as a social construct. Of course, in the writings of many speculative fiction authors, books remain books as we tend to know them nowadays; they have paper pages that can be turned by hand, and they can be read in the traditional way in which we read books. If, in such writings, the books of a speculative future differ from such description, then they usually do so in a manner that makes them more or less similar to films or maybe to our contemporary audiobooks. Examples for that include Isaac Asimov's *book-film*, which in his novel *Prelude to the Foundation* mostly resembles a mixture of a microfiche reader and a DVD player,[10] or Stanislaw Lem's vision of books as "crystals" that can be read with either an "opton," "which was similar to a book but had only one page between the covers [and a]t a touch, successive pages of the text appeared on it" (79), or "lectons," "which read out loud... [and] could be set to any voice, tempo, and modulation" (79)—future versions of our ebooks and audiobooks.

These and other similar fictional devices, although diverse in their appearance and design, all aim to facilitate a generalized, everyday reading process where the reader simply reads the book, with the book being a passive store of information. In contrast, Bradbury's description focuses heavily on an *interaction* between and involving the reader as well as the book itself, both being active agents in the process. The case Bradbury makes through such imagery is that quality reading requires a similar level of focus, concentration, awareness, and engagement as does playing a musical instrument. Reading is pictured here as far more than entertainment or collecting information: It is meditation, it is an art, and it is a deeply spiritual activity.

We have seen how the materiality, that is, the physical texture of books, is emphatic in Bradbury's works. Referring back to Faber's words about quality in a book being equal to "texture of information" (Bradbury, *Fahrenheit* 80), we find that texture is emphasized as probably the most important feature of books, that is, of texts. The original meaning of the word *texture* is *weaving*, that is, a textile production technique for making strong fabrics. Metaphorically speaking, in Bradbury's novel, books represent a texture of information, of knowledge, and thus, of a progressing and thriving society, a texture that is interlaced with itself, that can support itself and others as well.

This texture provides a background, a safe framework for human societies, and if this texture is removed, human societies become rootless, and thus defenseless against unreason, ignorance, tyranny, and the abuse of power. The removal of texture means the removal of the supporting system, the skeleton of a society. In turn, the individuals themselves in such societies become rootless, defenseless, and vulnerable, devoid of confidence, imagination, and willpower. Such individuals are not only exposed but they even voluntarily surrender themselves to those of power and authority and disclaim their individuality. The overwhelming majority of them do so out of desperation and a hope for protection and safety, while a smaller portion assume what Hannah Arendt calls the "mob mentality" (402) and do so out of fear and hate, a fear of things unknown and not understood, and a hate of the "society from which [they are] excluded" (138).

"*Fahrenheit 451* is speculative fiction. It's an 'If this goes on...' story" (Gaiman xii); Bradbury himself called it "political fiction [or] 'the art of the possible'" (Green 145). In the 1950s, when Bradbury wrote this novel, and *The Martian Chronicles* as well, the United States was still recuperating from the trauma of World War II and the Nazis, was fighting the Korean War, was struggling with the "Second Red Scare" and fully fledged McCarthyism, and was keeping one eye on Josef Stalin's USSR and the other on Mao Zedong's People's Republic of China. Throughout history, heavy censorship and even book burning were ways of getting rid of knowledge, ideology, memories, and general past that were considered subversive by oppressive regimes or agents of power. Bradbury's novel was primarily inspired by McCarthyism (Show 19), and it indeed was "the art of the possible" in that had McCarthyism escalated further, the outcome potentially could have been an oppressive totalitarian dictatorship.

In some cases, tactics have changed since the '50s. In the West, we are living in *post-truth*, or to formulate it more aptly, in the era of *weaponized narrative*. "Lead [sic] to trust little of what their leaders say, little their intelligence services say, little their professional media and fact checkers say, and little scientists say, individuals are being physically attacked. This is weaponized narrative at work" (Garreau 12). We can see it at work in the United States under Donald Trump, in Turkey under Recep Tayyip Erdogan, in Hungary under Viktor Orbán, and in Russia under Vladimir Putin, to name a few. Some go even further than sustaining verbal warfare against facts and confusing the truth, and take steps that are the digital era equivalents of book burnings: for example, Erdogan's authoritarian regime banned access to Wikipedia in Turkey, claiming that the website became "an information source acting with groups conducting a smear campaign against Turkey in the international arena" (Erickson).[11] There are signs, however, that people are not as quick to accept this new world order and weaponized narrative has not won the war yet: "It is heartening, for instance, that Orwell's *Nineteen Eighty-Four* rose to the top of Amazon's charts days after Kellyanne Conway urged Americans to embrace 'alternative facts'" (D'Ancona 101–02). Bradbury's works provide reassurance that the education, knowledge, critical thinking, and supporting texture provided by books must be the foundation of a morally upright society, and that "our imaginations could be used as a tool for better understanding, a vehicle for change, and an expression of our most cherished values" (Barack Obama, qtd. in Flood).

Notes

1. See, for example, Susan Spencer, Chapter 1 of Jonathan R. Eller's *Becoming Ray Bradbury*, and William F. Touponce's chapter in the present volume.

2. For Bradbury, the ability to read and write is not just the most fundamental goal to be attained through education, but also the doorway to and a catalyst for imagination and curiosity; see Kelley (152) and Klein (189).

3. Borges wrote the preface for the 1955 Spanish translation of *The Martian Chronicles*, published as *Crónicas marcianas* in Buenos Aires by Editorial Minotauro (Borges, "Ray Bradbury" 418-19). Borges also is widely considered to have provided a precursory idea of what we call *hypertext*—see Murray (4-5) and Bolter (147)—so much so that his short story "The Garden of Forking Paths" is included in MIT Press's gigantic survey volume on new media, *The New Media Reader* (Borges, "Garden" 29-34).

4. Texture is emphasized as probably the most important feature of books, that is, of texts. Texture is linked to texts intrinsically, with both nouns being derived from the Proto-Indo-European root *teks-, meaning *to weave, to fabricate, to make.*

5. It is hardly a coincidence that realism as a literary historical movement is traditionally considered to begin in the nineteenth century with the works of Marie-Henri Beyle, better known as Stendhal, the namesake of the chapter's protagonist, Mr. Stendahl.

6. Such a physical approach to the contents of books and the "consumption of value" is of course not a new idea. For example, Denis Diderot and other Enlightenment-era French encyclopedists provide an interesting precedent in the entry for the word *book*—*livre* in French—in the *Encyclopédie*, with regard to the different perspectives on the value of a book:

    The mercenary idea of "un livre qui se vend bien" ["a book that sells well"] goes to the heart of the inevitable conflict between a man of letters and a man of business: it is a matter of quality versus quantity. One can notice that in French, *un livre* (a book), ironically happens to be the same word as *une livre* (a pound – both the weight and the eighteenth-century monetary unit), though with a different gender and etymology. The thought of a work of literature, the first type of *livre*, being measured by mere price or weight, the second type of *livre*, is precisely what Enlightenment authors beheld with horror. (Tsien)

7. It is of particular importance regarding this section that the book in question is the Bible. Key related passages of the Bible are the ones where the Evangelists relate the story of the world as created by the word of God, and in connection with this, the Word's becoming physical, in passages such as "In the beginning was the Word, and the Word was with God, and the Word was God" (John 1:1) or "And the Word was made flesh" (John 1:14).

8. "Faber sniffed the book. 'Do you know that books smell like nutmeg or some spice from a foreign land? I loved to smell them when I was a boy" (Bradbury, *Fahrenheit 451* 78).

9. Characteristic examples can be found in both novels. *The Martian Chronicles* contains a "thin silver book" whose "pages [a]re tissue-thin, pure silver, hand-painted in black and gold" (*Martian* 81), while in *Fahrenheit 451* "The woman knelt among the books, touching the drenched leather and cardboard, reading the gilt titles with her fingers..." (35).

10. In the case of Asimov, it must be noted that I am only referring to this passage for an illustration of the use of *book-films*, and although this device appears on multiple occasions and in slightly different forms in his *Foundation* novels—see, for example, *Second Foundation* (246–47)

or *Foundation and Empire* (532)—he clearly utilizes this mechanism as a science fiction element to give the novels' worlds a more futuristic touch.

This assertion finds support for example in Asimov's essay "The Ancient and the Ultimate," where he describes, by essentially "reverse engineering" his own fictional device, how a book can substitute for, or rather is, any personal audiovisual projector, and also, similarly to Bradbury, emphasizes the interactive nature of the reading process:

> The book…demands cooperation from the reader. It insists he take part in the process…. When you read a book, you create your own images, you create the sound of various voices, you create gestures, expressions, emotions. You create *everything* but the bare words themselves. And if you take the slightest pleasure in creation, the book has given you something the television program can't. (269; italics in original)[11]

11. Other such atrocities include the Hungarian government's new discriminative law on higher education that specifically targets the Central European University in Budapest, which Prime Minister Viktor Orbán claims is an agent of billionaire George Soros that aims to "destabilize and weaken" Hungary and the whole of Europe (Karasz).

Works Cited

Aggelis, Stephen L., editor. *Conversations with Ray Bradbury*. UP of Mississippi, 2004.

Albright, Donn. "Interview with Ray Bradbury." Aggelis, pp. 139-44.

Allen, William B. "An Interview with Ray Bradbury." Aggelis, pp. 39-53.

Arendt, Hannah. *The Origins of Totalitarianism*. Penguin, 2017.

Asimov, Isaac. "The Ancient and the Ultimate." *Journal of Reading* 17, 1974, pp. 264-71.

———. *Foundation and Empire*. 1952. *Foundation, Foundation and Empire, Second Foundation*. Knopf, 2010, pp. 201-405.

———. *Second Foundation*. 1953. *Foundation, Foundation and Empire, Second Foundation*. Knopf, 2010, pp. 407-607.

Beschloss, Steven. "Object of Interest: Rube Goldberg Machines." *The New Yorker*, July 19, 2013. www.newyorker.com/tech/elements/object-of-interest-rube-goldberg-machines. Accessed 3 May 2017.

The Bible. Authorized King James Version. Oxford UP, 1998. www.biblegateway.com. Accessed 3 May 2017.

Berton, Pierre. "Ray Bradbury: Cassandra on a Bicycle." Aggelis, pp. 31-39.

Bolter, Jay David. *Writing Space: Computers, Hypertext, and the Remediation of Print*. Routledge, 2001.

Borges, Jorge Luis. "On the Cult of Books." *Selected Non-Fictions*. Edited by Eliot Weinberger. Viking, 1999, pp. 358-62.

———. "Ray Bradbury, *The Martian Chronicles*." *Selected Non-Fictions*. Edited by Eliot Weinberger. Viking, 1999, pp. 418-19.

———. "The Garden of Forking Paths." *The New Media Reader*. Edited by Noah Wardrip-Fruin and Nick Montfort. MIT P, 2003, pp. 29-34.

Bradbury, Ray. "A New Introduction." *Fahrenheit 451*. Simon, 2003, pp. 5-9.

———. *Fahrenheit 451*. 1953. Simon, 2013.

———. *The Martian Chronicles*. 1950. Simon, 2012.

D'Ancona, Matthew. *Post Truth: The New War on Truth and How to Fight Back*. Ebury, 2017.

Derrida, Jacques. *Of Grammatology*. 1967. Translated by Gayatri Chakavorty Spivak. Johns Hopkins UP, 1997.

Eller, Jonathan R. *Becoming Ray Bradbury*. U of Illinois P, 2011.

Erickson, Amanda. "Turkey Just Banned Wikipedia, Labeling It a 'National Security Threat'." *Washington Post,* Apr. 29, 2017. www.washingtonpost.com/news/worldviews/wp/2017/04/29/turkey-just-banned-wikipedia-labeling-it-a-national-security-threat. Accessed 4 June 2017.

Flood, Alison. "Ray Bradbury's influence on Our Culture Was Transformative, Says Barack Obama." *The Guardian,* June 7, 2012. www.theguardian.com/books/2012/jun/07/ray-bradbury-influence-barack-obama. Accessed 4 June 2017.

Gaiman, Neil. "Introduction." *Fahrenheit 451*, by Ray Bradbury.Simon, 2013, pp. xi-xvi.

Garreau, Joel. "Attacking Who We Are as Humans." *Weaponized Narrative: The New Battlespace*. Weaponized Narrative Initiative, Center on the Future of War, Arizona State University, 2017, pp. 10-13. https://weaponizednarrative.asu.edu/publications/weaponized-narrative-new-battlespace-0. Accessed 4 June 2017.

Gottlieb, Erika. "Dictatorship without a Mask: Bradbury's *Fahrenheit 451*, Vonnegut's *Player Piano*, and Atwood's *The Handmaid's Tale*." *Dystopian Fiction East and West: Universe of Terror and Trial*. McGill-Queen's UP, 2001, pp. 88-112.

Green, Judith. "A Few Words with Ray Bradbury: The 'Fahrenheit' Chronicles— It Did Happen Here." Aggelis, pp. 145-46.

Karasz, Palko. "Pressure Grows as Hungary Adopts Law Targeting George Soros's University." *The New York Times*, Apr. 11, 2017. www.nytimes.

com/2017/04/11/world/europe/hungary-george-soros-central-european-university.html. Accessed 4 June 2017.

Kelin, Joshua. "Ray Bradbury." Aggelis, pp. 184-90.

Kelley, Ken. "*Playboy* Interview: Ray Bradbury."Aggelis, pp. 150-69.

Kunert, Arnold R. "Ray Bradbury: On Hitchcock and Other Magic of the Screen." Aggelis, pp. 54-79.

Lem, Stanislaw. *Return from the Stars*. 1961. Translated by Barbara Marszal and Frank Simpson. Harcourt, 1980.

Milton, John. "Areopagitica." *The Major Works*. Edited by Stephen Orgel and Jonathan Goldberg. Oxford UP, 2003, pp. 236-73.

Murray, Janet H. "Inventing the Medium." *The New Media Reader*. Edited by Noah Wardrip-Fruin and Nick Montfort. MIT P, 2003, pp. 3-11.

Newcomb, Barbara. "It's Up, On, and Away." Aggelis, pp. 100-06.

Rabkin, Eric S. *Mars: A Tour of the Human Imagination*. Praeger, 2005.

Show. "A Portrait of Genius: Ray Bradbury." Aggelis, pp. 17-30.

Spencer, Susan. "The Post-Apocalyptic Library: Oral and Literate Culture in *Fahrenheit 451* and *A Canticle for Leibowitz*." *Ray Bradbury*, new ed. Edited by Harold Bloom. Bloom's Modern Critical Investigations Series. Infobase, 2008, pp. 129-40.

Tsien, Jennifer. "Diderot's Battle against Books: Books as Objects during the Enlightenment and Revolution." *Belphégor* 13 (2015). belphegor.revues.org/609. Accessed 2 May 2017.

Space and Translocality: Revisiting Ray Bradbury's Mars_
Imola Bülgözdi

The thing is, if you're in a climate of birth, if you arrive in a town that's birthing itself, then you are part of the birth process, and you are optimistic. It gets in your flesh, it gets in your mind. ... Tucson was very new, and everything was fresh, and nothing had been touched yet. The age of the car hadn't ruined it, and the age of space and jets hadn't touched it. ... So I felt new ... that's the thing I came away with. I was re-birthed along with the town. (Bradbury qtd. in Eller 12-13)

Much of Ray Bradbury's work produced in the 1950s has been interpreted primarily in terms of the context of the political climate of the era, and the analogy between the colonization of Mars and the nineteenth-century westward expansion of the United States would not be lost on the majority of readers either. The world of *The Martian Chronicles* (1950), the first science fiction novel to receive a front-page mention in the *New York Times Book Review* (Rabkin, "Ray Bradbury" 147), was conjured up based on both nonfictional and fictional sources, as pointed out by Wayne L. Johnson, who traces aspects of the geography of Bradbury's Mars back to the popular theories of American astronomer Percival Lowell (1855–1916), while also citing Edgar Rice Burroughs's adventure stories and Leigh Brackett's planetary romances as two main imaginary influences (30). The Martian world that thus came into being definitely qualifies as "soft" SF, and even sparked hot debate in the 1950s whether Bradbury, whose project to write an important book about Mars started as early as 1944, was a science fiction writer at all, given that his works focus much less on science or technology than on "the deeper human feelings and aspirations" (Johnson 32).

Eric S. Rabkin's overview of the cultural imagination of the Red Planet devotes a section to Bradbury and concludes that his Mars catered for those who were starved for "a simpler, easier time of hope and growth, for a time of personal and national youth, for a moment when the distant clouds were not atomic blasts towering over immolated cities but mists hovering above peaceful canals" ("Ray Bradbury" 147). Although this somewhat simplistic and idealized image of the Red Planet seems to have dominated the critical evaluation of Bradbury, the short stories, which present episodes from the colonization of the planet, place the far more multifaceted and problematic relationship of humans and Mars in focus. The analogy between real-world events, places, and attitudes and their Martian counterparts has long been the object of study; therefore, I propose to revisit Bradbury's Mars based on Robert T. Tally Jr.'s premise that "the literary cartography produced in narratives becomes a way for readers to understand and think their own social spaces" (6).

In *Spatiality*, Tally argues that especially in genres like utopia, science fiction, and fantasy, where the fantastic mode liberates the literary cartographies or geographies from certain aspects of realism (147), literature provides the mapping of both real and imagined spaces and the combination thereof, referred to by Edward Soja as *Thirdspace*. In other words, in science fiction the simultaneous mapping of "real-and-imagined" spaces, which combine "aspects of the 'real' and the 'represented' spaces while also going beyond them" (Tally 119), is more apparent. It is this specific feature of Bradbury's Martian short stories that I would like to explore in detail with the help of the concept of *translocality*, defined by Katherine Brickell and Ayona Datta as "a simultaneous situatedness across different locales which provide ways of understanding the overlapping place-time(s) in migrants' everyday lives" (4). When these approaches are combined, Bradbury's Mars becomes more than the speculative fiction author's playground that bears strong resemblance to certain aspects of our real world; it becomes the site of "embodied everyday experiences" (Brickell and Datta 3), all the while illustrating the cognitive mapping, a "practical reconquest of a sense of place," in Frederic Jameson's words (51), taking place during the individual's translocal experience.

Building on Bertrand Westphal's observation that the spatiotemporal revolution that replaced the perception of historical time with the laws of space-time took place around 1945 (13), Tally explores the practical consequences of World War II, which affected the perception of space:

> If the metaphor of time as a smoothly flowing river and the evolutionary theory of history as progressively moving from barbarism towards civilization could not be maintained in the aftermath of concentration camps and atomic bombs, other real historical forces also helped shape the heightened attention to space in the postwar era. Certainly the massive movements of populations—exiles, émigrés, refugees, soldiers, administrators, entrepreneurs, and explorers—disclosed a hitherto unthinkable level of mobility in the world, and such movement emphasised geographical difference; that is, one's *place* could not simply be taken for granted any longer. (13)

Although Bradbury's *Martian Chronicles* seemingly are concerned with time, as they were set in the future at the time of writing, the stories were conceived during a period that saw unprecedented restructuring of societies, followed by the emphasis on the dominant effect of space on the daily life, experiences, and cultural languages of the individual (Jameson 15). Whereas large-scale population movement, especially immigration, always has received statistical attention, the experience of the individual, which is at the heart of Bradbury's work, has not and could not be charted by such methods. It is exactly this aspect that translocal geographies are interested in. As highlighted by Brickell and Datta, these translocal geographies have opened the way to examine migration across other scales besides the most common one—the transnational—such as rural-urban, inter-urban, and inter-regional migration, and they even have succeeded in "bringing into view the movements of those supposedly 'immobile' groups…who negotiate different kinds of local-local journeys (both real and imagined)" (4).

Bradbury's short stories provide a variety of interactions between humans and the planet, from those who literally take the trip to Mars—the first explorers, the settlers, and even the refugees—to those who stay behind but with an imagination forever affected by the possibility of space travel, like the father in the short story "The Rocket" (1950), who cannot afford tickets to Mars for a family of six but spends all his savings on a model rocket to take his children on a make-believe trip to space they experience as real. Harold Bloom considers Bradbury highly inventive and humane, yet he also believes Bradbury's failure lies in his style, more specifically in the fact that "his language is thin, his characters are names upon the page" (1). Although the short stories do not feature complex characters, their involvement with space and place is significant and worth investigating, since several resonate with the tenet that "our identity—our sense of selfhood—is a geographical thing, it is characterised to some extent by our geographical and cultural context" (Anderson 56).

Johnson points out that the most prominent recurring motif to appear in *The Martian Chronicles* is that of metamorphosis, which he links to the planet functioning as a mythological place, in the vein of Burroughs and Brackett, though possessing a more classically Greek atmosphere in Bradbury's fiction (36). George R. Guffey discusses this aspect in detail as well, concluding that the book "is in reality a collection of atavistic daydreams, daydreams which derive much of their power from mythlike transformations" (152). Although Guffey makes a valid case for linking these transformations to Jungian psychology, I also would like to draw attention to the fact that they are prompted by the translocal experience, bearing in mind that in the human sciences emphasis has shifted on the spatial organization within societies, also pointing at "the degree to which geography conditions even the most mundane aspects of everyday life" (Tally 14). In my view, Bradbury's translocal narratives can be regarded as an attempt at clarifying the post-World War II spatial confusion caused by the various phenomena and effects collectively grouped under the label *globalization*, which according to Tally has conferred on mapping and other spatial practices the valuable role of providing an overview (14). Frederic Jameson, too, argues that a new historical situation requires new aesthetic practices, and the appropriate model of political culture "will necessarily have to raise spatial issues as its fundamental organizing concern" (51). Thus the term *cognitive mapping* links the process of identification to questions of power and space at the same time, since it "allows the individual to locate itself and to represent a seemingly unrepresentable social totality in the postmodern world system" (Tally 155).

Bradbury also has been accused of inconsistencies when it comes to his account of Mars, especially when not only the collection *The Martian Chronicles*, but also subsequently published short stories, are considered. The first phase of contact, the fate of the first three expeditions, is a linear narrative, but the origins, purpose, and fate of subsequent settlers are recounted in short stories that can be regarded as contradictory. For instance, "Dark They Were and Golden-Eyed" (1949) describes the transformation of Earthmen into Martians, of which there is no hint in the chronicles. Furthermore, the presence of a large African-American community on the planet after the nuclear war that has wrecked Earth in "The Other Foot" (1951) is nowhere mentioned in "The Million-Year Picnic" (1946), which describes the arrival of a white family of war refugees to a deserted Mars. This aspect of Bradbury's work is definitely not a sign of his inability to produce a consistent narrative; rather, it is an attempt at representing what Tally dubs above the "unrepresentable social totality" of the postmodern world, putting to good use the poetic license the genre permits.

Tally emphasises the role of space in the paradigm shift from the limited psychological interiority of modernism, which was not concerned primarily with real or imagined spaces beyond the self (35-36), to the rise of a new postmodern imaginary as a result of changing material and historical circumstances. This change necessitates "new cartographic approaches, new forms of representation, and new ways of imagining our place in the universe. Space, place, and mapping, then, are crucial to literary and cultural studies, just as these concepts and practices are required for living in an ever-changing social and geographical milieu" (42-43), lending far more scope to Bradbury's science fiction than a pulp adventure story with robots and aliens. Therefore, it is not the idyllic nature of his stories that caught the public imagination, but the characters' tentative process of searching for their places in the post-World War II world, a search that obviously has more than one route.

The existential angst that had considerable influence on the literary and popular culture of the period made cognitive mapping all the more desirable, and Bradbury's characters perform this in Soja's Thirdspace, due to the translocal experience that takes them to an imaginary place. The Martian stories provide a mixture of the real, the imaginary, and the possibility to interpret socially produced space, since, Soja argues, "spatial and social forms, relations, and processes...[are] mutually constitutive" (113). The past two decades have seen major developments in cultural geography, shifting the focus onto the role of place in identity formation, to suggest that "the notion of a sense of place leads us to consider how *who we are* is fundamentally connected to where we are. ...[O]ur identity...is a geographical and cultural thing, it is characterised to some extent by our geographical and cultural context" (Anderson 56; italics Anderson's). It is through these contexts, Anderson contends, that the individual's sense of place is established, leading either to a feeling of belonging, or not belonging, to a particular geographical site (62).

The fate of the first three expeditions, described in "Ylla" (1950) "The Earth Men" (1948), and "The Third Expedition" (1948), respectively, is sealed in a matter of hours or after spending a single day at the most on Mars. It is significant, however, that contact is established with the astronauts via telepathy before landing on all three occasions. In "Ylla," for example, a Martian woman involuntarily gets in touch with the captain of the rocket, and realizes that he and his crew were real and not a weird dream only after her jealous husband kills them upon arrival. "The Summer Night" (1948) recounts a similar phenomenon preceding the arrival of the second expedition: Musicians and children involuntarily perform alien music and nursery rhymes, and on the night side of the planet women wake up screaming with the knowledge that "something terrible will happen in the morning" and "is coming nearer, and nearer and *nearer*" (26; italics Bradbury's), but their concern and dread are not taken seriously.

Mars, prior to human contact, most often is regarded by critics as an idealized place of beauty and harmony reminiscent of antiquity, and Kimberley Fain more than sixty years after the publication of *The Martian Chronicles* claims that Bradbury interweaves the main themes of nostalgia, reinvention, and redemption in this work (117). However, the Martian world depicted before the arrival of the third expedition is not problem-free. Ylla's life and circumstances mirror those of the emotionally neglected postwar suburban housewives, for example, and her husband is portrayed as a despot. "The Earth Men" reveals more senseless violence, with one of the Martians getting so upset that he challenges to a duel the one who wasted his time by needlessly sending to his house the astronauts imagined to be locals suffering from psychosis. Traditional hierarchic power relations, bureaucracy, and the Martians' inability to step outside of their own frame of reference, which ultimately leads to the astronauts' deaths, are reminiscent of the conformity on the rise in post-World War II America.

The arrival of the third expedition in the eponymously titled short story also is preceded by telepathic contact: In order to lull the suspicions of the rocket's crew, the Martians project an elaborate fantasy of the captain's quaint 1920s hometown and "populated it with the most loved people from all the minds of the people on the rocket" (Bradbury, "The Third Expedition" 76). Even though capable of entering the minds of the crew, the Martians do not attempt to communicate, and instead ruthlessly kill all sixteen of them in their sleep. Fain's reading of the collection as a revelation of "the dual identity of Americans as both citizens and descendants of an immigrant legacy" draws a one-on-one equivalence between the American Dream and the Martian Dream of the future, and posits Mars as the new West (117), but when considered from the standpoint of translocality, the exploratory period already shows a more composite picture than this.

The members of the second expedition in "The Earth Men" are baffled by the locals' complete lack of interest in their feat, and even after several rude rejections the captain asks for attention: "We're from Earth, we have a rocket,...we're exhausted, we're hungry, we'd like a place to sleep. We'd like someone to give us the key to the city or something like that, and we'd like somebody to shake our hands and say 'Hooray' and say 'Congratulations, old man!'" (36). He craves appreciation so much that he resorts to begging for a handshake, finally bestowed grudgingly, then is blown away by the thunderous applause they receive from the crowd, which turns out to be a group of inmates in a lunatic asylum. Bradbury not only challenges the validity of the geocentric perspective that in this context is the equivalent of the Eurocentric one on Earth, but also puts to the test the astronauts' concept of their home planet. By means of introducing Martian inmates who claim to have come from Earth by the spirit of the body, the crew's heroic story and origin are reduced to merely one version out of several. "Earth is a place of seas and nothing but seas. There is no land," states one, while "Earth is a place of all jungle," including a civilization built of silver (41) claims the other. Translocality, as described earlier, entails simultaneous situatedness in more than one locale, and the astronauts' core identity, to which their sense of belonging on Earth is pivotal, is relegated to the status of mental illness.

The questioning of the validity of the sense of belonging to Earth continues in "The Third Expedition," when an idyllic version of a 1920s small town is projected onto the arrival site by the Martians, who also take on the role of deceased relatives of the crew. This mimicry yet again undermines the astronauts' identity. Captain John Black, an older and more experienced leader than that of the previous expedition, understands that even though they consider themselves explorers, they may be regarded "as invaders, as unwanted ones" (75) by the locals. He asks himself what would be the most efficient strategy against men in possession of atomic weapons, and concludes that their translocal experience, which is, contradictorily, also that of being at home, is the result of telepathy and hypnosis. The well-known home suddenly becomes uncanny:

> And wouldn't it be horrible and terrifying to discover that all of this was part of some great clever plan by the Martians to divide and conquer us, and kill us? Sometime during the night, perhaps, my brother here on this bed will change form, melt, shift, and become another thing, a terrible thing, a Martian. It would be very simple for him just to turn over in bed and put a knife into my heart. (77)

Thus on Mars, the secure home of Earth, seat of the crew's well-founded sense of belonging, becomes a source of terror and a disguise for death, which definitely undermines Rabkin's conclusion regarding the ending of *The Martian Chronicles*, that "the American myth comes clean again, small town life welcomes us all, and his Mars, undoubtedly, is heaven" ("Is Mars Heaven?" 103).

The death of Earthmen and the unintentional extermination of Martians caused by the chicken-pox virus contaminate the place, such that in "—And the Moon Be Still as Bright" (1948) the fourth expedition "landed on an immense tomb" where "a civilization had died" (80). The crew arrives with the same hunger for appreciation of their heroic deed, which manifests itself inappropriately considering the circumstances, and is reported with sarcasm from the point of view of the archaeologist, Jeff Spender: "The men shifted around. … They were not satisfied. They had risked their lives to do a big thing. Now they wanted to be shouting drunk, firing off guns to show how wonderful they were to have kicked a hole in space and ridden a rocket all the way to Mars" (81).

Translocality, however, affects Spender in a different way, for he recalls the history of colonization on Earth, which foreshadows a ruined Mars. He is so disgusted by the behavior of the crew that he leaves and immerses himself in the wonders of "a graceful, beautiful and philosophical people" (89), who "knew how to live with nature and get along with nature" (107), as well as how to reconcile science, art, and religion. This idealized image prompts Spender to try to defend the remnants of this civilization at all costs, proclaiming himself the last Martian and recalibrating his inner compass. He forswears his sense of belonging to Earth and proceeds to kill his crewmates, explaining, "I felt I was not only free of their so-called culture, I felt I was free of their frame of ethics and customs. I'm out of their frame of reference" (105).

Whereas the optimistic captain of the fourth expedition had claimed that the planet was "too big and too good" (88) to be ruined by the Earthmen, Spender's prediction is proved right in subsequent stories. In six months some ninety-thousand people come to Mars in locust-like rockets, intent on "beat[ing] the strange world into a shape that was familiar to the eye" (Bradbury, "The Locusts" 128), while in "The Off Season" (1948) Bradbury depicts the archaeologist's worst nightmare come true. However, Adam Lawrence's analysis of the encounter of a Martian and an Earthling in "Night Meeting" (1950) demonstrates that this story "characterizes hospitality as a form of *substitution* in which the identity of the self is challenged and, in a number of ways, transformed by the call of the other whose presence demands sensitive contemplation" (72; italics Lawrence's). While this short story shows both individuals taking a far more accepting and positive view of the other than the previous ones, substitution cannot be complete due to the translocal experience of the human; the Martian has access to his own present only, whereas Tomás not only sees the ruins of the very same thriving Martian town his companion describes, but also is on his way to Green City, built from "a million board feet of Oregon lumber and a couple dozen tons of good steel nails" (Bradbury, "Night Meeting" 132). He also saw the bodies, "black, in the rooms, in the houses, dead. Thousands of them" (137), and even tries to explain to the Martian that his planet has been invaded.

Walter J. Mucher investigates new identities in the framework of Edmund Husserl's phenomenology, but clearly privileges the role of time as regards to that of space in identity formation, as "time structures the constituting synthesis of perceiving the phenomena" (172). Mucher contends that Bradbury's imaginary world is built along this principle, and in his view, the last story in the collection closes the process of "colonizing" suffered by the identity when refusing to break its link with the past—that is, with Earth (180). In "The Million-Year Picnic," he claims, "this transposition of time over space reflects how one must deal with their 'new' identity. A total annihilation of their past selves is demanded for them to carry on... To establish the new self, all ties to the past must be broken" (180).

Even though the father's face looks like "one of those fallen Martian cities, caved in, sucked dry, almost dead" (Bradbury, "The Million-Year Picnic" 295) upon realizing that the last radio station on Earth has stopped broadcasting, the arrogance of the colonizer is still present when he grants cities to each of his sons and claims "the whole darn planet belongs to us, kids. The whole darn planet" (301). The father believes he burns a way of life in a ritual cleansing, finally tossing the map of the world on the fire, and yet Bradbury describes them as "King of the Hill, Top of the Heap, Ruler of All They Surveyed, Unimpeachable Monarchs and Presidents, trying to understand what it meant to *own* a world" (301; italics added). This family of refugees comes with the best intentions from an Earth destroyed by atomic warfare, but Bradbury makes it clear that the presence of Earth lingers in their new, Martian identity imagined when they glimpse their own reflections in the water of the canal. This new identity is the result of a conscious choice, just as it was in Spender's case; it is an attitude without which they would call themselves colonizers or possibly expatriates. The total annihilation of the past that Mucher argues for cannot take place, as they pass the already rotting remnants of a settlers' town, and the translocal experience will continue, their arrival from Earth becoming the foundational myth for the new inhabitants of the planet, resulting in simultaneous situatedness.

Lawrence also draws our attention to the hybrid nature of Mars, where the landscape "maps both colonization and a lingering doubleness" (80), a fact underpinned by Bradbury's choice to provide more than one possible scenario for the future of the settlers once the war on Earth breaks out. In *The Martian Chronicles*, the settlers go home, with only a handful of people being left behind, as described in "The Silent Towns" (1949) and "The Long Years" (1948), but the large community of African-Americans who fled Jim Crow South in "Way in the Middle of the Air" (1950) reappears in *The Illustrated Man* (1951), living and prospering on Mars without white interference for twenty years. The arrival of a white man from war-torn Earth sparks desire for revenge, but the news he brings rekindle thoughts of a distant home—"the towns and the places, the trees and the brick buildings, the signs and the churches and the familiar stores"—while the crowd listens, struggling "to imagine all of those places in ruins" (Bradbury, "The Other Foot" 61).

Although they claim "we're Martians instead of Earth people" (Bradbury, "The Other Foot" 49), their identity has been indelibly shaped by the traumas they suffered in the South, and, consequently, they put up signs to segregate the newcomers. The tide turns due to the new, incredibly detailed photographic map of Earth showing that the sites of humiliation and trauma, including the tree from which the father of the current lynch mob's ringleader was hanged, are gone and they realize there is nothing left to hate of the old Southern civilization built on white supremacy. The shift in the balance of power caused by the loss of a habitable home frees both the African-Americans and the whites of their prejudices, and the latter admit their past "stupidity and evilness" and offer to do all the menial jobs on Mars (62) in return for being rescued from radioactive Earth. The past that came flooding back is linked to place, and their sense of belonging is cut loose, since there is no place to anchor it, thus enabling everyone to "start all over again, on the same level" (67).

The other short story that describes the fate of a group of settlers stranded during the war focuses specifically on the transformation that the physical surroundings work on them from the very first moment. Harry Bittering's first experience is a wind that blows "as if to flake away their identities. At any moment the Martian air might draw his soul from him, as marrow comes from a white bone. He felt submerged in a chemical that could dissolve his intellect and burn away his past" (Bradbury, "Dark They Were" 56). This is neither the arrogant colonizer nor the fascinated archaeologist speaking, and Bittering has to face the consequences of translocality as his frame of reference changes. The rest of the people, including his own family, find the transformation natural, and do not even seem conscious about the fact that they turn into tall, slender, dark-skinned, and golden-eyed Martians. Moving to the far more comfortable Martian villas during the hot summer is completely reasonable, and the parents do not find it odd that the children start speaking a different language and ask for permission to change their names to something more appropriate.

The new frame of reference yet again is highlighted by the settlers' relationship to the map of Mars, which becomes irrelevant, as they revert to the old names "of water and air and hills" (Bradbury, "Naming of Names" 199). Bittering feels contaminated and first blames the air or some virus, perhaps some pollen, since whatever they plant is not the same as on Earth, and he even senses how "his bones shifted, shaped, melted like gold" ("Dark They Were" 64). In five years, the whole community is transformed completely, so much so that the new arrivals from Earth describe them as friendly "native life," and the Captain declares things must be set straight: "we'll have a job of remapping to do, renaming the mountains and rivers and such" (72). This story clearly illustrates how the embodied everyday experiences of translocality affect Bittering, who at first likens himself to "a salt crystal...in a mountain stream, being washed away" (57), and craves the safety of Earth. His sense of not belonging is assuaged very slowly through his cognitive mapping of his new environment and the enjoyment he finally finds when he accepts the inevitable: "Change. Change. Slow, deep, silent change" (66).

As Lawrence observes, "Earth has always been here (Mars), which means that it has never been there in reality: it has been a projection of Earth culture" (80), and Bradbury's stories make use of Soja's Thirdspace congenial to the genre to portray the painful postwar wayfinding. Mars in this case becomes a site to explore the new world order and sense of displacement, which entails cognitive mapping to achieve a sense of belonging. In a geocritical interpretation, Bradbury's stories can be regarded as a new cartography that includes embodied everyday experiences, without which it is impossible to make sense of one's place in the world. The short stories not only reflect on the American past and postwar problems, but also include the translocal experience of the individual, which inevitably has become part of the postmodern world. What often is remarked as Bradbury's lyrical quality also can be posited as the individual's mapmaking practice that gives rise to a new imagination to take shape on Mars.

Works Cited

Anderson, Jon. *Understanding Cultural Geography: Places and Traces.* Routledge, 2015.

Bloom, Harold. "Introduction." *Modern Critical Views: Ray Bradbury.* Edited by Harold Bloom. Chelsea, 2001, pp. 1-2.

Bradbury, Ray. "—And the Moon be Still as Bright." *The Martian Chronicles,* 79-117. 1950. Harper Voyager, 2008.

"Dark They Were and Golden Eyed." *The Stories of Ray Bradbury* vol. 2. Granada, 1980, pp. 56-73.

———. "The Earth Men." *The Martian Chronicles,* pp. 27-52.

———. "The Locusts." *The Martian Chronicles,* pp. 128-29.

———. "The Long Years." *The Martian Chronicles.* pp. 263-79.

———. *The Martian Chronicles.* 1950. Harper Voyager, 2008

———. "The Million-Year Picnic." *The Martian Chronicles,* pp. 290-305.

———. "The Naming of Names." *The Martian Chronicles,* pp. 199-200.

———. "The Off Season." *The Martian Chronicles,* pp. 226-43.

———. "The Other Foot." *The Illustrated Man.* 1951. Harper, 2008, pp. 47-67.

———. "The Rocket." *The Illustrated Man.* 1951. Harper, 2008, pp. 153-68.

———. "The Silent Towns." *The Martian Chronicles,* pp. 247-62.

———. "The Summer Night." *The Martian Chronicles,* pp. 23-26.

———. "The Third Expedition." *The Martian Chronicles,* pp. 53-78.

———. "Way in the Middle of the Air." *The Martian Chronicles,* pp. 178-98.

———. "Ylla." *The Martian Chronicles,* pp. 3-22.

Brickell, Katherine, and Ayona Datta. "Introduction: Translocal Geographies." *Translocal Geographies: Spaces, Places, Connections.* Edited by Katherine Brickell and Ayona Datta. Ashgate, 2011, pp. 3-20.

Eller, Jonathan R. "Miracles of Rare Device: Bradbury and the American Southwest." *Orbiting Ray Bradbury's Mars: Biographical, Anthropological, Literary, Scientific and Other Perspectives.* Edited by Gloria McMillan. Critical Explorations in Science Fiction and Fantasy Series 41. McFarland, 2013, pp. 11-23.

Fain, Kimberley. "Bradbury's Mars: Pathway to Reinvention and Redemption." *Orbiting Ray Bradbury's Mars: Biographical, Anthropological, Literary, Scientific and Other Perspectives.* Edited by Gloria McMillan. Critical Explorations in Science Fiction and Fantasy Series 41. McFarland, 2013, pp. 117-132.

Guffey, George R. "The Unconscious, Fantasy, and Science Fiction: Transformation in Bradbury's *Martian Chronicles* and Lem's *Solaris*." *Bridges to Fantasy*. Edited by George E. Slusser, Eric S. Rabkin, and Robert Scholes. Southern Illinois UP, 1982, pp. 142-159.

Jameson, Frederic. *Postmodernism, or, the Cultural Logic of Late Capitalism*. Duke UP, 1997.

Johnson, Wayne L. *"The Martian Chronicles* and Other Mars Stories." *Modern Critical Views: Ray Bradbury*. Edited by Harold Bloom. Chelsea, 2001, pp. 29-38.

Lawrence, Adam. "A 'Night Meeting' in the Southwest: Hospitality in *The Martian Chronicles*." *Orbiting Ray Bradbury's Mars: Biographical, Anthropological, Literary, Scientific and Other Perspectives*. Edited by Gloria McMillan. Critical Explorations in Science Fiction and Fantasy Series 41. McFarland, 2013, pp. 70-87.

Mucher, Walter J. "Being Martian: Spatiotemporal Self in Ray Bradbury's *The Martian Chronicles*." *Extrapolation* 43, 2002, pp. 171-87.

Rabkin, Eric S. "Is Mars Heaven? *The Martian Chronicles, Fahrenheit 451* and Ray Bradbury's Landscape of Longing." *Visions of Mars: Essays on the Red Planet in Fiction and Science*. Edited by Howard V. Hendrix, George Slusser, and Eric S. Rabkin. McFarland, 2011, pp. 95-104.

———. "Ray Bradbury: An American Fairyland." *Mars: A Tour of the Human Imagination*. Praeger, 2005, pp. 143-47.

Soja, Edward W. "Interview with Edward W. Soja: Thirdspace, Postmetropolis, and Social Theory." Interview with Christian Borch. *Distinktion: Journal of Social Theory* 3, 2002, pp. 113-20.

Tally, Robert T., Jr. *Spatiality*. Routledge, 2013.

Westphal, Bertrand. *Geocriticism: Real and Fictional Spaces*. Translated by Robert T. Tally, Jr. Palgrave, 2011.

Down to Earth: Mundane Concerns and Marginalized Individuals in Ray Bradbury's Rocket Stories_____

Andrea Krafft

While Ray Bradbury retains a central position in the pantheon of science fiction writers, some critics find fault with his work, citing a lack of technological accuracy. Damon Knight, for example, bemoans that "his spaceships are a joke" (4), while John Campbell, Jr. similarly censures Bradbury for writing about "fairy ship[s]" instead of "mechanical, operable devices" (qtd. in Seed 22). Bradbury indeed eschews functional explanations of rocketry, preferring instead to focus on the enduring impact that space travel and interplanetary colonization will have on ordinary individuals. For his everyday heroes, these technologies are "wonder-inspiring objects" that represent the "mythic significance" of carrying humanity into new and unexplored realms (Johnson 67). In this respect, he echoes the grand traditions of space opera and planetary romance that sparked the beginnings of his career when at age twelve he strove to imitate Edgar Rice Burroughs by writing sequels to *John Carter, Warlord of Mars* (Bradbury, "Introduction" 1). However, he breaks away from his science-fictional forefather by reminding us not only that his travelers are fallible and mortal but also that some people inevitably will be left behind due to the material realities of their earthbound situations. Bradbury's value does not lie in his scientific predictions but rather stems from his portrayals of how future advancements will alter the lives of those who are lucky enough to board the rockets and those who only experience such wonders from a distance.

3, 2, 1...Blast Off: The Power of Launch and the Wonder of Landing

The transformational potential of interplanetary technology for everyday people becomes apparent from the moment of liftoff, which Bradbury dramatizes in "Rocket Summer" (1950), a brief vignette that sets the events of *The Martian Chronicles* into motion. As a rocket prepares to depart for the first expedition to Mars, the heat from its engines melts the surrounding "Ohio winter," altering the climate to such an extent that it turns the snow into "a hot rain before it touched the ground" (Bradbury, "Summer" 1). Although the warmth of an artificial summer seems like a potentially happy reprieve from a deep winter, as Edward J. Gallagher has noted, "the power here is actually more display than benefit" (57). The small-town residents' sense of seasonal normalcy is forever changed, and not necessarily for the better, given that the machine can at any time disrupt their day-to-day lives. The environmentally destructive implications of the rocket become fully evident in a later story in *The Martian Chronicles* entitled "The Locusts" (1950), which describes how the vehicles "set the bony meadows afire, turned rock to lava, turned wood to charcoal, transmuted water to steam, made sand and silica into green glass which lay like shattered mirrors reflecting the invasion, all about" (107). The machine catalyzes multiple chain reactions within the Martian landscape, with apocalyptic results for any living things that lie in its path. Although the rocket enables the colonization of a new world, it also results in the careless decimation of its launch and landing sites, the side effects of which will remain for those people—and Martians—who lack the mobility to seek out new homes.

Despite the fact that the tools propelling Bradbury's characters into the future always are accompanied by significant costs, he insists on the necessity of such technologies by describing the spiritual effects they have on ordinary people. For example, in "The Gift" (1959), a young boy envisions the depth of space as a kind of sublime Christmas tree, as he witnesses for the first time "the burning of ten billion billion white and lovely candles" (140). In this case, the departure from Earth, which requires the abandonment of the boy's Christmas gift and the family's decorations, initially feels like being "deprived of the season" (Bradbury, "Gift" 138). However, the narrative affirms a new sense of fulfillment and celebration through the eyes of the child, marking Bradbury's "basic faith that we can adapt our central rituals and symbols" and transcend the losses that accompany the acceleration of modernity (Mogen 74). A similar pattern emerges in "The End of the Beginning" (1956), originally titled "Next Stop: The Stars," when two parents watch the departure of a rocket that carries their son and others who will "build the first space station" (22). Comparably to how the young boy in "The Gift" conflates outer space with Christmas, the mother here likens the anticipation of the launch to a grand Fourth of July picnic that will usher in "the end of old man Gravity" (Bradbury, "End" 23). Liftoff becomes the stuff of legend for the parents, marking a new age when "man will be endless and infinite" (Bradbury, "End" 24). However, the story is bittersweet, as the parents do not fully participate in the glories of the space age but remain gravity-bound and separated from their son. The story concludes not with the apotheosis of interplanetary travel but with the father resuming his task of mowing the lawn, as a rift now exists between his life and those of future generations.

Rocket Men: Bradbury's Average Astronauts

Just as those who are left on Earth experience simultaneous wonder and loss during the Space Age, the men who fly in Bradbury's rockets balance on a razor's edge between awe-inspiring achievement and the risk of a senseless death that might render their efforts personally meaningless. This tension becomes apparent in "The Golden Apples of the Sun" (1953) when the crew members of the triple-named *Copa de Oro-Prometheus-Icarus* attempt to harvest some of the sun's fire. Colliding with myths that represent technological might and swiftly delivered divine punishments, they complete their mission, but only after the first mate ironically dies from a suit malfunction that flash-freezes his body. "Kaleidoscope" (1949) represents the materiality of space in even more brutal terms, as an unknown object rips the various members of the crew from their ship. In this moment of abject failure, Bradbury reminds us that his astronauts are, first and foremost, average individuals with simple wishes, not all of which are admirable. For example, in their final moments, Hollis and Applegate work through a petty rivalry, calling to mind postwar organization men rather than fulfilling our expectations for interplanetary heroes. The narrative pulls us back to the concerns of mundane life, just as Hollis is dragged violently back into Earth's gravitational field, burning up in the atmosphere to become a "blazing white star" (Bradbury, "Kaleidoscope" 37).

For the eponymous protagonist of "The Rocket Man" (1951), the attractions of Earth are similarly inescapable, but they remain opposed to the majestic promise of outer space, resulting in irresolvable psychological and familial conflict. As David Mogen has observed, this particular astronaut "is at home in neither" his domestic life with his wife and son nor his lonely travels among the stars (67). Disillusioned by his impossible situation, he warns his son, Doug, not to follow in his footsteps, "because when you're out there you want to be here, and when you're here you want to be out there" (Bradbury, "Man" 106). Yet the father refuses to break the cycle, even though he both fully recognizes the multiple ways that he might die in outer space and observes the impact of his absenteeism on his family. The narrative further suggests that Doug may, despite the warnings, have the same feverish desire to explore other worlds, as he gleefully examines the cosmic dust from his father's uniform under a microscope. Like the optimistic boy in "The Gift," Doug celebrates a dreamlike vision of outer space, idolizing his uniformed father as a human embodiment of a "dark nebula, with little faint stars glowing through it" (Bradbury, "Man" 103).

Domestic Disruption and the Limits of Technological Mobility

As the rocket man becomes an incarnation of the Space Age, he destabilizes his family, leaving his wife and son to experience the nightmarish effects of his career choice. While George Edgar Slusser argues that "outer space drives a wedge between members of this family" (32), the father is the one who magnifies the separation by cutting off contact with them during his travels, adding insult to injury by bringing them no mementoes when he returns. Rocketry here functions not as a glorious means of mythic conquest but rather as a tool that amplifies the explorer's selfishness, as he argues that keeping his family in mind during his flights means that he "wouldn't be happy" (Bradbury, "Man" 104). The story ultimately becomes one of domestic fragmentation, as the mother and son strive to keep the rocket man at home, where he only remains for three days before leaving for months at a time. When his ship falls "into the sun" at the conclusion of the story, recalling the inherent dangers of the mission in "The Golden Apples of the Sun," he leaves broken people in his wake, and his family finds no comfort in his identity as an astronaut. Thus, Bradbury draws our attention back to Earth, as his stories of interplanetary colonization necessarily involve the abandonment of those people who cannot leave our home planet.

Like "The Rocket Man," "R is for Rocket" (1943), originally titled "King of the Gray Spaces," emphasizes that space travel involves the creation of an exclusive club of astronauts, the formation of which alienates those who cannot join the profession. In the universe of this story, rockets are commonplace but maintain a wondrous quality because "you cannot apply for space work" but "you have to be *chosen*" (Bradbury, "R" 4; italics Bradbury's). Furthermore, the profession is shrouded in secrecy because "nobody is to know you have been selected by the Astronaut Board," primarily to protect the reputations of those trainees who fail and then reenter ordinary society (Bradbury, "R" 10). When the fifteen-year-old Christopher is plucked from school for the program, the clandestine nature of his new life immediately separates him from his friends and his mother. As another astronaut explains it, Christopher's new identity is a kind of technological sainthood in that he will be "blessed" if he approaches it as a selfless task (Bradbury, "R" 11). But, by "relinquish[ing] his role on earth" (Mogen 66), he leaves real people "beyond the fence" of the launch site (Bradbury, "R" 15).

The fence that separates the rockets from the surrounding Florida town reminds us that space travel remains out of reach for nearly everyone else in the story other than Christopher and his new astronaut colleagues. In many ways, this reflects the reality of the nascent American space program of the time, as "President Eisenhower mandated that military personnel would fill all spaceflight positions" (Holderman 30). A major consequence of this decision was that women were not eligible to serve as astronauts, since the military did not allow them to become pilots in the first place. Additionally, people of color were left behind because of systematic limitations on their advancement to high-status positions (Holderman 34). While Wayne L. Johnson argues that "Bradbury is not directly concerned with" the exclusionary nature of space travel (51), "R is for Rocket" directly contrasts Christopher's privileged situation with that of his best friend, Ralph Priory. Like Christopher, Ralph yearns to become an astronaut, but the recruiter suggests that he is unsuitable for the job because he was raised in "one of those orthopedical stations" without any parents (Bradbury, "R" 7). The circumstances of his birth hold Ralph back, though he does find some small solace when Christopher's mother, Jhene, essentially adopts him at the end of the story. Jhene and Ralph, like the rocket man's family, are left behind, and Christopher recognizes that he "liked the rockets *more*" than them (Bradbury, "R" 15; italics Bradbury's). Once again, Bradbury shows us how earthbound individuals might become sacrificial lambs on the altar of the Space Age.

While "The Rocket Man" and "R is for Rocket" focus on the psychological and domestic effects of exclusionary technoscience, Bradbury also reminds us that advances in mobility often make the difference between life and death. In "The Taxpayer" (1950), the "wire screen" that surrounds the launchpad serves as an ominous barrier that locks Pritchard into a world scarred by "wars and censorship and statism and conscription and government control of this and that" (42). At the time, Pritchard seems like a paranoid madman and is carted away back toward "an ordinary Monday morning on the ordinary planet Earth" (Bradbury, "Taxpayer" 43). Yet as we witness the nuclear devastation of the entire planet later in *The Martian Chronicles*, it becomes evident that those who cannot board the rockets are doomed to mass extinction. Pritchard calls to mind the similarly stationary character of Hernando in "The Highway" (1950), who observes hundreds of cars driving past his home during the beginning of "the atom war" (60). Though the cars have a limited capacity for escape in comparison to the rockets, it is notable that Bradbury draws our sympathies to a simple farmer who does not understand the significance of the oncoming apocalypse and who has no choice but to remain rooted in his routine, though his ignorance shelters him to some extent.

For those marginalized characters who are unable to leave behind their mundane lives, the only possibility of participating in the Space Age exists in their imaginative capacity, which Bradbury glorifies in "The Rocket" (1950). In this story, Fiorello Bodoni, who owns a struggling junkyard, spends each night watching rockets in the night sky and dreams about riding "up in one someday" (Bradbury, "Rocket" 246). He is, to quote the original title of this narrative, an "Outcast of the Stars," bound to a simple life in the midst of what his neighbor sarcastically proclaims to be "the world of the future" (Bradbury, "Rocket" 246). Undeniably, this world is built on the backs of men like Bodoni, who spends the day transforming scrap metal into "usable ingots" that might make their way back into the technologies that he is unable to afford (Bradbury, "Rocket" 250). Even when he manages to scrape together the money for a luxury rocket trip to Mars after six years, it remains unclear whether this is the best use of resources for a family that has been "on the insane edge of poverty for twenty years" (Bradbury, "Rocket" 250). As it has done before, the rocket threatens to tear the family apart, as Bodoni can send only one of them on the trip, and they desperately need the money to make improvements to the junkyard.

Bodoni's solution to his quandary is a creative one, as he purchases a "full scale model" of a rocket and fills it with colored films, mirrors, and car engines to make a one-time simulation of outer space for his entire household (Bradbury, "Rocket" 250). Though his children thoroughly enjoy the "journey," the story reminds us that Bodoni's construct that sits "in the center of the junk yard" is merely an imitation of the real experience of space (Bradbury, "Rocket" 255). Furthermore, by his own admission, Bodoni is "a great fool," as he spends the entirety of his savings building the rocket, potentially dooming his family to ruin, since they will not be able to pay for necessary junkyard equipment (Bradbury, "Rocket" 250). Given that it will take years for the family to recover their financial footing, the question arises as to whether the taste of space was worth it, especially since they may never set foot on a rocket ever again. However, Bradbury suggests that momentary contact with wonder is better than turning away from technological progress, as even the false memory is something that the Bodoni children "will never forget" (Bradbury, "Rocket" 257). Similar to the single night of privilege that a group of Mexican-American men enjoy in "The Wonderful Ice Cream Suit" (1958), the brief trip of the Bodoni family presents a speculative vision of what might occur if marginalized people were able to access the technologies that otherwise remain out of reach.

Reclaiming Rockets and Breaking Down Boundaries

The dream of affordable technology becomes a reality in "Way in the Middle of the Air" (1950), demonstrating how widespread access to rocketry might achieve the utopian goal of disintegrating racist tensions and class disparity. In this optimistic vision of the future, the disenfranchised African-American population of a small Southern town bands together, saving their money to secretly build rockets that they use to travel to Mars. Their collective spirit leads not only to technoscientific innovation but also to the end of what is essentially indentured servitude, as they pay off the debts of various members of the community so they can "*all* get free" (Bradbury, "Air" 644; italics Bradbury's). Though their goals of opening hardware stores and building houses may seem understated or make them appear to be "servile stereotypes" (Gallagher 71), we cannot underestimate the significance of how space travel will radically reframe the lives of this group. Specifically, Bradbury emphasizes the violently racist environment that they are leaving behind, embodied by Samuel Teece, the hardware store proprietor who expresses himself with racial epithets and regularly goes out on lynching raids. The rocket once again provides an escape from a life-or-death situation, both for the characters in the story and for young African-American readers such as Isiah Lavender III, for whom the narrative left an "indelible impression" about the alternatives to segregation and violence (5).

As the arguable sequel to "Way in the Middle of the Air," "The Other Foot" (1951) continues its predecessor's optimism about how widespread access to the glories of the Space Age might lead to the erasure of racial marginalization. Set twenty years after the previous story, "The Other Foot" initially reads as a narrative of fearful invasion, as the rockets occupied by white men approach the African-American settlement on Mars. In response, the community joins together to establish familiar patterns of segregation, agreeing that they will subject the new migrants to the experiences they suffered in the past. When it is revealed that an atomic war has devastated Earth, leaving behind roughly "five hundred thousand people," the populace abandons their desire for vengeance, agreeing to use their rockets to shuttle the survivors to Mars ("Foot" 50). In this moment of charity, they tear down the old systems of power and agree to "start all over again, on the same level ("Foot" 54). Unlike "R is for Rocket" and "The Taxpayer," in which unscalable walls trap huge portions of the population on Earth, "The Other Foot" illustrates Bradbury's desire to transcend these divides so that everyone might participate in a promising and inclusive future.

Rockets are just the first step towards evolving away from a world based on inequality and separation, as Bradbury envisions the future of humanity in terms of a blurring of boundaries between not only races but also species, leading to posthuman hybridity with the alien. "Night Meeting" (1950) signals the beginning of this process, as Tomás Gomez encounters the ghostly Muhe Ca when traveling the Martian roads at night. Rather than shrinking away from the alien creature or attacking it—as occurs elsewhere in *The Martian Chronicles*—Tomás communicates with it. He, too, understands what it means to be a lonely outsider within an imperialist culture and thus rewrites the stereotypical script of the alien contact narrative and makes no assumptions about whether the other's intent might be malevolent. The story is further complicated by the fact that both characters experience different chronological perspectives regarding the Martian landscape, making it unclear who is from the past and who is from the future. Rather than insisting on the dominance of their respective viewpoints, they "agree to disagree," leaving one another in mutual respect (Bradbury, "Night" 118). As Adam Lawrence notes, the story is one of "hospitality and peaceful cultural exchange," and heroism here stems not from a mastery of technology and violence but from "the willingness to embrace the strange" as if it were just another ordinary moment (72, 78).

In a similar vein, "Dark They Were, and Golden-Eyed" (1949), originally published as "The Naming of Names," blurs the line between the average individual and the unfamiliar other, conflating the categories so that their distinctions become unimportant. At first, this story reads as a confirmation of xenophobia, as Harry Bittering fears that his body, his family, and their home will become victims of a hostile takeover, believing that Mars "would eat them" (Bradbury, "Dark" 97). Bittering desperately tries to maintain a kind of purity by eating only "food from our Deepfreeze" rather than the fruits of the Martian garden that begin to change color and grow into unfamiliar shapes (Bradbury, "Dark" 101). But as a consumer of artificially preserved foods, he is clinging to unnatural practices that soon prove to be unsustainable in the new environment. Bittering's transformation is not a violent one but occurs gradually and peacefully, and he and his family take new names and abandon the Earth settlement in favor of symbolic unity with their new home. They change not just psychologically but also physically, as their bodies appear "burnt almost black by the sun" (Bradbury, "Dark" 101). The racial dimension of this story is impossible to ignore, as it seems that the future of space colonization in Bradbury's fiction lies not in the hands of the majority but with symbolically marginalized individuals who merge the past with unfamiliar traditions and thus imagine "racialized *becoming* in place of racialized *othering*" (Dillon 65; italics Dillon's).

Such a transformation concludes *The Martian Chronicles*, as the young family in "The Million-Year Picnic" (1946) searches for the native inhabitants of the planet, only to find their own reflections staring "back up at them for a long, long silent time from the rippling water" of a canal (268). However, Bradbury remains ambivalent about this group of settlers, as they threaten to reinstate isolationism and paranoia rather than truly erasing boundaries. The father, William Thomas, views Mars as a unique opportunity to start anew "and form our own standards of living," but he restricts the new community to two families (Bradbury, "Picnic" 268). Furthermore, as he burns newspapers and digests that describe the war on Earth, he foreshadows the ominous censorship of the firemen in *Fahrenheit*

451. The father in this story attempts to reshape the Red Planet in his own image, treating Mars simply as a vehicle for his political ideology rather than as a fluid and collaborative space. Of course, this does not guarantee that his new society will revert to the old ways of Earth, but reminds us that the shutting down of borders runs counter to the pioneering spirit that Bradbury's rockets so frequently embody.

Celebrating Marginality and Seeking the Stars

Just as his stories about space travel celebrate the removal of constraints between privileged individuals and outsiders, Bradbury's larger opus explores how average people encounter grotesque or sublime events, pushing them to redefine their understanding of normalcy. Indeed, the number of his works that revolve around haunting, carnival freaks, and otherworldly beings are too numerous to list here. Bradbury celebrates these liminal sites because their occupants all too frequently are metaphorical representations of real people who are treated as alien and relegated to the margins of society. The full implications of this become evident in his realistic explorations of tenement life in midcentury Los Angeles, particularly "I See You Never" (1947), in which a quiet tenant, Mr. Ramirez, is deported to Mexico. As Mr. Ramirez exclaims, "I don't want to go back," he reminds us what happens to ordinary people when we fence off national boundaries or limit their access to life-saving and transformative technologies (Bradbury, "Never" 65). Bradbury remains "a foot soldier in the war against marginalization" by pushing us to consider how we might traverse the structures that separate us from one another and by mourning for those people who otherwise would remain invisible (Barr 54).

Rockets are just one possible tool with which Bradbury hopes we will break through the boundaries of life on Earth and explore a new age of humanity marked by egalitarianism and joyous achievement. At Comic-Con in 2010, one of his final public appearances, he again expressed his passion for space exploration, arguing that it will give us "a chance at living forever," particularly if we colonize the Moon and Mars ("Ray Guns" 6). Even though he has acknowledged the inherent dangers of interplanetary travel and explored the psychological risks that affect astronauts as well as people who remain within the Earth's gravitational field, Bradbury consistently has treated the Space Age as an opportunity whose benefits will outweigh the costs. Perhaps this is why so many of his stories about rockets involve children who remain optimistic about the radical possibilities encapsulated within the engines of the spacecraft. As Bradbury states in the epigraph to *The Martian Chronicles*, "Space travel has again made children of us all" (xv), offering us a way to slip the surly bonds of Earth and evolve into new and fantastic creatures of the future.

Works Cited

Barr, Marleen S. "Prescient Border Crossing: 'I See You Never' and the Undocumented Mexicans Americans Prefer Not to See." McMillan, pp. 39-56.

Bradbury, Ray. "Dark They Were, and Golden-Eyed." 1949. Bradbury, *Medicine*, pp. 94-109.

———. "The End of the Beginning." Bradbury, *Medicine*, pp. 21-26.

———. *Fahrenheit 451*. 1953. Simon, 2013.

———. "The Gift." Bradbury, *Medicine*, pp. 138-40.

———. "*The Golden Apples of the Sun*." Bradbury, *Golden*, pp. 148-56.

———. *The Golden Apples of the Sun and Other Stories*. 1953. Avon, 1990.

———. "The Highway." Bradbury, *Illustrated*, pp. 56-61.

———. *The Illustrated Man*. 1951. Harper, 2011.

———. Introduction. *S is for Space*. Bantam, 1966, pp. 1-2.

———. "I See You Never." Bradbury, *Golden*, pp. 63-66.

———. "Kaleidoscope." 1949. Bradbury, *Illustrated*, pp. 26-37.

———. "The Locusts." Bradbury, *Martian*, pp. 107.

———. *The Martian Chronicles*. 1950. Harper, 2011.

———. *A Medicine for Melancholy*. 1959. Bantam, 1977.

———. "The Million-Year Picnic." Bradbury, *Martian*, pp. 256-68.

———. "Night Meeting." Bradbury, *Martian*, pp. 108-18.

———. "The Other Foot." Bradbury, *Illustrated*, pp. 38-55.

———. "Ray Guns, Robots, and Rockets: The Influence of Ray Bradbury on the Future." *Ray Bradbury: The Last Interview and Other Conversations.* Edited by Sam Weller. Melville, 2014, pp. 1-22.

———. "R is for Rocket." 1943. *R is for Rocket.* Bantam, 1965, pp. 1-15.

———. "The Rocket." 1950. Bradbury, *Illustrated,* pp. 245-57.

———. "The Rocket Man." Bradbury, *Illustrated,* pp. 97-111.

———. "Rocket Summer." Bradbury, *Martian,* pp. 1-2.

———. "The Taxpayer." Bradbury, *Martian,* pp. 42-43.

———. "Way in the Middle of the Air." 1950. *Bradbury Stories: 100 of His Most Celebrated Tales.* Harper, 2003, pp. 639-50.

———. "The Wonderful Ice Cream Suit." 1958. Bradbury, *Medicine,* pp. 27-50.

Dillon, Grace. "Bradbury's Survivance Stories." McMillan, pp. 57-69.

Gallagher, Edward J. "The Thematic Structure of *The Martian Chronicles.*" *Ray Bradbury.* Edited by Martin Harry Greenberg and Joseph D. Olander. Writers of the 21st Century Series. Taplinger, 1980, pp. 55-82.

Holderman, Angie. *"It's a Man's, Man's, Man's World:" Popular Figures and Masculine Identities in 1960s America.* Dissertation, California State University, 2007.

Knight, Damon. "When I Was in Kneepants: Ray Bradbury." 1956. *Modern Critical Views: Ray*

Bradbury. Edited by Harold Bloom. Bloom's Modern Critical Views Series. Chelsea, 2001, pp. 3-8.

Johnson, Wayne L. *Ray Bradbury.* Recognition Series. Ungar, 1980.

Lavender, Isiah, III. Introduction. *Black and Brown Planets: The Politics of Race in Science Fiction.* Edited by Isaiah Lavender III. UP of Mississippi, 2014, pp. 3-11.

Lawrence, Adam. "A 'Night Meeting' in the Southwest: Hospitality in *The Martian Chronicles.*" McMillan, pp. 70-87.

McMillan, Gloria, editor. *Orbiting Ray Bradbury's Mars: Biographical, Anthropological, Literary, Scientific, and Other Perspectives.* Critical Explorations in Science Fiction and Fantasy Series 41. McFarland, 2013.

Mogen, David. *Ray Bradbury.* Twayne's United States Authors Series 504. Twayne, 1986.

Seed, David. *Ray Bradbury.* Modern Masters of Science Fiction Series. U of Illinois P, 2015.

Slusser, George Edgar. *The Bradbury Chronicles.* Borgo, 1977.

RESOURCES

Chronology

1920	Ray Douglas Bradbury born August 22 in Waukegan, Illinois
1926-1933	Bradbury family moves back and forth between Waukegan and Tucson
1931	Bradbury begins writing stories on rolls of butcher paper
1934	Family moves to Los Angeles
1936	First poem published August 18: "In Memory to Will Rogers," in *Waukegan News-Sun*
1938	Graduates from high school
1938	First story, "Hollerbochen's Dilemma,"published in January in Forrest Ackerman's fanzine *Imagination!*
1939-1940	Writes and publishes fanzine *Futuria Fantasia*
1941	First paid story, "Pendulum," coauthored with Henry Hasse, published in August in *Super Science Stories*
1944	Writes second half of *Lorelei of the Red Mist* for Leigh Brackett
1947	*Dark Carnival* published by Arkham House
1947	Marries Marguerite Susan McClure
1947	Receives O. Henry Award, Best First-Published Story, "Homecoming" in *Mademoiselle*
1948	Receives O. Henry Award, Third Prize, "Powerhouse" in *Charm*

1949	First of four daughters born, Susan Marguerite
1950	*The Martian Chronicles* published by Doubleday
1950	October, review of *The Martian Chronicles* by Christopher Isherwood in *Tomorrow*
1951	February, "The Fireman" published in *Galaxy Science Fiction*
1951	*The Illustrated Man* published by Doubleday
1951	Second of four daughters born, Ramona Anne
1953	*The Golden Apples of the Sun* published by Doubleday
1953	Film *It Came from Outer Space* released, directed by Jack Arnold
1953	Film *The Beast from 20,000 Fathoms* based on "The Fog Horn" released, directed by Eugène Lourié
1953	*Fahrenheit 451* published by Ballantine
1953-1954	Bradbury works on John Huston's film *Moby Dick* in Ireland
1955	*The October Country* published by Ballantine
1955	Third of four daughters born, Bettina Francion
1956	Film *Moby Dick* released, directed by John Huston
1957	*Dandelion Wine* published by Doubleday
1958	Fourth of four daughters born, Alexandra Allison
1959	*A Medicine for Melancholy* published by Doubleday

1962	*R is for Rocket* published by Doubleday
1962	*Something Wicked This Way Comes* published by Simon and Schuster
1964	*The Machineries of Joy* published by Simon and Schuster
1964	*The Anthem Sprinters* published by Dial
1966	Film version of *Fahrenheit 451* released, directed by François Truffaut
1966	*S Is for Space* published by Doubleday
1966	*Twice 22* published by Doubleday
1969	*I Sing the Body Electric!* published by Knopf
1969	Film version of *The Illustrated Man* released, directed by Jack Smight
1971	Lunar feature named Dandelion Crater by Apollo 15 astronauts
1972	*The Halloween Tree* published by Knopf
1973	*When Elephants Last in the Dooryard Bloomed* published by Knopf
1976	*Long After Midnight* published by Knopf
1977	Receives World Fantasy Award, Life Achievement
1978	*Long After Midnight* published by Knopf
1980	Receives Gandalf Grand Master Award from World Science Fiction Society

1980	*The Stories of Ray Bradbury* published by Knopf
1983	Prometheus Award, Hall of Fame, from Libertarian Futurist Society
1985	*Death Is a Lonely Business* published by Knopf
1988	*The Toynbee Convector* published by Knopf
1988	Bram Stoker Lifetime Achievement Award, Horror Writers Association
1989	Damon Knight Memorial Grand Master Award from Science Fiction and Fantasy Writers of America
1990	*A Graveyard for Lunatics* published by Knopf
1992	*Green Shadows, White Whale* published by Knopf
1992	Newly discovered asteroid named 9766 Bradbury
1994	Receives Daytime Emmy for screenplay of animated *The Halloween Tree*
1996	*Quicker than the Eye* published by Avon
1997	*Driving Blind* published by Avon
1999	Bradbury suffers stroke
1999	Inducted into Science Fiction and Fantasy Hall of Fame
2000	Receives Medal for Distinguished Contribution to American Letters, National Book Foundation
2001	*From the Dust Returned* published by Morrow

2002	*One More for the Road* published by Morrow
2002	*Let's All Kill Constance* published by Morrow
2002	Receives Star on Hollywood Walk of Fame
2003	Bradbury's wife dies
2003	*Bradbury Stories* published by Morrow
2003	Receives honorary PhD from Woodbury University
2004	Receives National Medal of Arts Award from National Endowment for the Arts
2006	*Farewell Summer* published by Morrow
2007	Receives French Commander *Ordre des Arts et des Lettres* medal
2007	Receives Arthur C. Clarke Special Award
2008	Receives Rhysling Award, Grand Master Poet, from Science Fiction Poetry Association
2009	Receives honorary PhD from Columbia College Chicago
2012	June 5, Bradbury dies in Los Angeles
2012	August 22, Curiosity Mars rover touchdown named Bradbury Landing

Major Works

Novels, Including Fix-Ups
The Martian Chronicles, 1950
Fahrenheit 451, 1953
Dandelion Wine, 1957
Something Wicked This Way Comes, 1962
The Halloween Tree, 1972
Death Is a Lonely Business, 1985
A Graveyard for Lunatics, 1990
Green Shadows, White Whale, 1992
From the Dust Returned, 2001
Let's All Kill Constance, 2002
Farewell Summer, 2006

Story Collections
Dark Carnival, 1947
The Illustrated Man, 1951
The Golden Apples of the Sun, 1954
The October Country, 1955
A Medicine for Melancholy, 1959
R is for Rocket, 1961
The Machineries of Joy, 1964
S is for Space, 1966
Twice 22, 1966
I Sing the Body Electric! 1969
Long After Midnight, 1976
The Stories of Ray Bradbury, 1980
The Toynbee Convector, 1988
Quicker than the Eye, 1996
Driving Blind, 1997
One More for the Road, 2002
Bradbury Stories, 2003

Poetry Collections

When Elephants Last in the Dooryard Bloomed, 1973
Where Robot Mice and Robot Men Run Round in Robot Towns, 1977
The Haunted Computer and the Android Pope, 1981

Drama

The Anthem Sprinters and Other Antics, 1963
The Pedestrian, 1966
The Wonderful Ice Cream Suit and Other Plays, 1975
Pillar of Fire and Other Plays, 1975

Bibliography

Acklam, David M. "The Exploration of Mars: An Unintentional Invasion?" McMillan, ed., pp. 164-75.

Allen, Howard. *The Illustrated Man Illustrates Our Future.*" McMillan, ed., pp. 211-17.

Barlow, Aaron. "If We Own It, We Can Destroy It: *Fahrenheit 451* and Intellectual Property." McGiveron, ed., pp. 200-11.

——. "Loss in the Language of Tomorrow: Journeying through Tucson on the Way to 'Usher II'." McMillan, ed., pp. 105-16.

Barr, Marleen S. "Prescient Border Crossing: 'I See You Never' and the Undocumented Mexicans Americans Prefer Not to See." McMillan, ed., pp. 37-56.

Beaumont, Matthew. "Stumbling in the Dark: Ray Bradbury's Pedestrian and the Politics of the Night." *Critical Quarterly* 57.4, 2015, pp. 71-88.

Bloom, Harold, editor. *Ray Bradbury*. Bloom's Modern Critical Views Series. Chelsea, 2001.

——, editor. *Ray Bradbury*, new ed. Bloom's Modern Critical Views Series. Infobase, 2010.

——, editor. *Ray Bradbury's Fahrenheit 451*. Modern Critical Interpretations Series. Chelsea, 2001.

——, editor. *Ray Bradbury's Fahrenheit 451*, new ed. Bloom's Modern Critical Interpretations Series. Infobase, 2008.

Bogár, Ádám T., and Rebeka Sára Szigethy. "Bradbury, Technology, and the Future of Reading." McGiveron, ed. 212-29.

Bould, Mark. "Burning Too: Consuming *Fahrenheit 451*." *Essays and Studies* ns 58, 2005, pp. 96-122.

Bradbury, Ray. *Bradbury Speaks: Too Soon from the Cave, Too Far from the Stars.* Harper, 2005.

Brown, Joseph F. "'As the Constitution Says': Distinguishing Documents in Ray Bradbury's *Fahrenheit 451*." *The Explicator* 67, 2008, pp. 55-58.

Bülgözdi, Imola. "Knowledge and Masculinity: Male Archetypes in *Fahrenheit 451*." McGiveron, ed., pp. 152-66.

Cokinos, Christopher. "The Desert is Earth and Mars: An Ecocritical, Bachelardian Exploration of 'And the Moon Be Still as Bright' and *It Came from Outer Space*." McMillan, ed., pp. 133-55.

Connor, George E. "Spelunking with Ray Bradbury: The Allegory of the Cave in *Fahrenheit 451*." Extrapolation 45, 2004, pp. 408-18.

Cote, Paul. "De-Alienating the Alien: The Limits of Empathy in NBC's *The Martian Chronicles* Miniseries." McMillan, pp. 193-210.de Koster, Katie, editor. *Readings on Fahrenheit 451*. Greenhaven Literary Companion Series. Greenhaven, 2009.

Dillon, Grace L. "Bradbury's Survivance Stories." McMillan, ed., pp. 57-69.

Dimeo, Steven. "Man and Apollo: Religion in Bradbury's Science Fantasies." Greenberg and Olander, pp. 156-64.

Diskin, Lahna. "Bradbury on Children." Greenberg and Olander, pp. 127-155.

Dugan, Charles L., Jr. "A Martian Chronicle." McMillan, ed., pp. 176-80.

Eller, Jonathan R. *Becoming Ray Bradbury*. U of Illinois P, 2011.

―――. "Miracles of Rare Device: Bradbury and the American Southwest." McMillan, ed., pp. 11-23.

―――. *Ray Bradbury Unbound*. U of Illinois P, 2014.

―――. "Speaking Futures: The Road to *Fahrenheit 451*." McGiveron, ed., pp. 77-91.

Eller, Jonathan R., and William F. Touponce. *Ray Bradbury: The Life of Fiction*. Kent State UP, 2004.

Espinoza, Ari. "Why Does Mars Beckon Us?" McMillan, ed., pp. 157-63.

Fain, Kinberly. "Bradbury's Mars: Pathway to Reinvention and Redemption." McMillan, ed., pp. 117-32.

Feneja, Fernanda Luis. "Promethean Rebellion in Ray Bradbury's *Fahrenheit 451*: The Protagonist's Quest." *Amaltea: Revista de Mitrocrítica* 4, 2012, pp. 1-20.

Filler, James. "Ascending from the Ashes: Images of Plato in Bradbury's *Fahrenheit 451*." *Philosophy and Literature* 38.2, Oct. 2014, pp. 528-48.

Forrest, Wolf. "*Fahrenheit 451* and the Utopic Dystopia: Bradbury's Vision Compared to Those of More, Orwell, Huxley, Wells, and Dick." McGiveron, ed., pp. 107-22.

―――. "The Sorcerer's Apprentice: How the Lives of Three Regional 'Weird Fiction' Writers Became Creatively Entangled." McMillan, ed., pp. 24-37.

Forrester, Kent. "The Dangers of Being Earnest: Ray Bradbury and *The Martian Chronicles*." *The Journal of General Education* 28, 1976, pp. 50-54.

Gallagher, Edward J. "The Thematic Structure of *The Martian Chronicles*." Greenberg and Olander, pp. 55-82.

Greenberg, Martin Harry, and Joseph D. Olander, editors. *Ray Bradbury*. Writers of the 21st Century Series. Taplinger, 1980.

Grossman, Kathryn M. "Woman as Temptress: The Way to (Br)Otherhood in Science Fiction Dystopias." *Women's Studies* 14, 1987, pp. 135-45.

Guffey, George R. "*Fahrenheit 451* and the 'Cubby-Hole' Editors of Ballantine Books." *Coordinates: Placing Science Fiction and Fantasy.* Edited by George E. Slusser, Eric S. Rabkin, and Robert Scholes. Alternatives Series. Southern Illinois UP. 99-106.

———. "The Unconscious, Fantasy, and 'Science-Fiction': Transformations in Bradbury's *The Martian Chronicles* and Lem's *Solaris.*" *Bridges of Fantasy: Essays from the Eaton Conference on Science Fiction and Fantasy Literature.* Edited by George E. Slusser, Eric S. Rabkin, and Robert Scholes. Alternatives Series. Southern Illinois UP, 1982. 142-59.

———. Hall, Martin R. "Silver Locusts on the Silver Screen: Bradbury's Western Mars Confronts 1960s British Art-Cinema." McMillan, ed., pp. 218-28.

Hoskinson, Kevin. "*The Martian Chronicles* and *Fahrenheit 451*: Ray Bradbury's Cold War Novels." *Extrapolation* 36, 1995, pp. 345-59.

Huntington, John. "Utopian and Anti-Utopian Logic: H. G. Wells and his Successors." *Science-Fiction Studies* 9, 1982, pp. 122-46.

Johnson, Wayne L. *Ray Bradbury.* Recognition Series. Ungar, 1980.

Kelley, Timothy E. "'Where Ignorant Armies Clash by Night': Love, War, and the Women of *Fahrenheit 451*." McGiveron, ed., pp. 138-51.

Krafft, Andrea. "'The House All Burnt': Disintegrating Domesticity in Ray Bradbury's *Fahrenheit 451*." McGiveron, pp. 123-35.

Laguna-Correa, Francisco. "Illustrating Otherness: Crossing Frontiers in *The Illustrated Man.*" McMillan, ed., pp. 88-103.

Laino, Guido. "Nature as an Alternative Space for Rebellion in Ray Bradbury's *Fahrenheit 451*." *Literary Landscapes, Landscape in Literature.* Edited by Michele Bottalico, Maria Teresa Chialant, and Eleonara Rao. Carocci, 2007, pp. 152-64.

———. "Reading Montag as a Postmodern Don Quixote." McGiveron, pp. 167-82.

Lawrence, Adam. "A 'Night Meeting' in the Southwest: Hospitality in *The Martian Chronicles.*" McMillan, ed., pp. 70-87.

McGiveron, Rafeeq O. "Bradbury's *Fahrenheit 451*." *The Explicator* 54, 1996, pp. 177-80.

———, editor. *Critical Insights: Fahrenheit 451.* Critical Insights Series. Salem, 2013.

———. "'To Build a Mirror Factory': The Mirror and Self-Examination in Ray Bradbury's *Fahrenheit 451*." *Critique: Studies in Contemporary Fiction* 39, 1998, pp. 282-87.

———. "'Do You Know the Legend of Hercules and Antaeus?' The Wilderness in Ray Bradbury's *Fahrenheit 451*." *Extrapolation* 38, 1997, pp. 102-9.

————. "From 'Government Control of This and That' to 'The Whole Culture's Shot Through': Behavior, Blame, and the Bomb in *The Martian Chronicles* and *Fahrenheit 451.*" McGiveron, ed., pp. 62-74.

————. "'They Got Me a Long Time Ago': The Sympathetic Villain in *Nineteen Eighty-Four*, *Brave New World*, and *Fahrenheit 451.*" *Critical Insights: Dystopia.* Edited by M. Keith Booker. Critical Insights Series. Salem, 2013, pp. 125-41.

————. "What 'Carried the Trick'? Mass Exploitation and the Decline of Thought in Ray Bradbury's *Fahrenheit 451.*" *Extrapolation* 37, 1996, pp. 245-56.

McHugh, Anna. "The Argument about Memory in *Fahrenheit 451.*" McGiveron, ed., pp. 183-99.

McKay, Christopher P., and Carol Stoker. "The Naming of Names." McMillan, ed., pp. 181-91.

McMillan, Gloria, editor. *Orbiting Ray Bradbury's Mars: Biographical, Anthropological, Literary, Scientific and Other Perspectives.* Critical Explorations in Science Fiction and Fantasy Series 41. McFarland, 2013.

————. "Teaching Martians in Tucson." McMillan, ed., pp. 229-41.

McNelly, Willis E. "Ray Bradbury—Past, Present, and Future." Greenberg and Olander, pp. 17-24.

————, and Keith Neilson. "*Fahrenheit 451.*" *Survey of Science Fiction Literature* 2. Edited by Frank Magill. Salem, 1979, pp. 749-55.

Mengeling, Marvin E. "The Machineries of Joy and Despair: Bradbury's Attitudes toward Science and Technology." Greenberg and Olander, pp. 83-109.

————. *Red Planet, Flaming Phoenix, Green Town: Some Early Bradbury Revisited.* 1stBooks, 2002.

Mogen, David. *Ray Bradbury.* Twayne's United States Authors Series 504. Twayne, 1986.

Moskowitz, Sam. *Seekers of Tomorrow: Masters of Modern Science Fiction.* World, 1966.

Mucher, Walter J. "Being Martian: Spatiotemporal Self in Ray Bradbury's *The Martian Chronicles.*" *Extrapolation* 43, 2002, pp. 171-87.

Nichols, Phil. "'Classics Cut to Fit'? *Fahrenheit 451* and Its Appeal in Other Media." McGiveron, ed., pp. 92-106.

Nolan, William F. *The Ray Bradbury Companion.* Gale, 1975.

Pell, Sarah-Warner J. "Style Is the Man: Imagery in Bradbury's Fiction." Greenberg and Olander, pp. 186-94.

Pierce, Hazel. "Ray Bradbury and the Gothic Tradition." Greenberg and Olander, pp. 165-85.

Plank, Robert. "Expedition to the Planet of Paranoia." *Extrapolation* 22, Summer 1981, pp. 171-85.

Rabkin, Eric S. "Is Mars Heaven? *The Martian Chronicles, Fahrenheit 451*, and Ray Bradbury's Landscape of Longing." *Visions of Mars: Essays on the Red Planet in Fact and Science*. Edited by Howard V. Hendrix, George Slusser, and Eric S. Rabkin. McFarland, 2011, pp. 95-104.

———. "To Fairyland by Rocket: Bradbury's *The Martian Chronicles*." Greenberg and Olander, pp. 110-126.

Reid, Robin Anne. "Genre, Censorship, and Cultural Changes: Critical Reception of Ray Bradbury's *Fahrenheit 451* from the 1950s to 2000s." McGiveron, ed., pp. 37-49.

———. *Ray Bradbury: A Critical Companion*. Critical Companions to Popular Contemporary Writers Series. Greenwood, 2000.

Reilly, Robert. "The Art of Ray Bradbury." *Extrapolation* 13, 1971, pp. 64-74.

Seed, David. "The Flight from the Good Life: *Fahrenheit 451* in the Context of Postwar Dystopias." *Journal of American Studies* 28, 1994, pp. 225-240.

———. *Ray Bradbury*. Modern Masters of Science Fiction Series. U of Illinois P, 2015.

Sisario, Peter. "A Study of the Allusions in Bradbury's *Fahrenheit 451*." *English Journal*, Feb. 1970, pp. 210+.

Slusser, George Edgar. *The Bradbury Chronicles*. Mitford Series, Popular Writers of Today 4. Borgo, 1977.

Smolla, Rodney A. "The Life of the Mind and the Life of Meaning: Reflections on *Fahrenheit 451*." *Michigan Law Review* 107, 2009, pp. 895-912.

Sommers, Joseph Michael. "The Phoenix and the Fireman: Dialogistic Inversion in Ray Bradbury's *Fahrenheit 451*." McGiveron, ed., pp. 50-61.

Spencer, Susan. "The Post-Apocalyptic Library: Oral and Literate Culture in *Fahrenheit 451* and *A Canticle for Leibowitz*." *Extrapolation* 32, 1991, pp. 331-42.

Stupple, A. James. "The Past, the Future, and Ray Bradbury." Greenberg and Olander, pp. 24-32.

Touponce, William F. *Lord Dunsany, H. P. Lovecraft, and Ray Bradbury: Spectral Journeys*. Scarecrow, 2013.

———. *Ray Bradbury and the Poetics of Reverie*. Studies in Speculative Fiction 2. 1981. UMI, 1984.

———. "Some Aspects of Surrealism in the Work of Ray Bradbury." *Extrapolation* 25.3, Fall 1984, pp. 228-38.

Touponce, William F., and Jonathan R. Eller, editors. *The Collected Stories of Ray Bradbury: A Critical Edition, 1938-1943*. Kent State UP, 2011.

Watt, Donald. "Burning Bright: *Fahrenheit 451* as Symbolic Dystopia." Greenberg and Olander, pp. 195-213.

Weller, Sam. *The Bradbury Chronicles: The Life of Ray Bradbury*. Harper, 2005.

———. *Listen to the Echoes: The Ray Bradbury Interviews*. Melville, 2010.

Wolfe, Gary K. "The Frontier Myth in Ray Bradbury." Greenberg and Olander, pp. 33-54.

Zipes, Jack. "Mass Degradation of Humanity and Massive Contradictions in Bradbury's Vision of Humanity in *Fahrenheit 451*." *No Place Else: Explorations in Utopian and Dystopian Fiction*. Edited by Eric S. Rabkin, Martin H. Greenberg, and Joseph D. Olander. Alternatives Series. Southern Illinois UP, 1983, pp. 182-98.

Rafeeq O. McGiveron holds a BA with Honor in English and History from Michigan State University, an MA in English and History from MSU, and an MA in English from Western Michigan University. Having taught college-level literature and composition for many years at a number of schools, in positions that have allowed his scholarship to be driven by personal interest and the serendipity of the classroom rather than by necessity, he has published several dozen articles, chapters, and reference entries on the works of authors ranging from Ray Bradbury and Robert A. Heinlein to Willa Cather to Shakespeare, most recently editing *Critical Insights: Fahrenheit 451* (2014) and *Critical Insights: Robert A. Heinlein* (2015) for Salem Press. Currently he works in student services at Lansing Community College, where he has served since 1992. He also dabbles in fiction, occasionally poetry, and mobile art. His website is www.rafeeqmcgiveron. com, and his novel *Student Body*, the sensual, allusive, and introspective tale of a glib yet secretly troubled young professor-to-be and the women who love him, was released in 2014.

Contributors

W. C. Bamberger has published essays on topics ranging from Wonder Woman comics to the death of Kierkegaard, the poetry of Anne Carson, the composers Mauricio Kagel and Christos Hatzis, and the role of eggs in the writings of Samuel Butler and Friedrich Nietzsche. He edited *Routine Disruptions: Selected Poems and Lyrics* by Kenward Elmslie, and *Guy Davenport and James Laughlin: Selected Letters*. Recent translations include *The Unruly Bridal Bed* and *My Papa and the Maid of Orleans*, both by the German Expressionist author Mynona (Salomo Friedlaender), and *Two Draft Essays from 1918*, by Gershom Scholem. He has published book-length studies of novelist William Eastlake, musician Don Van Vliet, and perceptual theorist Adelbert Ames, Jr. He lives in Michigan.

Ádám T. Bogár (MA, Karoli Gaspar University, 2012) is an independent scholar and translator. His main research interests are the works and thought of Kurt Vonnegut, speculative fiction, and technology and society. He so far has published over a dozen articles in various volumes and journals, including the 2013 essay "Bradbury, Technology, and the Future of Reading" in *Critical Insights: Fahrenheit 451*. He has coedited a volume of papers from "The Arts of Attention" conference (Karoli Gaspar University, 2013), which has just been published by L'Harmattan Press. Bogár also writes poetry, and translates poetry and prose to and from Hungarian, English, and Spanish.

Imola Bülgözdi is an assistant professor teaching American Literature and Cultural Studies at the University of Debrecen, Hungary. She specializes in the cultural embedding of the creative process of Southern women writers, also branching off to the comparative analysis of Southern novels and their film adaptations. Her recent publications include "Myths of Youth and Gendered Ageing in *August: Osage County* by Tracy Letts" (*albeit*. 2016) and "Girls in Search of a Viable Identity in Eudora Welty's *The Golden Apples*" (*Critical Insights: American Short Story*, 2015). She is a devoted reader of fantasy and science fiction, as attested by her publications in this field: "'Some Genetics are Passed on Via the Soul:' The Curious Case of Susan Sto-Helit" (*Gender Forum*, 2015), "Artificial Intelligence and Gender Performativity in William Gibson's *Idoru*" (*Navigating Cybercultures*, 2013) and "Knowledge and Masculinity: Male Archetypes in *Fahrenheit 451*" (*Critical Insights: Fahrenheit 451*, 2013).

Karen S. Garvin holds a master's in history from the American Military University and a bachelor's in communications from the University of Maryland University College. She is an independent historian and freelance writer and works as a copy editor for a Washington, DC, think tank. She writes on a wide range of historical topics, but her main area of interest is nineteenth-century European history and technology. She is an avid Victorianist and a Steampunk aficianodo, with one foot planted firmly in the nineteenth century and the other in the twenty-first century. Forget the flying car; where's her airship? Her current projects include several novels, anthologies, and nonfiction projects, and she is a partner at Corrugated Sky LLC, a small publishing company that she formed with a group of fellow writers.

Timothy E. Kelley holds a BA in English and an MA in English/Creative Writing from Michigan State University. His areas of scholarly interest include moral and religious philosophy, American Constitutional history, and twentieth-century American fiction. He is currently an assistant professor of English and course coordinator for Composition I at Lansing Community College, where he has taught writing since 2002. Previous publications include an essay titled "Where Ignorant Armies Clash by Night: Love, War, and the Women of *Fahrenheit 451*," which appeared in *Critical Insights: Fahrenheit 451*. His first book, a novella titled *Solid Contact*, awaits publication as he works on an experimental crime novel set in northern Michigan.

Andrea Krafft is a Marion L. Brittain postdoctoral fellow and the Assistant Director of the Writing and Communication Program at Georgia Tech. She earned her PhD from the University of Florida in 2015 with a dissertation about the intersections of speculative fiction with pop cultural fantasies of post-World War II domesticity. Her recent work appears in the edited collections *Shirley Jackson: Influences and Confluences* and *Critical Insights: Fahrenheit 451*. Science fiction is integral not only to her research but also to her pedagogy, as she has developed courses such as "Future Wars: Military Science Fiction" and "Discovering *Dune*." Her additional research interests include multimodal pedagogy, gender studies, and contemporary American popular culture.

Guido Laino is an independent researcher working in Italy both as a critic and as creative artist. He received his PhD in American Literature from the University of Salerno with a study on the shapes of utopia in postmodern fiction, with a specific analysis of the work of Thomas Pynchon and Don DeLillo. In more general terms, his main research interests (and part of his obsessions) have always been focused on utopian and dystopian fiction, its narrative strategies, and its philosophical features. He has published more than twenty-five essays and articles on literature and all those things that can be connected to literature (i.e. almost everything), and has produced artistic and theatrical work on a wide range of themes, doubts, and dilemmas (obviously including utopia). He has published various articles on Ray Bradbury and has been part of the *Critical Insight* volume on *Fahrenheit 451.*

Anna McHugh is a writer and teacher in Sydney, Australia. She completed a PhD in medieval literature at the University of Sydney and a second PhD in medieval history at Oxford, where she taught in the English faculty. She has published on literature and history in the Middle Ages, and contributed to Salem Press's volumes on *Fahrenheit 451* and *Robert A. Heinlein*, also edited by Rafeeq O. McGiveron.

Phil Nichols recently completed his PhD on the screen works of Ray Bradbury, holds an MA in Screenwriting, and is course leader for Film & Television Production at the University of Wolverhampton in the UK. He is a Fellow of the UK Higher Education Academy, and serves on the Advisory Board of the Center for Ray Bradbury Studies (Indiana University), and the Editorial Board of *The New Ray Bradbury Review*. His previous writings on Bradbury have appeared in *The New Ray Bradbury Review, The Radio Journal*, and the books *Science Fiction Across Media, Visions of Mars*, and *Critical Insights: Fahrenheit 451*. His website at www.bradburymedia.co.uk catalogs and reviews Bradbury's work across all media.

Robin Anne Reid, PhD, is a professor in the Department of Literature and Languages at Texas A&M University-Commerce. Her teaching areas are creative writing, critical theory, and marginalized literatures. She teaches graduate and undergraduate creative writing courses in fiction, undergraduate courses in technical writing, women writers, and popular culture, and graduate courses in stylistics, gender theory, and digital studies. She published *Ray Bradbury: A Critical Companion* (2000) with Greenwood Press, and "Genre, Censorship, and Cultural Changes: Critical Reception of Ray Bradbury's *Fahrenheit 451*" for Salem Press's *Critical Insights: Fahrenheit 451* (2013). She is the editor of Greenwood's *Women in Science Fiction and Fantasy* Encyclopedia.

William F. Touponce (1948-2017), PhD in comparative literature, University of Massachusetts, 1981, was Emeritus Professor of English at Indiana University. He was the author of several critical studies on science fiction and fantasy authors, including Frank Herbert and Isaac Asimov, as well as two books on Ray Bradbury. In 2004 he published a comprehensive survey of Bradbury's life and career: *Ray Bradbury: The Life of Fiction*, coauthored with Jonathan R. Eller, and published by the Kent State University Press. From 2007 to 2012, he directed the Center for Ray Bradbury Studies. During that time he was general editor of *The Collected Stories of Ray Bradbury* and edited a yearly journal devoted to Bradbury, *The New Ray Bradbury Review*, now in its fifth volume of publication. His most recent publication was *Lord Dunsany, H. P. Lovecraft and Ray Bradbury: Spectral Journeys* (Scarecrow Press, 2013).

Index

117, 118, 164, 178, 179, 180,
182, 183, 184, 186, 188, 189,
190, 191, 192, 193, 199, 200,
201, 202, 203, 213, 217, 218,
219, 220, 221, 227
"Mars is Heaven!" 58
The Martian Chronicles v, vii, viii,
xi, xii, xv, xvi, xvii, xviii, xxii,
xxiii, xxiv, xxvi, xxxi, xxxiii,
3, 5, 7, 8, 9, 10, 11, 12, 17, 19,
20, 21, 22, 25, 26, 28, 32, 33,
35, 43, 44, 50, 58, 59, 63, 65,
66, 67, 75, 104, 105, 120, 135,
139, 140, 163, 164, 166, 168,
170, 172, 173, 174, 176, 178,
181, 182, 184, 186, 188, 191,
192, 193, 194, 198, 201, 202,
204, 210, 215, 218, 219, 220,
221
McCarthyism 13, 172
McCarthy, Joseph 13
McClean, David 94
McClellan, Clarisse 13, 43
McClure, Marguerite Susan xxxi,
209
McKuen, Rod 27
mechanical hound 90
Medal for Distinguished Contribution
to American Letters xxxiii,
212
A Medicine for Melancholy xxxii,
210, 215
Melville, Herman 45, 63, 74, 139,
166, 222
Merwin, Sam 21
metamorphosis 181
metaphor in literature xi, 64, 65, 72,
203
Metropolis vii, xiv
Meyrink, Gustav 91
"The Million-Year Picnic" x, 106,
116, 117, 182, 187, 202
Moberg, Esther Marie xxviii

Moby-Dick 63, 122
Moby Dick (film) xxiii, xxvi, xxxii,
161, 210
modernism 182
Moffett, James 147
Moirai 108, 109
Mon Oncle 93
Montag, Guy 13, 43, 47, 76, 87
Montag, Mildred 36, 38
moral/morality xviii, 7, 25, 48, 53,
56, 78, 85, 88, 106, 107, 118,
119, 226
Morgan 131, 132, 133, 134
Morrow 65, 75, 212, 213
Moskowitz, Sam 25
Mr. Big 43
Mr. Bigelow 51
Mr. Dark 70, 72, 84, 85
Mr. Electrico 6
Mr. Garrett 53, 166
Mr. Jonas 81, 82
"Mr. Pale" 112
Mr. Pale 112
Mr. Ramirez 203
Mrs. Braling 39
Mugnaini, Joe 67
The Mummies of Guanajuato xxxiii
mundane xii, 11, 46, 113, 128, 181,
195, 199
"The Murderer" xi, 101, 122, 124,
127, 135
myth v, x, 30, 70, 85, 93, 100, 106,
107, 109, 110, 111, 112, 113,
114, 115, 116, 119, 120, 140,
186, 188, 195, 225

Nagasaki 107
Naked Lunch 93, 104
"Naming of Names" 190
The Nation 15, 120
National Medal of Arts Award 213
Nazi Germany 46
Nebbs, Lavinia 81